MY SEVEN-YEAR DIRTY WEEKEND

BY PHILIP NYE

INTRODUCTION

A warm welcome to you, as I extend an invitation to join me on a journey through what has been a turbulent and exceptionally long mid-life crisis. The words 'mid-life crisis' might lead you to believe that things went horribly wrong, but I have to say that what I went through during my time in Dirty Weekend gave me some of the most memorable, enjoyable and exciting times in my life. If this is what a crisis has to offer, then I, for one, say bring it on.

In the years that followed, the band would have a direct impact on my working life as well as my personal life. After twenty-five years working in supermarket management, I would walk away and find a job supporting adults with learning difficulties (with no clue what I was doing at first) and that this would then lead on to working with children in the social care sector? Believe it or not, the world of music would become a great help to me in coping with the challenges I would encounter within these working environments.

It would allow me to have opportunities to engage with a completely new set of people who have now become some of my closest friends.

It opened doors I never knew existed to my own creativity and passions. I never thought I would be writing my own songs, learning instruments and structuring melodies. I also never imagined I would start promoting live music events, go on to produce a local music magazine, help build rehearsal studios, manage a band of teenagers, make an album and play live in front of 200,000 people (wait for the Pride chapter). It has given me the chance to be a part of events that have provided me with memories of some of the biggest laughs I have ever had, and at times it has put me in situations that have frustrated the hell out of me.

It would give me with the means to bring joy to lots of people, but it would also invite ridicule from a few. I have seen first-hand the profound effect that music can have on people's lives. Music has a special power that really does not care about age, gender nor ability; it is only people who have agendas who care about such things (wait for Music Mafia chapter).

So, this is for all the people who have helped me reach this stage. I would estimate that this mid-life crisis is in its twelfth year now and is showing no signs of abating. During the weird times of Covid and the lockdowns, my avenues to perform or to spectate were curtailed. So, I panicked and thought, "No fucking way. I'm going to write a book." Does this make me an author? In a way it does as I am writing words on to a page, but as to whether they are worthy of being read is not my call and I am ready for the bouquets or brick bats that may be heading my way.

As I always like to point out, this is my personal experience: what I saw and what I felt. I am aware that others view things through their own lens and their interpretation of events is not wrong but is their truth. I will try to give you a feel of what it all meant to me, and I do this knowing it is the most accurate account that I can give. I am sure there will be an element of poetic licence, but it will not be far from the truth and – as you will find out – I do not lie very well.

I am always amazed by the connections we make in life. How one event can take you down a certain path until the next gives you the choice to go left or right, and so on. I have concluded that some of the worst days in my life have eventually led me to experience some of the best, and that the people I now call my friends would not be my friends if things had taken a different course.

Do not fret, this book is not going to be that deep. In fact, it will be an account of what turned out to be a lot of fun. You will be introduced to quite a few people along the way. Nobody is perfect and, as is always the case, when you become close to someone over a long period of time a few flaws will be exposed. We all have good days and bad days, and we all have strengths and weaknesses. I have been fortunate, in the main, to surround myself with people who have good hearts and good intentions. Admittedly those intentions might not have always been executed in the correct manner, but nothing was too serious.

I chart the story with chapters focusing on key events and as we go through I will add some footnotes that will offer a bit more depth and give a bit more background on the characters involved. Also, from time to time, I will include what I will call a Big Footnote. This will not be a synopsis of the mighty Sasquatch but instead will be a slightly longer detailed account of a place, a person, a song meaning, or something else related to the chapter in hand.

To set the scene, let me give a brief description of myself. At the beginning of this story, I am a 42-year-old with no experience of the music scene apart from the odd drunken karaoke performance from time to time. I had recently departed from a failed marriage and had one mental breakdown to my name after which I was diagnosed with acute depression. (There was nothing cute about it.) I am 5ft 8in and I look like the product of a Ronan Keating, Jimmy Somerville and Tin Tin love triangle. My partner who goes by the name of Tree tells me she does not see the Ronan Keating resemblance. (Bitch)

So, grab a beer, chill the fuck out and join me on my Dirty Weekend.

CHAPTER 1 – THE MORNING GLORY

Well, here I am in Brighton walking down the street towards the Latest Music Bar. The year is 2011 and it's a beautiful day down here on the south coast with most of the population heading towards the seafront to while away the day on the beach or waste some money in a multitude of different amusement arcades. As I approach, I can see a small melee of people hovering by the door of this fairly impressive building. The outside is slightly tatty but inside the building exudes a feeling of fun and artiness.

The Latest Music Bar is a venue that has quite a history of live entertainment, and over the years thousands of bands and performers have appeared here. From music to comedy, and cabaret to special events, as well as being the studio for the local TV channel Latest TV. It's a Sunday and as the clock hands reach midday, I find myself waiting for the doors to open into what will either be a waste of my time or a bit of a laugh. I haven't got anything else on, so have nothing to lose I suppose. Admittedly this is not the usual time to be attending a gig, normally at this time on a Sunday I am just about coming round from whatever mess I got myself into the night before, but here I am.

I guess I am here for two reasons. Firstly, I have absolutely fuck all else to do. After all, it's late on a Sunday morning and the alternative activities I might partake in are not exactly forthcoming. Secondly, a friend has asked me to come and support him as he tries out a new avenue of so-called pleasure which has something to do with him trying to make sweet music.

I had bumped into Tony the week before in a pub that I was helping to run. I haven't known him for long, but we seem to have a rapport and conversing with him was easy. I found him good company and considered him to be an alright chap. We chatted in the normal way that two blokes do, just going through the normal pleasantries asking how he had been and what he was up to now. He then mentioned he recently joined a rock band. It took me a little while to process this piece of information being offered to me. This was not how I was expecting the course of the conversation to go and to be polite I asked him a few questions about it. I was not just being polite though. I was being bloody nosy. He informed me they had their first ever gig coming up the next week and would be performing a set of five songs. I was impressed he was talking about doing gigs, which made me assume they must be decent. I asked if the band had a name, and he was proud to announce they were called Morning Glory.

I did my best to suppress my giggles and wondered if he was winding me up. This was the first time I had heard of his musical prowess. Was he being serious? After all, he was now in his early forties. I wondered if maybe I wasn't the only one here going through the old mid-life crisis. The more he told me about it, the more I realised he was being totally serious. He explained he had been having drum lessons and that he and some fellow music students were being taught how to play as a band together. He mentioned that a chap called Wama was also in the band and when he mentioned this my ears pricked up.

I had known Wama for many years. We were not necessarily that close as he was a bit older than me, but we did move in similar circles and had similar interests, namely pubs, football and, in Wama's case, scrapping. His actual name was Wayne and many years ago he had been known to me simply by his surname, Marmont. He was now Wama and apparently he played rhythm guitar. (More on his name change later, as it is a subject that warrants some explanation).

They also had a bass player called Mark and a lead guitarist called Clive, neither of whom I knew at that point in the proceedings, but they both go on to become major characters in this story. Lastly, they had a lead singer called Lockie who I knew slightly from his long-standing relationship with Wama. They had been friends for many years as well as having a connection through the work they both did in the world of upholstery.

Tony began to elaborate as he told me more about the drum lessons that he had been having with a guy called Graham, who in Tony's words was "some sort of percussive genius". Said drum genius had a friend called Alex, who apparently also turned out to be some sort of electric-guitar-teaching guru and between them they had started up a music teaching business in Brighton which went by the name of Rock School.

As far as I could ascertain, it consisted of bringing individual students that they taught together to form bands and to teach them how to make music together whilst all working on a number of different songs. The teaching facility was based on the third floor of a building that was the headquarters of a security firm. They had two fairly large rooms upstairs and as it was a standalone building, they didn't have any noise complaints from neighbours. Alex was a youngish master lead guitarist of Italian heritage with a goatee beard and a hairline that was struggling to hang on in there.

He had his own band called Thieves by the Code, with mates Steff on bass/synth and Nick on drums. They were very heavy in sound with good original material. He was also involved in several function bands, with the main one being the awesome South Coast Soul Revue. Doing this in conjunction with his teaching helped to pay the bills and allowed him to try and eke out a living doing something he clearly loved. Graham went under the shortened name of G. He was a percussion genius who taught at a local music college and has his own band AKDK, which is a truly spectacular act comprising two drumkits, synths and loads of technical shit that, quite simply, I have no clue about. Both of them were very accomplished musicians and complemented each other in their teaching. G could be almost zen like in his approach and Alex could be a fiery Latino when he wanted to be. It was also handy that G was there to work as an interpreter for Alex as well (only joking, Alex). They taught a number of different age groups, including a collective with an average age of about 12, another made up of older teenagers, and then Tony and Wama's lot which could only be described as old and having 'missed the boat' with nothing better to do. I must remember to ask them one day which group was the hardest to teach.

The general format was a two-hour lesson every week where they would learn a song and break it down to be able to play it together as a band. Then every six months G and Alex put on a gig where each band has a twenty-minute set and they perform five songs each. This is in a proper venue with a stage, professional sound and lighting. The event is generally supported by lots of eager and adoring mums and dads watching their offspring and trying to figure out whether they will turn into mini rock stars.

The tension is beginning to build as I approach the bar. And thank goodness the bar is open, and they are serving alcohol, so it won't be a complete waste of my day. It is half an hour before the scheduled start and looking around the room I feel a bit out of place. Most of the adult audience members appear to be drinking tea or coffee. The younger members of the audience, who make up a large proportion, are on a different selection of soft drinks. This is definitely a Fruit Shoot sort of crowd and I soon become aware that all the kids have exotic names like Tarquin or Destiny. This is perhaps an unfair assumption, but I guess it's likely the parents are loaded to not only afford the cost of instruction for their young maestros, but they all look to be part of the new "mocha coffee" crowd that is beginning to blight the real and genuine side of Brighton. I stick out like a sore thumb standing there clutching my second pint of Foster's. I am at a gig for goodness' sake, but this has the feel of an early morning Sunday school crowd as far as I'm concerned. The performance areas are on two levels. You walk into the upper bar, where the audience will mingle before being given the green light to descend the stairs into the basement performance area. It is actually quite exciting going down into the darkness of the basement for the very first time. There is no natural light to be had and as soon as you immerse yourself in the room you wouldn't know whether it was midday or midnight.

The room itself is quite impressive. It has a capacity of just over a hundred, not the biggest, but it has an intimate, theatrical feel about it. The stage is quite big for the size of the room. There is a long bar on one side, which is where I intend to install myself for the duration. The surrounding walls have a city skyscraper mural painted across them. The buildings have hollowed out windows which, with the aid of back lighting, give it an exceptionally beautiful and stylised look. You could imagine this sort of place being ideal as an illicit drinking den during Prohibition, were we in America. One more glance around the room and it's back to reality as I remember I'm surrounded by the coffee and Fruit Shoot drinkers and suddenly the illicit drinking den has melted away into the ether.

The room is slowly beginning to fill up and there is a flurry of activity on the stage as a busy sound engineer finishes setting up. It looks like he is struggling a little, but that is understandable when trying to control this many newbies. I cannot even begin to imagine how he was feeling whilst doing the soundcheck. My guess is he has earned his money today. I ponder the thought that he has chosen this line of work as he must have a love of music. I would like to know whether that love has been dented in the two hours leading up to this moment or whether it has inspired him, knowing that having performed his duties today, he has acquired superhero status.

Just off stage I can see Tony and Wama standing with what I assume is the rest of the band. I catch Tony's eye and gesture to him to say "hi". He gestures back, smiles a little smile and then returns to his conversation with the others. He and the guys have a look about them that can only be described as 'shitting themselves'. This fills me with a sense that I am about to witness something special indeed and that my punt on coming along is going to bear fruit after all. Just to the back of the stage I notice Alex and G surrounded by a group of kids. They are deep in conversation, and I assume this is a rallying call to their little troopers before they go for the final push over the top. These kids are the first act on, and I wonder if they are to be cannon fodder. There are six of them with an average age that I estimate to be around 11 or 12. One of them is Tony's daughter, who is a talented guitarist and vocalist. I think she may be the main reason that Tony got into this music lark. I am sure I remember him telling me he used to take the kids to have music lessons and he would wait outside the room. One day, whilst one of his children was having drum lessons, he was finally invited in to have a go on the drums himself. From that moment he was hooked, and his musical journey began. I will tell you this, the money he has spent on music lessons and instruments for himself, and his kids could equal the budget of a small country.

Anyway, back to the gig. The young band has a setup that consists of drums, vocals, keyboard, bass and two guitars. It appears some of the kids are welcoming the last-minute instructions and words of encouragement, whilst a couple of them look like they are about to do a runner. Looking closely at one poor girl you can see she is on the verge of either passing out or throwing up with nerves. She is being strong-armed to stand behind the keyboards. The flurry of activity onstage is reaching its climax and suddenly the main lights in the room begin to dim. The kids are primed and ready to rock as they take up their starting positions. The silence is broken by the occasional twang of instruments being given their final tuning. There is a noticeable hum coming from the crowd as they anticipate that the future Hendrix's in front of them are about to unleash musical hell.

Alex appears at the front of the stage. Microphone in hand, he welcomes everyone to the show. He gives a speech in his thick Italian accent, that we mostly understand, on how he and G had spent months teaching the techniques of Rock School and that this is to be the first of many showcases. He then explains his feelings of pride as he charts the progress his students have made and goes to great lengths to reinforce the knowledge they have gained in such a short time period. My brain translates this to mean, "prepare yourself for some truly appalling noise and try to smile as if you are enjoying yourselves, and remember I am not a bloody miracle worker".

Alex then asks the audience to give the kids a rousing welcome. The audience responds enthusiastically and makes plenty of agreeable noise. The lights go down and permeating through the darkness comes a familiar bass line. It is slower than usual, but you can recognise that this is 'Seven Nation Army' by The White Stripes. Each member of the band gradually joins in with their instruments until we reach a point of maximum destruction.

As the first song ends the gathered audience members, who are mostly relatives, give a rather over-the-top round of applause and the odd "whoop-whoop". Then again, maybe I am being too harsh and on reflection it was a valiant effort. At this point I swear the young girl on the keyboards throws up. It looks like she is just about to pass out and has to be led off the stage for a sit down. Looking at her I have the impression she has not enjoyed the experience and future pop stardom is perhaps not part of her life plan. I also suspect she has thrown a sickie just to get the hell out of the firing line and so I order another pint of Foster's to toast her good health.

What happens next is something I find to be utterly amazing. The little chap playing guitar goes on to the keyboard, the bass guitarist goes on to drums, the rhythm guitarist is now the lead singer, and the drummer is now playing bass. The next song starts and although it is not exactly a masterpiece, you have to really admire the fact that these youngsters are not only performing live but are also willing to learn all the instruments. They carry on changing around during their next four songs and when their set comes to an end the applause is thunderous and well deserved. Out of the corner of my eye I can see Tony and Wama looking on, appearing more and more concerned as their set is fast approaching. Alex arrives onstage again and is giving the first group some warm praise indeed. Keyboard girl is still alive, and any traces of vomit are not noticeable. He is about to announce the arrival of the next act. I shall call this ensemble the Teenagers as they don't have an official name. They are a four piece that consist of the classic line-up of drums, bass and two guitars, with one of them doing the main vocals. My guess is their average age is 16. They all look the part and have an array of swishing hair and smouldering angsty looks. They obviously really fancy themselves as rock stars, as you can tell they have worked really hard to achieve a look that is both moody and miserable. There's a smattering of their friends in the audience who look like they might wet themselves with excitement, some are obviously girlfriends of the band, and you have the impression they feel they have lucked out to be associated with such rebels. You can tell that the lead singer/guitarist really thinks a lot of himself. He has the looks but can he back it up with the goods? The lights start to dim, and their set begins to come to life. It is obvious that the parents of these guys and girls have had a serious musical influence on them, as the tunes they cover are in the main from the heady days of the early 70s – Clapton and Hendrix, with a bit of experimental prog rock thrown in for good measure. These are not working-class kids, I suspect. They all play to a fairly high standard, and all have the maximum amount of rock gurnage pouring from their faces. The lead singer/guitarist has it all, quite frankly. The looks, the voice, the guitar skills and an on-stage charisma that belies his years. To be honest with you I cannot stand the guy. I can in hindsight only put this down to complete and utter jealousy.

A quick look to my left and I spy Tony and Wama looking on from the side of the stage and it is a pleasure to see their reactions. I swear I can see the colour draining out of their faces. With Wama I sense that he is looking on in admiration rather than fear. Wama is always like that really, he tends not to have any fear and is quite gifted at not stressing about what others think of him. He has a depth to him that I admire.

The intrepid angst-ridden rock gods finish their set to warm applause from the audience and accept the adulation as only teenagers can: they quite frankly cannot care less as they flounce off stage to be with their mates. It is hard to tell whether they enjoyed the experience or not, but I am sure their street cred has gone up and the lead singer is definitely getting laid later.

Time now for a small interval as the third and final band make their last-minute preparations. This means me going to the bar (there is no queue) for yet another beer, and the rest of the audience frantically trying to get another cup of tea from upstairs. I watch the guys scurrying around onstage getting ready. Tony is positioning and then repositioning every single piece of his kit, over and over again. Clive the guitarist is just noodling away doing that really irritating thing guitarists do, playing random notes with no discernible melody completely oblivious to anyone else in the room. (He has not changed much to be fair; some call it annoying; some call it perseverance).

Mark the bass player is looking studiously at the knobs on his amp and is in deep conversation with Tony on drums. It looks almost like they are arguing with each other, but it is just the normal relationship between drum and bass, as they see themselves as the engine room of the band and a separate entity. I think that comes from the fact they are always kept at the back, and everyone assumes they are talentless and ugly. In such circumstances a siege mentality comes over them and the thin line between love and hate starts to emerge. It probably doesn't help that they are both extremely anal and robotic about the timings of songs and are constantly glaring at each other and blaming one another for any hiccups that occur.

Wama is standing there just taking it all in, projecting a sense of calm. I think that is what he is doing, although it is hard to read the thoughts that are going through his head as he is wearing a very dark pair of sunglasses. Looking like a curly-grey-haired Bono, the impression he gives is that he seems relaxed, although in truth he is probably bricking himself. All in all, though, you have to hand it to him for his wardrobe and accessory choice. He had obviously considered the fear factor, hence the masterstroke of wearing a pair of brown trousers as well.

Lockie the lead singer is shuffling through some pages in front of him on a music stand. He has the look of a man who knows what he is doing. He appears to be doing vocal warm-up exercises whilst positioning the mic stand into the optimal vantage point on the stage. No nerves visible, this man is a pro.

The room is beginning to fill up again with eager anticipation. Obviously, the caffeine and E numbers in the Fruit Shoots are beginning to work their magic. It seems to be less busy than it was for the first band. I can only assume that once the parents of the little cherubs had seen their performance, they had obviously fucked off to a garden centre or something similar, which probably had a shorter queue to get themselves a nice latte.

Alex the Latin Adonis appears on the stage and welcomes the crowd back. He remarks on how well the previous bands have done and explains that he and G are happy with the enthusiasm and progress that has been made by all concerned. He tells us that it is his honour to welcome the last act. Unlike the other two bands, this one has a name – Morning Glory. In truth it never occurs to me why they are the only band with a name, and I begin to wonder where the inspiration for this has come from.

The name obviously conjures up expectations of some kind of Oasis tribute band or they may be venturing down the Christian evangelical route, who knows. All I know is that the first band had an average age of 12, band two an average age of 16 and by the looks of this lot the average has shot up to probably being in the region of 45. With this in mind, I am expecting that with this level of experience they must be half decent to put themselves through this ordeal, surely. Alex introduces us to the next big thing and with the lights going down and a notable buzz circulating the room, the first chords are struck. I kind of recognise the chords and eventually realise that it is 'The Man Who Sold the World' by David Bowie. This is played at a tempo that I had not realised was possible. The best way of describing it is as follows. Imagine you are having the worst day of your life and you try to shoot yourself, but you have left your gun at home. But wait, the vocals now kick in and you realise that you know where you live, you get in a taxi, pick up said gun and then blow your brains out. This song is not long, but the way the Morning Glory boys perform it makes it appear to be the length of 'Bohemian Rhapsody'. I am supping on my beer and loving every minute of this cabaret. I survey the room to gauge audience reaction. All I can see is lots of faces looking on in slight confusion and pity. The first song finally comes to a crescendo and as the final note is hit there is a round of slight, gentle applause that resonates more pity. I am clapping enthusiastically and loving it. I swear I am even crying a little with joy. I order another Foster's to celebrate my find.

The band, at this point, appear to be in shock as they launch into the next tune. Tony on drums looks like someone has emptied a bucket of water over his head, he really is sweating that much. I do not think this is because of heat, but due to sheer fear. The next tune is an original composition called something about a highway. I remember how bold I thought it was to do an original number and if memory serves me well the lyrics and tune are actually surprisingly good. It doesn't go down greatly with the audience, though, mainly driven by the fact the rhythm section has now gone on strike, the singer is tone deaf and the audience just do not give a fuck. The end of each song is greeted by lower and lower levels of appreciation, and you can see panic etched in the eyes of all the band members – except Wama.

That is only because his use of dark glasses is an inspirational and practical accessory, but I am sure beneath them panic is probably making itself at home there as well. What can I say? The guy's a fucking genius. As the panic sets in the mistakes creep up. As the mistakes creep up the panic levels rise, and the cycle goes on and on. Nearing the end of the set, Tony on drums looks like he has stepped out of a swimming pool. His choice of a light grey T-shirt is now beginning to look like a faux pas in the wardrobe department. Mark is just staring at Tony in disgust. Clive is hiding at the back of the stage. Wama is soldiering on blindly and Lockie the frontman is fronting it out as if his life depends on it. He seems oblivious to what is going on around him and I am fairly sure that he feels they are doing a great bloody job. The final note of the final song is eventually struck and the collective sigh from the crowd can be felt. A lacklustre ripple of applause ensues and looking at the band it appears they now know what it must have felt like to be at Rourke's Drift staring at Zulus, thousands of them. I drink my beer, order another and try to think of a recent time when I have had such a good day out. The crowd starts thinning as some of them meander off. The band are onstage and in the process of breaking down the instruments. There doesn't appear to be an awful lot of conversation between them as they toil away. I approach Tony by the front of the stage and give him a cheery, "Hello, mate." He looks directly at me for a while and then laughs. He asks me what I thought. I quickly change the subject and catch Wama's eye. We haven't seen each other in quite a while, and he tells me how good it was of me to come along and support. He doesn't appear to be perturbed, but you get the impression he is glad it is over; however he also seems to have really enjoyed it. You also sense that this is just the start for him. The one thing you will learn about Wama is when he has a passion for something, he is all in. I am introduced to Clive, and he appears to be a very pleasant and unassuming fellow. To look at him you would have thought he was some kind of hard-nosed, gruff old rocker who would take no prisoners at all. It turns out he is one of the nicest human beings with the biggest of hearts. (More about him as we progress through the story.) I then meet Mark for the first time and have a brief chat with him, before I say a quick hello to Lockie who I know but not that well. I tell them all I have really enjoyed myself without going into too much detail. I decide to say my goodbyes and make my exit. The reason for my avoidance is because I have a trait that some find hard to handle. I can be pretty forthright and cannot be arsed to lie. Consequently, I can come across as a bit of a blunt dickhead. I don't mean to be like this, but I unfortunately inherited this from my father. Also, when I was young, whenever I told a lie I would go bright red in the face, which in turn earned me the nickname 'Beetroot'. I decided early on that lying was just not worth the grief that ensued. I finish my beer and climb the stairs from the bowels of the Latest Music Bar and step into the street. It is an early Sunday afternoon and the sun is streaming down upon me. I feel a little pissed and I head towards the seafront happy with how the day has started. Little do I know that this is a day that will shape the next years of my life.

FOOTNOTES

ALEX – Still an amazing musician pushing the boundaries of his art. Still teaching and venturing into film score music. A good friend.

KEYBOARD GIRL – Took up bass guitar for fun. Has nearly finished her second year at Uni studying something really brainy. Lovely individual.

TEENAGE COOL GUY FRONTMAN – Turned out to be a very modest chap. Absolutely superb guitarist who managed to avoid the diva bug.

THIEVES BY THE CODE – This is Alex's originals band. The first time I saw these guys live they played dressed up as ghoulish pirates. They had full on makeup, which took ages to skilfully apply and looked magnificent. Nick on drums wore eye patches over both eyes, and the crowd marvelled at his skills and technique whilst not missing a single beat on the drums. What the crowd did not know was that Nick was blind and this was not stretching his skills in any way at all. True performers.

BIG FOOTNOTE

WAMA/WAYNE – I first met the man many years ago in my late teenage years. He was a few years older than me and although we drank in the same pubs we were not part of the same crowd. I knew him by his surname at the time and would always refer to him as 'Marmont'. He was a very brash and uptight character in my eyes and was well known for having something of a short fuse. Whether this is fair or not, my opinion of him was that he was a hooligan that was always getting involved in situations that led to scrapping. If truth be known I always thought he was a bit of a dick, and I had no real wish to get to know him better. I am sure he would say the same about me, but then again he probably never thought that about me as I was not the same big character to others that he appeared to be.

The first meaningful conversation I ever had with him was on a football pitch when we were playing for the same pub team in a charity match. Every time he had the ball I would scream out, "Marmont, Marmont give me the ball!" He would completely blank me and pass to someone else. This went on for the entire first half, with me relentlessly screaming and him completely ignoring my requests.

The whistle blew for half time and as we walked off the pitch he came running over to me.

In an extremely aggressive voice he said, "What's your fucking name."

"Phil."

"Do I fucking call you Nye."

"No."

"Well my fucking name is not Marmont, it is Wayne and don't you ever fucking forget it."

That was our first ever meaningful conversation, and from that point on we tolerated each other and eventually got on with one another. Many years later I moved out of the area and lost touch with the day-to-day things going on in some people's lives. I was in Brighton at a pub and standing at the end of the bar I saw a face that I recognised. It was Wayne and I was pleased to see him after so many years. I went over to catch up with my old mate to see what he had been doing.

I tapped him on the shoulder and as he turned around I said joyfully, "Wayne, how the fuck are you."

He then replied, "My name is not Wayne it is fucking Wama."

There are a lot of contemporaries of ours who never understood the name change and lots of them who had known him from childhood found it hard to call him by his new name. It took me a little time to get used to it but that was his wish, so it was no big deal. I remember asking him about his reasons for the change and it is something that I admire. He wanted to kind of reinvent himself as he didn't see anything in his current life that pertained to the way he was when he was younger. He will openly admit that he used to get into all sorts of stuff that he was not particularly proud of, and now he had a philosophy of trying to look forward.

He is a different character now. I liked him a bit years ago, but I admire him a lot these days and he was the catalyst to many things that I would go on to do. A good friend, a good role model and a frustrated lead guitarist.

CHAPTER 2 – *ET TU, BRUTE?*

Nearly two weeks had passed since the Morning Glory gig and my life at this time was not moving forward in many positive ways. I had not really thought too much about the gig in all honesty. It was an enjoyable event to witness, but it didn't make any impact upon my day-to-day life at this stage. I had no affiliation to it, no skin in the game so there was no reason it would have had any influence onto how my life was going to proceed going forward.

 At that moment in time I was living with some personal problems, such as a separation in my marriage that I was struggling to cope with. This would result in experiencing issues relating to depression that were affecting my performance at work and this in turn would find me struggling at times whilst I was adapting to a new way of living day to day. It was proving much more difficult to manage than I could have anticipated as now I had more spare time on my hands, with no discernible structure in my home life at all. I was living the single life and once the initial period of so-called freedom had worn off the reality of the situation kicked in. In all honesty I felt completely lost with no clue with what to do next. It had some superficial advantages, but I recognised that I missed having a partner. The silence of your own company with no background noise can really begin to make you question quite what the point is in being able to do what you want when you want. My only constant at the time was work where I was working as a retail manager, and although I had some great colleagues my love for the job was beginning to wane.

A recurring theme would begin to emerge where I was to become quite the risk-taker and more than willing to have a go at any madcap idea that crossed my path. This was partly fuelled by a need to have a bit of excitement, but if I am being completely honest it was mostly driven by boredom. I soon found myself becoming less and less fulfilled by day-to-day life and needed to seek out situations that could provide me with some sort of instant buzz. I became heavily influenced by a Polish chap who was one of the guys that I was sharing a house with. He went by the name of Serge. Just to give you have a little bit of background information, Serge is one of the craziest yet happiest individuals I have ever met. He was employed as a cleaner at the store that I worked at. He was constantly smiling, nothing was too much bother for him and if you needed his assistance he was always happy to help. I ended up in a house share with him for a short amount of time and he was simply one of the most eccentric people I had ever met (in a good way). He had a limited range when it came to English vocabulary, but to be fair it was far superior to my knowledge of the Polish language by quite a large margin. I tried to get him to teach me some Polish for my own dubious reasons once. I remember there was a lovely Polish girl I really liked, and I asked Serge to teach me a few words so that I could pay her a compliment and impress her. He taught me to say, "I like your arse" in Polish, which turned out to be of no use at all to me as I was trying to tell the Polish girl that I fancied that she had beautiful eyes. I remember thinking at the time that I couldn't understand why she looked so upset when I delivered such a beautiful compliment to her and didn't fully comprehend why Serge was pissing himself laughing as she responded in a forceful tone and flounced off. What always stuck with me most about Serge though was that if anyone ever asked him why he did this or that, or shall we do this or that, his answer was always the same: "WHY NOT?" He would then simply smile and crack on with whatever had been suggested to him.

"WHY NOT?" had become the answer to every decision I was now going to make from this moment forward. Now whether that is a good thing or not is open to debate, but that was where my mind was at the time, and I was going for it.

So, anyway, there I was in the pub that I helped to run as well as doing my day job (there is a random tale of how I got here, but maybe that is another book), not really knowing what I was doing but giving it a go and learning as I went along. That night we had arranged for someone to come in and run a karaoke event, which was quite a popular night out at the time. As we edged towards the beginning of the festivities, the pub was beginning to fill up with an assortment of locals that were a mixture of wannabe Beyoncé's, Madonna's, Elvis's, etc, etc. The place in question was a small local boozer that we called the Midway at the time. It had been the hub of the community for some time that had been better known as The Little Cricks in its glory days. Nothing grand about it, simply good people having a no-frills good time.

As was usually the case at these events it struggled to get going at first as the punters were filled with a mixture of nerves and sobriety, which hindered any thoughts of getting up to perform straight from the off. They required a certain amount of Dutch courage to get their creative juices flowing, so it was always a battle of attrition trying to entice the first few to make fools of themselves. It is never easy to engage a sober audience, and this is something I would encounter many times in the years ahead.

In this sort of situation, I can be a bit of an asset. Not only had I been in the pub for many hours drinking several pints of Dutch courage, but I also had my "WHY NOT" mantra on which to rely upon. I was the first to volunteer and, like a lamb to the slaughter, I then proceeded to sing a couple of numbers in order to move things along. I can't recall the tunes, but they can't have been too bad as no one had thrown anything at me, and I had received only a few friendly insults for the effort I had made. My bravado appeared to have had the desired effect as the compere was greeted with an avalanche of slips requesting that the freshly emboldened patrons have their time to bask in the karaoke spotlight. I had either given them the confidence to get up or I was the victim of an organised coup d'état as I had been so bad that anyone who followed was to be a definite improvement as far as they were concerned.

I returned to my place by the bar, propping it up whilst chatting with some mates who were giving me some interesting feedback on my performance. I then noticed that sitting at the table to the rear of the pub were Tony and Mark from the band. I walked over to say hello. We exchanged the usual pleasantries, and I sat down at their table to join them for a minute or two. They started discussing the gig from the week before and were now probing me on my thoughts and asking me lots of questions in order to get some feedback. In my head I was looking for a way out of having to answer anything that may require a direct honest answer, but soon concluded that it would be rude to cut the conversation dead. I tried to be as vague as I could, but then Tony said, "Don't worry, Phil, we know it was shit."

We all laughed. The atmosphere had instantly become a lot more relaxed, and we began swapping stories about the gig and chatting with more ease about all the funny stuff that happened on the day. Tony told me how he had felt on the day, he went on to describe in graphic detail all his feelings of sheer terror whilst the performance was taking place. As he was talking and describing his experience, we found ourselves laughing so loudly that we were getting a few stares from the karaoke crowd as our noise was drowning out the would-be Liam Gallagher giving his all to 'Wonderwall'. I swear to you we were practically crying at one stage as he was recalling his own private hell. The conversation flowed and remained quite light-hearted, and I enquired where and when their next gig would be. I was informed that they were not quite sure what they were going to be doing going forward and with a wry smile I told them that I would definitely be there to watch again. I was just about to wrap up the conversation and join my other friends when Tony said that he wanted to put a proposal to me. He then said, "How do you feel about coming along to the rehearsals and joining the band as a singer." At that point I was thinking that he must be either drunk or joking. Why would he think that I would possibly want to do that? I decided at this point to remind him of the bleeding obvious and went on to inform them that they already had a singer. Tony said it would be a good idea to have two singers in the band as this would allow for harmonies to be introduced and it would give the whole thing a different feel. Mark then told me that after what he had seen of me on the karaoke, I would easily be able to do it and then he said the words that made my ears prick up, "If nothing else it will be a laugh."

I told them that I would think about it and asked if the other band members knew about this change in direction. The reply was no, but I was assured that I had nothing to worry about as they would be having a word with the other guys in the next few days. I remember thinking at the time that I considered this to be slightly odd, but I was sure that things were fine. They gave me the time, date and address of the next practice session and I said I would think about it as I was a little interested. I said my goodbyes and then went to re-join my mates at the bar.

So, several days later I found myself standing outside a three-storey building in the middle of Portslade, which is roughly three miles west of Brighton. The signs on the door told me that this was home to a security company by day and the building appeared to be deserted apart from some lights shining out of the upstairs windows. As I stood there wondering if I had come to the right place, Tony pulled up in his car and greeted me enthusiastically. He was smiling and appeared to be quite relaxed. He took the lead and I followed as he climbed the stairs to the top floor to a small reception area, which had a small kitchen to the right and two doors in front of us. I could hear music coming from the other side of the closed doors in front of us. We were then joined in the waiting area by Wama, Clive, Mark and eventually Lockie. They were welcoming enough, but I did sense that Lockie was not 100 per cent happy. The door in front of us opened and out stepped the teenagers I had seen play the week before, followed by Alex and G. They had just finished their weekly lesson and now it was time for the Morning Glory boys to have their time with the professionals. Alex and G gave me a nice welcome and we made our way into the studio to begin the masterclass.

Now, before we progress any further into what happened in the initial rehearsal, I feel it would help to give you some context as to who knows who, and how their relationships were formed.

From what I can gather the band was created by Tony and Mark. They had been having music lessons with Alex and G, and they then invited

Wama, and another guitarist called Tim to join. They then decided to try and get a singer, Wama suggested his friend Lockie. Apparently, he had seen him performing in the semi-final of a karaoke competition at the old Nellie Peck pub in Brighton, and he thought at the time that he was competent. Lockie knew Tony already due to them being in the same line of work. Tim, the original guitarist, had already left the band and Lockie had put forward his childhood friend Clive to replace him. Clive had never met any of the others before he joined the band.

Now to give you a bit of context as to how I know everyone at this point. I didn't know Clive or Mark at all and the only time I had ever seen them was at the first gig that they had played. I had only known Tony for about a year, and this was as a casual acquaintance from drinking in the same pub. Lockie I knew to say hello to through a small number of mutual acquaintances, which leaves Wama, the one I probably knew the best, but not in a really close pal kind of way. So, if you can make sense of that we shall now move back into the rehearsal room.

Everyone gathered around, there was a quick chat about how everyone was doing and then talk turned towards the gig the previous week. Alex and G were supportive and complimentary with their comments, and they thought that the boys did very well in their opinion. Wama seemed happy with the way it went, Clive appeared to agree with everything and Lockie thought it had gone pretty well. All fairly positive so far, and the atmosphere can only be described as cordial. However, Tony and Mark were not of the same opinion, and soon there was a bit of an awkward vibe filling the air. I stood to the side and was thinking to myself, *What the fuck am I doing here?* There was a definite feeling of tension hanging in the air and different factions working against each other. A few grievances were aired, and I began to second guess what I was told and was now thinking that this didn't appear to be the fun time I had been promised. Alex and G brought the temperature in the room to a more civilised level by going through the performance and focusing on the good points. Any elements that were not so good were talked about and dealt with in a proactive way, which had the desired effect of bringing things to an amicable conclusion.

Focus now shifted towards me. Unbeknownst to me it appeared not everyone in the band had been informed I would be coming along. In later years Wama admitted he remembered how awkward he felt at the time, especially as he had introduced Lockie into the band. He also reminded me that at that time we were not really friends. We were never nasty to each other, but there was a kind of, "Oh no, not him again" whenever we would come into contact in shared social circles.

The discussion then turned to what the plan was regarding me, and Tony suggested I might do some singing. Lockie remarked: "What am I, the fucking teasmade?" That raised the temperature of the room again somewhat. It was suggested that I would provide some backing harmonies and maybe sing a lead on one or two songs going forward, but Lockie was still the lead singer. It didn't bother me as I was quite happy to see how things might pan out. I would happily just go with the flow. The guys started going through their repertoire and I took a back seat to watch them at work. Alex and G were working through the dynamics of a song bit by bit, and just by watching them I was getting an appreciation of how song structure worked and what exactly goes into performing with other players.

This went on for a while and I was encouraged to join in with some backing vocals to see if they complemented the overall feel of the song. I thought it was going OK, but I had never done this before and as such was not totally sure. There was no denying there was a very strange atmosphere in the room and I got the sense that not all were completely happy campers. Alex suggested that maybe they do some work on one of the songs they had performed at the gig, as in his mind it was always good to look at where they could make some small improvements. The band proceeded to work through 'The Man Who Sold the World' by David Bowie. As they were progressing through the verses, Lockie was struggling a little with the timing and the formulation of the lyrics. There were several starts and stops, as over and over again they tried to make some progress. You could see that Lockie was looking agitated and was beginning to become slightly tetchy. Tony and Mark were facing each other and rolling their eyes, and not in a very disguised way either. I noticed the distinct lack of smiles on the faces of any of the guys and sensed that something was about to give.

Suddenly, mid-song, Lockie stopped and shouted, "Fuck it!" What followed was a short period of silence before he bellowed, "It's no good! There are too many words in it, it doesn't fucking fit in."

Some more silence followed before someone said, "Well, Bowie managed it".

More silence, before Alex realised he needed to bring everything back on track and suggested that we move on and come back to it another time. I bet if you asked Alex now, he would tell you that teaching the kids was a lot easier and certainly not as dramatic.

Alex steered us towards working on 'Maggie May' by Rod Stewart. It was suggested that I give it a go and I was fine with that. Maybe we were doing this to give Lockie time to cool off, but I can't help thinking this was probably winding the poor sod up even more. I was handed the lyrics, and as I had obviously heard the song many times before, what could possibly go wrong? Lockie stood over to the side of the room and didn't appear to look happy about this at all. He didn't say anything, but deep down I knew he was festering inside and maybe thinking up different scenarios for my death. The rest of the boys played, and I sang. It was enjoyable and although it might not have been great, I am happy to report that it wasn't a complete disaster either. I managed to get all the words in, and out of the corner of my eye I could see Tony and Mark nodding slightly at each other in approval. I thought they must be easily pleased, but future events would prove this was not a correct assumption to make. We went through the song a few more times and each time appeared to be an improvement on the last. So, I had passed my first little test and I enjoyed the experience much more than I expected to. Lockie was then summoned back to the mic (from the naughty step) and the guys spent the rest of the session practising some of the other tunes. I was back to looking on from the side-lines and thinking that it was quite an eye opener to see how a band functions and develops musically. It was also fascinating to me to see how a band can function emotionally and quite easy to underestimate the politics in play. Lots of bands are made up of differing levels of ability, over-inflated egos and high levels of sensitivity. Forming alliances and political manoeuvring amongst a group is certainly not as rare as you would imagine, and it can be akin to some of the best Greek tragedies or modern-day soap operas. In hindsight, many lessons were learnt at this stage. This would eventually give me a greater understanding of how to proceed with future projects, but I realise I am getting ahead of myself at this point, so let us return to where we were.

The session came to an end. I received some kind comments, and all was reasonably good as I said my goodbyes to the guys. Afterwards, I went for a beer with Tony. As he quizzed me about what I thought and whether I would give it a go, I found myself weighing up the pros and cons. I did think it was fun and at that moment in time the alternatives for things to do on a Tuesday night were limited. At least it would keep me out of the pub for a few hours. The guys, on face value, seemed alright. Clive was a nice chap, Wama was not the complete knob I was expecting, Tony and Mark were supportive for some reason, and Lockie did not kill me. I remembered the mantra that Serge had instilled into my psyche, and I answered, "WHY NOT?"

So, for the next few weeks I turned up, got to know the guys a bit more and found that I was being asked to do a bit more week on week. As the weeks were going by it was noticeable that Lockie was becoming more and more tense, and he didn't seem to be finding the experience much fun at all. A few artistic disagreements (squabbles) between him, Tony and Mark didn't necessarily help the situation either.

The next week Lockie didn't turn up for practice and it turned out he was no longer in the band. At the time I thought this was a decision he had made, and that Wama had been in touch with him to try and convince him to change his mind. To my knowledge Clive was also trying to sort out the situation, but to no avail. Lockie had made up his mind. That is how I had read the situation for all these years, and it is only in gathering information for this chapter that I found out Lockie was informed by text message that he was no longer required by the band. Talk about savage! You hear stories of boyfriends or girlfriends being dumped by text and although it is never easy splitting up from a lover, at least have the guts to do it face to face.

Et tu, Brute? It amazes me how we can all have differing interpretations of events and there is no absolute truth, but only your own take on an event that happens in your life.

The following week I turned up to the rehearsal to find out I was the new lead singer of Morning Glory. But not for long, as I was determined to change that stupid bloody name.

FOOTNOTES

PUB – The pub in question was at that time called the Midway but it will always be known to me as its previous name, which was The Little Cricks in Church Road, Portslade. It was run by for many years by the wonderful couple Sue and Gerry Lawlor. Gerry was a thickset no-nonsense Irishman who did not suffer fools at all. When he called you a 'coont' it was a term of endearment.

QUOTE – I asked Clive many years later about his initial thoughts when I first turned up at the rehearsal. He said, "Thank fuck for that. He's not a guitarist." This would have a funny context later as you will find out.

ALEX – He once remarked to Wama that band politics were harder than a romantic relationship.

'THE MAN WHO SOLD THE WORLD' – In independent tests carried out all over the world, all studies have concluded that you *can* fit all the words in.

AK/DK – This is the name of G's originals band. I give them a mention not just because of knowing Graham, but also into maybe pushing a few of you readers to go and check out their stuff. Ed and G are a double-drum and double-synth duo who produce what is simply described as energy-packed noise. They tour extensively in the UK and Europe where they are invited to grace the stage of many great festivals. The whole show is a feast for the eyes as well as the ears and the spectacle that is generated lends to an out-of-body experience.

BIG FOOTNOTE

DAVID BOWIE – A very tenuous link to the band but an interesting story as far as I am concerned. Bowie is treated like a god by quite a few of the members and I myself have nothing but the greatest admiration for the man. We've covered a few of his songs in our time and I wrote an original number about the great man the day after he died. We only performed it a couple of times live, but we did record it on our album so it cannot have been completely shit. The story I have of the idol is that whenever I am asked about the best and worst live gig I have ever been to, I reply I saw both of these one after the other and Bowie falls into the worst category.

I went many years ago to the Phoenix Festival that was held in Stratford-upon-Avon. There were some genuinely great acts on that year, but the fact that Bowie was headlining one of the nights was the decisive factor in going along to this hedonistic weekend. It lived up to a lot of expectations and it reached a point of pure Nirvana when I witnessed a performance from a relatively unknown newcomer who had just released her first album. That newcomer was Alanis Morrissette and the performance she put on was one like I had never witnessed before. It had everything. The songs were banging, the musicianship was quality and the way she expressed herself in every song is something that will stay with me for all time. By the time she had finished I knew I had witnessed the greatest gig I had ever been to.

Friends find it surprising when I tell them that at the same festival I also witnessed the worst gig I had ever been to, and they are even more surprised when I tell them it was David Bowie. At the time he was experimenting with a new sound, and he did this under the guise of the band Tin Machine. It was a festival for fuck's sake and 40,000 people had not paid all that money to listen to an hour and a half of what he had been working on in his garage for the last six months. It was shit and the biggest let-down I had experienced at a live event. I admired him a little bit for breaking new ground and not caring what the masses thought about his art, but I also thought it showed total disregard for the event and the audience. It didn't stop me admiring him, but I selfishly wished he could have played a few songs for me to drunkenly sing along to.

CHAPTER 3 – OUR FIRST DIRTY WEEKEND

So, it was a new dawn, and the first order of play was to get rid of that bloody awful band name. Many ideas were discussed and although I don't recall many of the alternatives, I can testify that most of them were either complete garbage or plain obscene. We eventually agreed on the name 'Dirty Weekend'. I am fairly sure it was my idea, but if others want to come forward with compelling evidence to the contrary I am more than happy to concede. Wama was particularly happy with this choice as it encompassed the whole idea around his beloved hometown of Brighton. Later on, it would inspire him to write one of his first songs. Anyway, this was how we progressed. It was a Tuesday night, and we all met up just before half past seven to have our two-hour lesson with Alex and G. The average age of the band at this point was a very sprightly 47. Not exactly a boy band I know, but we had grander plans than just being pin-ups on some teenage girl's bedroom wall. The old adage goes, "You can't teach an old dog new tricks" – well, we were about to find out whether Alex and G were up to teaching these old dogs. This would certainly be a test of not only their teaching abilities, but also their levels of patience putting up with general bullshitery. They would either dine out on our success for years to come or pretend they didn't know us. I did wonder what they genuinely thought of us at the time. Were we a project that they derived some pleasure from or just some shmucks who helped to pay the bills?

At the next lesson, the atmosphere in the room seemed to be a little bit friendlier and definitely much more stress-free. This I put down to the fact that some random unknown had not been brought into the room and declared to be a second drummer or bass player.

The general plan was formulated around the next Rock School showcase gig. This meant there would be something real for us to aim towards and would make us more serious about how we approached things. It would be a similar format to the previous gig with a setlist of up to six songs. I was the newbie and needed to be brought up to speed as the other guys were pros compared with me and had been in the game for at least four months. I had to get up to speed fast and after about half an hour I think I had reached their level. They already had a few songs in the bank, but it was important to start working on a few new ones so the setlist would be a bit different. I was glad I was getting to know Clive a little better. He was a big bloke and from a distance looked slightly menacing, but that all disappeared as soon as he opened his mouth. He came across as such a gentle soul. He was fairly new to the guitar and up until this point had been pretty much self-taught. I would learn lots more about him as we went on. Apparently, he was a founder member of the B52s, which was an American football team based in Brighton. He had a black belt in some sort of martial art shizzle. He was a mad fanboy of the ultra-heavy German band Rammstein, and on top of that he was the biggest Harry Potter geek I had ever come across. I was sure that one day he would become as accomplished with his guitar as he was with his wand.

With his newfound love of guitar playing, it obviously took time for him to take in the information and techniques being taught, which meant progress could appear slow at times. It was the same for Wama, as he too was something of an apprentice in the noble art of axe-wielding. At the time I didn't really know this was probably quite a weird time for Clive. It is only now, on reflection, that I realise he was introduced into the band by Lockie, so when Lockie left he really didn't know any of the other guys very well at all. I wouldn't have blamed Clive if he had treated me with some sort of distain. I can tell you now, though, that I think he was incapable of doing that, because that is not in his nature. The world would be a far better place if there were more Clive's in it. The format of the teaching tended to go like this: Alex, being the guitar guru, would focus his teaching time with Clive and Wama; whilst G, the drum genius and multi-instrumentalist would concentrate more on Mark and Tony. It was not apparent which one of the pair had the harder task or the thinner end of the wedge. I would sit to the side and just read the lyrics to whatever song we were working on, trying to memorise them but failing miserably. Most of my time in the lessons was spent waiting around and I would disappear out the back every so often to not only have a cigarette on the flat roof, but also to escape some of the god-awful din that you were bound to get when something was being murdered (learnt) for the first time. This would be the pattern for the first hour of the lesson and then the last hour was spent trying to perform what had been learnt as a band.

In the main, this was done in a fun and easy-going way, but if a particular song were proving tricky it could become a little tiresome going over and over the same thing time and time again. Listening to the same bar of music being repeated 50-odd times can feel quite soul destroying, although many of today's biggest artists seem to make a reasonable living out of it. It felt at times that Clive was being singled out for criticism. It was not really verbal at this stage, but you could pick up gestures and body language that was a tad negative.

Once practice was over, more often than not, Tony and I would find ourselves going to a pub called the Harbour View to chill out and chat about what we had been practising. After a couple of weeks, Mark on a started joining us, and it was at this point that the Harbour View pub became our unofficial headquarters. There was no sinister reason why Wama and Clive didn't join us, as Clive needed to get back to the other side of Brighton and Wama usually had an early start for work the next day. This place would soon begin to have a major influence on future events. We would have a couple of pints and generally just discuss the usual subjects of work, relationships, interests, etc. We would talk about music that we liked and would suggest different songs that could be good for us to cover. It was noticeable even at this early stage that our tastes in music were remarkably diverse and we didn't necessarily like all the same stuff. I was beginning to wonder whether this was a good or a bad thing as most bands tend to concentrate on a certain sound or genre. I didn't mind doing covers, but I really didn't want to do all the clichéd numbers that the cheesy function bands did. In fact, I didn't want to be seen as a function band at all. Cover band I was happy to do, function band could fuck right off.

I concluded it was a good thing that we didn't like the same stuff and many a Tuesday night in the Harbour View was spent coming up with lots of different suggestions of songs to learn. We spent a lot of money in the jukebox trying to convince each other why we should cover a certain song. I'm fairly sure this is where we formed the basis of our future setlists as we were quite happy to do songs people knew but that you didn't hear many bands play in pubs.

Also, with our setlists there was something for everyone. One minute you would be listening to something that may not float your boat, the next you could be moshing your head off and this could be followed by an anthemic lighters-in-the-air moment.

The Harbour View was a large traditional boozer located on the coast road in Portslade, about four miles west of Brighton. It was positioned on the corner of a block that was dominated by the empty shell of a warehouse which will have some relevance a little later on in our story. The factory had been deserted for many years, and this behemoth of a building was left to sit and decay as various planning applications for its use were considered and rejected. There was some talk that it might just be demolished to make way for a massive block of flats. There were rumours of it becoming a leisure complex with an ice rink, as well as various other plans that never got the nod of approval. So, in the years it sat there doing nothing, its only function seemed to be to provide a home for pigeons and rats.

The pub itself had been there a long time, built in the Victorian era to service workers from the nearby port and gasworks, and I would imagine that it had been busy back in the day… Like most boozers it had gone through a number of different guises over the years. It was probably best known when it was named The Alexandra and it was a favourite hangout for bikers from the 1970s onwards. It effectively became their clubhouse and there were many photos showing large numbers of hairy Vikings standing beside their shiny metal horses.

It was now being run by a chap called Sam, alongside his partner Penny. Sam was of Iranian heritage and had a dry wit. He was not everyone's cup of tea as he didn't really tolerate idiots and unfortunately the levels of racism even in 2011 were a lot higher than they are today. It wasn't a busy pub at all, as this place – like many – was to fall victim to the changing trends and restrictions the pub game was buckling under. It didn't seem fashionable any more to go out to a pub like this, so it just about scraped by with the patronage of its small band of regulars. Passing trade was not going to sustain this business as it was positioned in an area that was mainly commercial businesses such as garages, furniture-makers and the like. At the top of the road was a big modern building that was the headquarters of some new Christian church movement – and they were certainly not big drinkers.

Walking through the doors of the pub you were greeted by a parrot sitting in its cage in a sizeable conservatory that had views on to the busy coast road. As it was called the Harbour View, I can only assume that maybe 50 years ago there was such a view before the ugly structures over the road had been built. There was a long traditional wooden bar that stretched more than half the length of the pub. Beyond that was a large area at the back where you would find the pool table, dartboard and jukebox. I hadn't realised that this space would have such a big impact on the band's life. It was soon to become our own Wembley Stadium, and it would provide us with a chance to improve our musical prowess as well as giving us the opportunity to make many happy memories. The toilets flanked the back wall and if you carried on past the ladies' loo you were led out to the back area. I call it the 'back area' as it certainly bore no resemblance to a garden unless you think weeds and tarmac constitute a floral display. It was quite a large space in which was housed no more than two benches and, inexplicably, one of those old springy horses that you find in a children's playground, which was happily rusting away. This was maybe an attempt to become the Disneyland of Portslade, but it didn't seem to be having the desired effect of bringing in the crowds. This space was quite frankly used for one reason only: smoking, whether it be normal tobacco or something slightly more exotic. If you had an exotic fag the springy horse was something to avoid.

I had been coming in here from time to time in the past, but I was certainly not what you would call a regular. I had started to visit the pub a couple of years before when our beloved Gerry and Sue from the Little Cricks around the corner had retired and sold the pub to a management company, which then succeeded in turning what was a thriving and jovial place, into a den of dickheads who were far more preoccupied with getting as much marching powder up their noses as they could. The Little Cricks' regulars used to do a charity quiz every Sunday. This had been running for many years and the money they had raised was indeed very impressive. They were a bunch of the nicest down-to-earth people you could wish to meet and had got to the stage where they had had enough of mixing with idiots. They needed a new home and Sam at the Harbour View was happy to home them, which in turn led by default to the decent people from the Little Cricks slowly migrating over. It wasn't quite the same, but it wasn't far off either. This is what led me here on a regular basis and I soon became quite friendly with Sam.

So, anyway, there I was with Tony and Mark on Tuesday nights having a pint and a debrief about practice, and as we were usually the only ones in, Sam took an interest and was soon joining in with our conversations. He would prove to become quite pivotal in our future progression. Throughout the year I had had a number of changes in my own personal circumstances. I don't mind admitting that in the previous year or so I had what can only be described as a mental breakdown. In this day and age, we call them mental health issues, but however you wrap it up it was a fucking awful part of my life. I was now living on one of the floating platforms on the Marina, which is bearable during the summer months, but during the winter the place is a ghost town, and it's not a lot of fun bobbing up and down all night when the weather is slightly inclement. I was still working for Asda – it had been 20-plus years – and I was currently one of the night managers of the store situated at Brighton Marina. Working nights was not ideal for my lifestyle, but I was on a rather good salary thanks to the years I had put in.

My mum became unwell. She had been diagnosed with cancer. With this news I moved back into the family home in Hove that she shared with my brother Ian. It was decided that with me helping to cover Ian's wages we were in a position where he could take up to six months off work using a benefit called a 'career break'. This meant he could stay at home and provide some much-needed day-to-day care and assistance for Mum. Mum was going downhill fast and to see the decline in her memory, and the changes in her behaviour first-hand were heart-breaking. It needs to be pointed out that I had the luxury of being able to take myself away from this by going to work each day. My brother didn't have the same luxury and was there for the majority of the hard graft. It is ridiculously hard to truly express my admiration for my brother, but it came as no surprise to me the way he stood up and dealt with the situation. The man has the purest of hearts and lives life in a simple black-and-white kind of way. He has his weird mannerisms and can be a complete pain in the arse, which have served him well being a Manchester United supporter.

Above all this, he is himself and I am proud to have him as my brother. Sadly, Mum passed away within a couple of months and in a way, it was maybe better that her illness didn't cause her pain for a longer period. I won't go into too much more detail as this is a book about the band after all, so I will just leave it as a matter of fact that my brother was a fucking superstar and I love him dearly.

So, there I was, living back in Hove and visiting some of my old haunts. I was a frequent drinker in the pub over the road called the Three Graces and as well as catching up with some old faces I began to meet a few new ones as well. With my new interest in music, I was starting to have some interesting conversations with like-minded characters. I became very pally with one particular older gentleman by the name of John Hickey who was in his early 60s and had an abundance of tales from when he was in a band in his younger days. I'm making this introduction now, as John H will feature as we go further into the story.

The pub had recently undergone some changes and was under new management. It was now being run by two girls, one from Derby going by the name of Tree (another introduction to a recurring character in the book). I instantly warmed to her. The other was Kiri, a pretentious, up-her-own-arse bitch, who was such a waste of space that I will spend no more time writing any words about her. Whilst I am introducing some people I might as well mention that they employed a young barman by the name of Adam, who turned out to be some sort of thrash-metal-kind-of-wannabe rock god, another one who will contribute to this rich web of intrigue.

So that is a snapshot of where I was, but let us get back to the band. We had a date for my first foray into the world of showbiz, and we were informed by Alex and G that the next Rock School extravaganza would take place in July at the Latest Music Bar. It was a little while off yet, so there was no real sense of panic setting in at that particular point in time. The first step was to work out what we were going to play. I would like to tell you that we went through an extensive process of narrowing down our best songs from a catalogue of critically acclaimed classics, but as we didn't know many songs the narrowing-down process was not going to take an awful lot of time.

We finally decided on our setlist, which would consist of five covers and, bravely, one original that had been written by Wama.

The covers, if I remember rightly, were the obligatory 'Maggie May', of course; Bruce Springsteen's 'Dancing in the Dark' (which would be sung by Wama); 'When You Were Young' by The Killers; 'Creep' by Radiohead; and, lastly, a song called 'No Excuses' by Alice in Chains. Not one of us had ever heard of this last song and I am quite sure it was an attempt by Alex and G to show off how hip they were and how Avant Garde they could be with their teaching. Deep down I am sure that we all thought it was the biggest load of pretentious crap we had ever heard but we all kept it to ourselves for fear of losing any street cred. Rehearsals of these songs progressed pretty well in the main, and I remember feeling particularly confident with how The Killers song sounded. Years later I would change my opinion, but I digress. 'Creep' was a tour de force, and I was actually surprised to find that I possessed what I was led to believe was called a vocal range (who knew?). 'Maggie May' was a piece of piss, as I had done this before, and the Alice in Chains song was just three minutes of embarrassment where I had to look like I was earnestly feeling every word of this angst-ridden drivel.

Wama was bringing his Springsteen to life and making Bruce's voice seem more like a young Charlotte Church in comparison. My god could Wama get that swallowing-razor-blade voice going. When he sang 'Dancing in the Dark', you really did know what it was like to wake up in the morning after one of the heaviest nights out and all you want is that glass of water to ease your weary tonsils. But bravo to him for also trying to incorporate a bit of harmonica into it as well. I didn't suspect it at the time, but this was the first stage of what was to become his fetish for accessorising and showmanship. This was the birthplace of Wama T. Barnum.

That left us with the original we were going to do. I see this is my opportunity to dedicate a little space in this book to give you an insight into the tune that was a major launchpad for the band. It was called 'Brighton March'. I know it as 'the hooligan song' and to this day I maintain that it was not a Dirty Weekend song. Instead, I insist it was a Morning Glory song as that was the name of the band when it was recorded, and it was before my time. No doubt Wama will disagree, but the facts are on my side. (I persuaded Wama to write a piece about this song, which I have included in a footnote at the end of the next chapter.) Back to the plot. We had spent a long time rehearsing and refining our setlist. It hadn't been all plain sailing and there were moments where a few heated debates did crop up. To be fair, this was mainly between Mark and Tony as they were prone to throw many toys out of the pram and at each other. It was mainly to do with timing. It sounded all right to me, but what did I know? They were the engine room of the band, apparently. Clive was progressing OK, but you felt sometimes it was not at an acceptable rate for some people. Wama was keeping his head down to concentrate on his parts and would occasionally appear with some new pedal to use. It seemed that quite a bit of the session was being taken up with Alex giving Wama a lesson on his new toy as he would carefully explain how to set it up. It seemed wasted on him, as the following week we would wait for Wama as he faffed around still not knowing how to attach it properly.

I still had all my lyrics on bits of paper on a cheap and tacky music stand, and I was not making any progress in retaining the words in my head at all. In the main, though, spirits were fairly high and there was a lot of fun and laughter to be witnessed at these sessions. We practised the set over and over again, and we finally got to the stage where we were happy that we were not going to get it much better. I remember I was having a lot of fun with what we were doing and that the band had become a nice distraction from reality.

As a group of individuals, I also thought we had bonded well and that I could now consider these fellow old gits good friends. It almost felt like the band was bordering on family as there were arguments as well as laughter, and over the last month or so we had spent quite a lot of time together. As well as the regular weekly lesson we were also meeting up several times a week to practise the setlist continuously. All the hard graft had been put in and that coming weekend was the gig at the Latest Music Bar, so now was the moment to see if we were to become the next big music sensation.

The morning of the gig finally arrived, and I wasn't feeling particularly nervous. I didn't know whether this was a good or a bad thing. I had nothing to really compare it with apart from some work events when I had to speak in front of a large group of people. I was aware today's crowd were not exactly going to be akin to the one the Beatles experienced at Shea Stadium in America. (For younger readers think of Jedward playing at Croke Park in Ireland.)

I had arranged to have my daughter Madelaine with me on the day. She was 11 years old and for some reason I had harboured the illusion that this was going to be an excellent way to have some daddy–daughter bonding time. I mean, how cool must it be for her to have a father who is the lead singer of a hard-hitting and non-conforming local rock band. I imagined that she would go into school on Monday and would hold court as all her friends surrounded her asking for the latest update on what the band were working on, or what their favourite crisp flavours were. Do they prefer puppies or kittens? (On second thoughts probably not particularly good examples of questions).

So, as I say, how cool must it be? Well, apparently, not very cool at all based on her complete lack of excitement. We made our way into town and were accompanied by another brother of mine, Kev. I had asked him to come along so I had someone to keep Maddie company whilst I was off doing rockstar stuff. He was very agreeable to do this, which came as a pleasant surprise, and I was grateful towards my brother for stepping up to help me in my hour of need. On reflection, I now realise his motives were not so Christian. If I were in his shoes and I was presented with the opportunity of a front-row seat to watch him make a complete tit of himself then wild horses could not have dragged me there fast enough.

We arrived at the venue and went downstairs to the performance area so we could soundcheck before the baying crowds were let in to rush for their places at the front of the mosh pit (one can dream).

Maddie was looking suitably unimpressed as she surveyed her dad's new church. I sauntered over to the other guys and said my hellos. Everyone appeared to be looking fairly relaxed at that point, although it was mid-morning, and they were probably not yet awake enough to fully grasp that they were standing at the scene of the last crime they committed. We were first to soundcheck as we were the last ones performing. This was my first ever soundcheck and I imagined it was going to be an exciting insight into the razzmatazz of the biz. It started with Tony being asked to sit behind the drumkit and to hit his bass drum at short intervals over and over again. This was because all the drums are miked up and the levels had to be altered. This exercise was repeated for every single fucking piece of equipment he had on the kit. Anyway, after what seemed like a fortnight, we finally got to the end of the drum's setup. I was now realising the art of the soundcheck was not as sexy as I had imagined. The sound engineer went through the other band members one by one, and it seemed he was losing the will to live as he gave Clive, Mark and Wama instructions. Clive, especially, seemed to be having a staring contest with his amp – and he was winning. Wama was staring at his amp a lot as well but seeing as he was sporting his now obligatory dark glasses it was hard to ascertain the result.

It was finally my time to shine, and I started doing the old, "One, one, one, two, two, one, two, two, two, one, one; check, check, check." I couldn't even get THESE bloody lyrics right. I glanced over and spotted Maddie looking at me, and I tried to work out if this was in admiration or pity. Once we were all individually sound checked, the band were asked to play a bit of a song that we would be performing, including any backing vocals. Wama would be doing some BVs (technical term) as the others didn't seem that keen to have a microphone in front of them and they had obviously decided that Wama was the best singer, which was a worry in itself.

Tony counted us in and to my utter surprise everyone came in at the same time. We did a verse and a chorus of 'Maggie May' before being asked to stop. To my mind it sounded passable, and I thought we might just get away with this. I glanced over to Maddie and Kev who were both smiling and chatting to each other. I went over and asked Maddie what she thought, and she answered with one word, "Loud." I was quite pleased with that critique in all seriousness and in the realms of one-word answers it wasn't the most offensive I have heard. The rest of the band seemed pleased and there was a bullish can-do attitude starting to emerge. Wama asked me (not for the first time) if I really did need to use the music stand as in his opinion it made us look amateurish. My reply was, "Yes I bloody do," as my lyrical retention superpower was yet to see the light of day. In terms of looking 'amateurish' I thought the fact that this was my first gig and his last one was not exactly Pink Floyd live from fucking Pompeii, meant he should shut the fuck up.

One of the other bands were preparing to do their soundcheck and I saw this as an ideal opportunity to get out of the war zone, go upstairs, order a beer, and go outside and smoke a hundred cigarettes. With this in mind I abandoned my child into the care of my idiot brother and announced I needed some time to prepare myself.

The upstairs part of the venue was beginning to fill up and the coffee machine behind the bar was working overtime as the parents of the younger bands were discussing 50 different things to do with an avocado. I recognised a few faces and realised that some of the guys from work were there, as well as one or two old mates. They were obviously here to support me in the same way crowds in Roman times flocked to the colosseum to witness a good kill. I thanked them for coming and then made my way downstairs to prepare with the rest of the gang.

The usual format ensued, and once again Alex and G welcomed everyone to the show, passing a comment about being able to witness the improvement everyone has made. I assumed they were including us in this and was supremely confident we would live up to this seeing as the bar had been set so low at the previous gig.

The first band up were the incredibly young pretenders. Still no band name, which to me just smacked of plain laziness on their part. Keyboard girl was back looking positively numb with excitement and I did hope she would last the course this time. They went through their set, and much like last time the end of their show brought thunderous roars of approval. They were followed by the teenagers (again no band name) and again the travelling fan base gave them the royal thumbs up – although judging by the band's reaction you wondered why they bothered supporting this bunch of miserable, hormone-addled, angst-ridden gits.

A short interval, and very soon it would be us strutting our stuff. I looked around at the band and recognised a look that I had seen before. It wasn't the look of love but one of fear. We took to the stage and hit the ground running with the Springsteen number. Wama was singing lead and I was doing backing vocals. I realised it was quite hard to stand on a stage without an instrument unless you are some great dancer, or you look like a supermodel. I should point out that I am not a great dancer so only 50 per cent down (ha ha). We got through the song and the applause was just enough to not strip our souls from our bodies. The next song was The Killers track, and we were joined onstage by Alex for this one. The reasoning for that was that, whilst rehearsing, it was agreed that the main guitar part was "rather technical", and we found out that we were not yet at the technical stage. This was the first song with me on lead vocals and armed with my piece of paper and my shitty music stand I had everything I required. A good workman does not blame his tools and mine were fully functioning.

It is hard to describe the feeling of being up there. I couldn't see much as the lights were shining into my face and as such it was tricky to gauge the audience's reaction during the song. All I can say is that when it finished, and we received what I considered to be loud claps and cheering, I felt like I was in another body. You do get a major adrenaline rush that can only be akin to some kind of surge that you might get from certain drugs. My confidence grew after that song and the rest of the set went by in a blur. When we came to the end, the audience were supportive and many were cheering, clapping and, above all, smiling. I looked around at the other guys and they were smiling as well. They still looked scared and nervous, but they didn't look beaten and deflated. We hung around for a little bit afterwards and talked a little about the show, but we would leave the full debrief until we all met at the next practice. This was probably the first time my brother Kev had met the members of the band and was also the first time I had met Linda, Gill, Wendy and Alison – the partners of Clive, Wama, Tony and Mark, in that order. I was the only single person in the band so I looked forward to being the only one who would be able to enjoy the company of the hordes of groupies that would be heading in our direction. I had dallied with some exotic relationships recently, but in all honesty my single-life experience was not really filling me with joy. I was a little jealous of the other guys as their partners seemed really nice and looking at how they supported their menfolk make tits of themselves brought a little tear of joy to my eye.

We all said our goodbyes as everyone had other commitments. It was still only about three o'clock as we stepped out into the Sunday Brighton sunshine, and I suggested to Kev and Maddie that we make our way back to Hove to get something to eat.

We hopped on to the bus and were soon walking into The Three Graces pub where we could get a roast. We found a table and I went to the bar to get some drinks. Tree was serving as I knew she would be, and I was telling her about the gig and how it went. I ordered the food and returned to Kev and Maddie at the table. We were generally having a good laugh talking about the gig when Maddie asked me why we had come into this pub. Kev pointed at Tree who was over the other side of the room and said, "I think you will find it's because of her." Maddie smiled, Kev laughed, and I went bright red. It had been quite a day. My very first gig, and this was just the start.

FOOTNOTES

LITTLE CRICKS QUIZZERS – Over the years this bunch of reprobates were responsible for raising thousands of pounds for several charities. The quizzers included Nick, Kaye, Neil, Linda, Julian, Dave, Samir, Ian, Stuart and some others whose names I cannot remember, but they were all great individuals.

GERRY AND SUE LAWLOR – Landlord and landlady of the Little Cricks in Portslade who provided us all with so many good memories. Sadly missed, but never forgotten.

ADAM SEDGEWICK – Frontman and guitarist of a band called King Leviathan, which specialised in death thrash metal. I often said to him that I couldn't stand his band, but I knew they were exceptionally good at what they did.

'BRIGHTON MARCH' – An original song by Morning Glory, so don't go expecting to see it on any future Dirty Weekend greatest hits album.

TREE McCAULEY – Future squeeze perhaps? I am the first person she met when she came down from Derby. How unlucky is that?

MADDIE NYE – Long-suffering daughter who wonders when I will grow up. I said in the introduction that this book is my perception of how things transpired. After writing my version of the gig I rang Maddie and asked for her memories of it. I showed her a draft of this chapter and she sent me this following message:

"That was bloody brilliant. It is interesting though as from your perspective you had the impression that I didn't really care about it. My memories are of me being nervous for you and I had a feeling of being a bit sick, but as soon as you did The Killers song, I felt myself well up and I was really proud of you. I was surprised really as I thought it was half-decent. It was a relief in all honesty."

CHAPTER 4 – ROCKIN' WITH THE ROMANS

Riding the tidal wave of euphoria we had experienced from the first gig (poetic licence) and celebrating the fact we were still talking to each other, we set out to further improve our skills and to build the foundations for the ensuing world domination.

We resumed our lessons with our musical Svengalis on a Tuesday night and the format of the sessions didn't alter too much. The goal at this stage was to get better at mastering our instruments, but also to increase our catalogue of songs because our setlist was slightly limited to say the least. The small selection of cover songs we were working on at the time included the likes of 'Pinball Wizard' by the Who, 'Satisfaction' by the Rolling Stones and others that seem to escape me for some reason. It could be that they were so bad that I have developed some kind of mental block to erase the memory of my contempt for them.

Things seemed to be going quite nicely and we were fairly happy with the pace at which we were learning, so this made for an incredibly happy camp indeed. This oasis of calm was soon to be shattered though, when Wama delivered some news that would throw a major spanner into our current mood of tranquillity – he informed us that he had secured us our first proper gig. Now, I know you may be thinking the whole point of our existence as a band was to aim towards occasions such as these and that it should have come as good news, as well as something that was both exciting and challenging. The issue was not that we finally had a gig, but that it in four weeks and we had maybe six songs locked in and probably about another five on the go.

With my limited knowledge of how many songs were required I felt we were a good 12 songs short at the very least. I suppose we could do the 12-inch remix versions of the covers to pad them out a bit, but I was fairly sure we weren't going to get away with Clive and Wama doing five-minute guitar solos in each song. God only knows what kind of merry hell that would sound like as I imagined smoke bellowing from the amps as well as the audience's ears. There was no other way around it. We were going to have to go into overdrive and start taking this shit seriously in order to not only sound respectable, but to do a show that lasted more than half an hour.

This meant that as well as our usual practice night on a Tuesday we were now going to have to put in the heavy graft and start practicing several nights a week at the very least.

At that stage in my personal life things had taken a turn in the romance stakes. I had been going out with Tree, the girl from the pub across the road, for a little while and was wondering if these extra practice sessions would have a detrimental impact on my Casanova wooing opportunities. When I say I was seeing her; in truth the courtship was not quite as embedded as I have led you to believe. We would go out on a Monday night to any dive bar that had a pool table and play a competition for two little trophies. One of these had been bastardised to say 'winner' on it, whilst the other said 'loser'. I think the loser one was a little golf trophy

I had provided, and Tree provided the winner one. The winner trophy had been won for Irish dancing, allegedly. To this day I have never seen any evidence of said Irish dancing skills, but anyway, I digress, back to the band.

So, the hunt was on to scour the back catalogues of our musical memories to find songs that would assist us in padding out the set. When selecting songs it is important that you do so with integrity because they appeal to your creative side, you get pleasure out of playing them, or you have an affinity with the story they tell. However, sometimes you just have to be practical and recognise your current predicament, and this was definitely one of those times. We all agreed that we were an upbeat, fast-paced and loud kind of band, and as such there was no point in learning something beyond our capabilities. As such we looked for numbers that were simplistic yet still had the energy required. Ideally not too many chords and most certainly something that was not going to rely on long solos, be it on drums or guitar. From my own selfish point of view, I most certainly didn't want to entertain anything too wordy either – as I have already pointed out, my memory had now reached a legendary status when it came to non-retention of any kind of lyrical content.

And so, we set about formulating a shortlist that we hoped to turn into a medium list and then potentially a longlist. The songs we chose included the following: 'Should I Stay or Should I Go?' by The Clash, 'Ziggy Stardust' by David Bowie, 'Rock and Roll' by Led Zeppelin, 'Start' by

The Jam, 'Pinball Wizard' by The Who, 'Creep' by Radiohead and a load of others that I cannot remember at the time of writing this. From the very beginning the thing I liked most was that once we had chosen a song to cover, we would then go about transforming it to sound like our own. When we did covers no one could accuse us of doing carbon copies. We would perform them in a particular style and, as I used to describe it, we would take a song and then "Dirty Weekend it".

For the next few weeks, we practised the shit out of the material we now had, and all in all I think we gave it a bloody good stab. It got to the point where I was finally beginning to believe we might just be able to pull this off, but I was secretly worried we were still a long way off the numbers we required. From attending gigs over the years in various clubs and pubs the basic formula as far as I had witnessed was this. Band comes on, does 45 minutes and then fucks off to the bar for a drink. Fifteen minutes later, band comes on, does 45 minutes, pretends to end, does encore of ten minutes, says goodnight and then goes to the bar to get shitfaced. With the songs that we had under our belts and by using my extensive calculations I realised we would be getting shitfaced at least half an hour too early.

The answer to our problem was solved, however, as Wama announced he had found a band to support us, and this would eat up around half an hour at the start of the performance. Not only was this great news and a massive relief to us all, but it also meant we were now the headlining act. It was only our first gig and already we were top of the bill.

The day of the gig was fast approaching, and many things had moved on apace. Meanwhile, my many nights of laying the groundwork playing drunken pool with a washed-up Irish dancer had borne fruit and myself and Tree McCauley were now officially what could be classed as boyfriend and girlfriend, and who can blame her? Not everyone has the chance to date a would-be international rock god in the making, and it was clear that her ship had finally come in. I considered I should be keeping this information quiet from the fan base to avoid provoking the kind of anger that was similarly felt towards Yoko Ono when she got together with John Lennon. Yoko and Tree are similar, both about the same height, name contains four letters and when Yoko said to John, "Give peace a chance," Tree my northern Yoko had said, "Give mushy peas a chance." (Still, will never get them… yuck.)

The gig was now upon us and was to be held at a pub in nearby Southwick, just west of Brighton, called the Romans. Aptly named, I would suggest, as one can imagine many a battle in there every Saturday night. This happened to be just along the road from where I used to live. My daughter Maddie was still living there with her mum and, technically speaking, my wife Christine (Chris). Chris and I had been separated for roughly five years and we had never really got around to the admin side of the split – i.e., the divorce papers. We were very amicable with each other, and I would say we were really good friends. We had a lot of good years and a couple of bad ones, and Maddie was obviously a common bond that we both had, and I think we both felt any bad blood was counter-productive and certainly wouldn't be in Maddie's best interests. The fact the gig was so close to the family home was good in one way as I knew Maddie wanted to come along and support and, if she did, she would be accompanied by Chris. Admittedly this might prove a tad awkward for Tree as she had never met Chris, but I decided I would cross that bridge when I came to it and would come up with a cunning plan to make the meeting as manageable as possible.

The pub itself was a large building that took up a good-sized plot on the corner of Manor Hall Road. It was an exceptionally large two-storey building, and the inside comprised of a long front saloon bar and a very good-sized sports bar to the rear of the building. The gig was to take place in the back bar, which I estimated was capable of housing around 130 eager punters longing to witness musical Nirvana. It was being run at the time by a really decent chap by the name of Chris Pobjoy (POBS). He was dressed in a pretty flamboyant shirt that appeared to totally complement his equally flamboyant waistcoat. There could be no doubt this man was way ahead of Gareth Southgate in mastering the camp snooker-player look. He turned out to be an old friend of Wama's from school, which made me suspect we hadn't got this gig on our own merits at all. Also, I assumed maybe he too was curious to see just what the hell his old mucker from school was doing with his life now. The gig was advertised to commence at eight o'clock that evening and for some reason Wama had arranged for us to meet at the pub and start setting up at six. He was eager to make sure all bases were covered and to work on some finishing touches that at the time we had no idea about. Setting up early was to become a recurring theme with Wama, and more often than not he would rope in a lovely chap called Rod Montague to help him cart all the gear in and out of vans and venues at the gigs. Technically you could say Rod was our first roadie and I am not sure if he wears this as a badge of honour, but I do know we were thankful for his generous support in those early days. We entered the arena (bar) and said our hellos to our host for the evening. Pobs then showed us to the space that was to become our playground for the night. I was both surprised and impressed as I was expecting just an area on the floor, but no. Pobs was spoiling us. He led us towards a reasonably sized stage that he had constructed by slotting blocks together. I remember thinking this was way above my expectations, and it would be good to have us towering over the audience giving a much more theatrical effect. I say towering above, but in reality, it was only 2ft in height and I would estimate 8ft depth by 15ft width. Pobs informed me it had set him back about £2,000 and I started to think he had bought it just for this gig, which in my head was a rubber stamp of confidence in us as a band. Back to reality, he shattered my ideas of grandeur and self-importance when he told me he bought it some time ago as the pub did actually hold quite a lot of functions these days.

Tony pulled up in his car and started to unload the multitude of bits and pieces that would be put together to make up his drumkit. I pondered what a ball ache it must be to be a drummer, all that stuff to cart around in a car, meaning that you couldn't drink after the gig. Where was the fun in that? He took ages as he anally set up each piece, bit by bloody bit. Putting one stand down then stepping back and looking on forensically, before stepping forward and moving it one inch to the left before stepping back and pondering its new position. This was repeated over and over again, and it looked like Wama's idea of getting there early was perhaps an inspired call after all. The others had to wait for this process to reach its mind-numbingly boring conclusion before they could contemplate which part of the remaining territory onstage was left for them to claim. I figured I had plenty of time to kill so made the executive decision to go to the bar and chat with my brother Kev, who had come early to take the piss.

It was then I noticed Wama walk past with a hammer, some nails and a large roll of vinyl under his arm. He went to the back wall and unfurled a 10ft banner with the band name and a drawing of a scantily clad lady. This was something of which I had no prior knowledge, and this unexpected little detail was to become another example of Wama going the extra mile and would in my mind be the starting point of him turning into the media whore that he is today. I was fairly sure he hadn't asked Pobjoy for permission to start whacking his walls with a hammer, but he carried on regardless in arranging the backdrop. Once said banner had been nailed into position, Wama then proceeded to position some disco lights on either side of the stage. He stood back and cast a critical eye over his workmanship – you could tell by his expression that he was pleased. He left the stage area and walked over to where his belongings were and placed his Thor like mallet back into a small satchel.

He then delved into the satchel and took out a large wad of papers. These turned out to be some flyers he had prepared in advance that explained all about the band and also featured a brief biography of the support act as well. He placed the flyers for the gig all around the bar. Once he had peppered every inch of the room with the paraphernalia he went into the other bar and continued placing the flyers on to every table in there as well. This was to become the first recorded example of Wama's slow descent into the murky world of self-promotion, and it was reminiscent of a cross between P. T. Barnum and Rupert Murdoch.

Tony finally finished setting up and was reasonably pleased that everything was done to his exacting standards. The rest of the lads started to position their amps around the drums. As they were plugging in and attaching an assortment of pedals, I watched as this not so finely tuned operation unfolded in front of me and was now totally convinced that they did not have a clue as to what they were doing. They didn't have the luxury of our teacher Alex being there to oversee things but, in all fairness, the finished product looked good enough to me. Eventually it fell to me to do my technical bits. I put a microphone on to the stand, put my lyric book on a stand and then went back to the bar with Kev. Its hard work being a singer, you know.

It was still only seven o'clock and there were a few punters milling about in the bar. They weren't there for the band, they were just regulars that would usually frequent this place on a Saturday evening. I began to wonder what sort of crowd we would get. I was confident it would be well attended as I knew quite a few friends were turning up, out of a mixture of kindness and curiosity. Obviously, the band had family members coming, whether they had wanted to or not. Poor Gill, Linda, Wendy and Alison were almost duty-bound to stand by their men, even if their men were publicly dragging their families' good names through the gutter. Tree was soon to become a member of this select group and this would be a real test to see if she was a keeper. If she could put up with this shit, she could put up with anything. As well as the aforementioned groups there was also an unknown quantity to consider. Around this time, the Morning Glory song 'Brighton March', which Wama had written and recorded, had a video on YouTube that had managed to rack up about 5,000 views. It had gained some traction and there was a little bit of interest bubbling away amongst some of the local football fans. I was wondering if we would be playing to a large mob of baying Brighton & Hove Albion fans and if we should have considered some form of crowd control. I had visions of police horses galloping down Manor Hall Road on their way to the gig, which would have been great publicity, but unfortunately this did not come to pass.

The pub soon filled up and it was good to see lots of familiar faces as this would mean playing to a bit of a home crowd, which can be a plus and a minus rolled into one. There were also a lot of unfamiliar faces, which did raise the levels of anxiety. Unlike the gig we had done with the kids, this crowd weren't complete strangers so we could be open to some ribbing and ridicule from our nearest and dearest. The support act was getting ready onstage, doing last-minute preparations. I didn't know the chap or the young woman who were supporting us – and unbeknownst to me at the time one of them was to have a major impact on the band in the years to come.

The support act was a young duo comprised of singer Rose-Anne Raymond and guitarist Joe Colburn. Joe was the son of Wama's close friends Mandy and Mark. They had known each other for years and Joe was like a son to Wama. I think due to the fact Wama had three daughters Joe had provided some much-needed testosterone in Wama's life. He was 21 and guitar playing had been his life for as long as anyone could remember. He had been in a number of bands. One in particular was called Thank You Anyway and at one stage it looked like they could potentially make a breakthrough to a higher level within the music business.

Joe had teamed up with Anne who was a singer/songwriter, and as a duo they were going to do a small set of around five songs to get the evening going. At the start of their set the pub was reasonably busy but not full. They started off and played some good stuff, some of which was their own material. As you can imagine, as there were only the two of them, it was pretty tame and although the crowd were fairly generous in their applause and appreciation it was not exactly rapturous. If they had been playing this set at some bohemian open-mic night at some trendy bar in the Brighton Lanes they would have gone down a storm. Instead, their audience this night was made up of a variety of our middle-aged mates and a smattering of football hooligans. To give you a sense of the room they were playing to, I have a vivid memory that made me laugh. There was a chap we knew called Phil Daly there that night. He was a no-nonsense kind of character who had a love of life and liked to wind people up. In this day and age, some of his humour could be deemed as politically incorrect and to be honest I doubt he has changed much. I remember him telling a filthy/dirty joke to a sweet-looking girl who looked like butter wouldn't melt in her mouth; she replied, "Fuck off you perv or I'll mace you then stab you." I think she would have made an ideal songwriting partner for Wama.

It was now about ten minutes before we were due to go on, and through the door of the bar I could see my daughter Maddie arrive accompanied by Chris. I knew they were coming, but I think I may not have informed Tree about this. They came over to the table we were sitting at, close to the front at the right-hand side of the stage. I welcomed both of them and ushered them to sit down with us. At this point I made some introductions.

I said, "Tree, this is my wife, Chris. And Chris this is my girlfriend, Tree. Must go now as we are starting in a minute."

I then left them to it and joined the boys onstage. That was about the full extent of how cunning my plan was to deal with this situation. Some may call it stupidity, some may say cowardice, some may dub me rude, but I like to think it was spontaneous and inspired.

We had started a little later than advertised, which in hindsight I think worked to our advantage – the audience were getting well and truly oiled. One thing I have discovered over the years is that a sober crowd is a tough crowd. With a drunk crowd you can play any old shit and just about get away with it, whereas a sober crowd can hear every mistake and have ways of reacting that can suck every last ounce of confidence from your soul. The last thing you want when starting out is to set standards too high. Set the bar low and if you over-achieve then everyone is happy.

We have lift off and, as the old saying goes, "Go big or go home." We started large by going full throttle into 'Rock and Roll' by Led Zeppelin and that led straight into 'Ziggy Stardust' with no break in between. As Ziggy ended the crowd went wild. I am not even joking… they really did go wild. (The power of alcohol can be a beautiful thing.) In the front saloon bar at the time there was a pre-arranged party going on for somebody's birthday and it was a joy to witness an influx of these people pile into the back bar. I wish I could describe the adrenaline buzz, but all I can say is I was on cloud nine and was engaging in an out-of-body experience. I looked over towards Tree, Maddie and Chris and it appeared that they were enjoying it and smiling, and that gave me an added feeling of complete relief. We carried on through the set and although I certainly didn't have what some would describe as 'stage craft', I did have a bit of a gift for banter in between the songs. I was very self-effacing, and I loved taking the piss out of the others in the band. Their obvious discomfort was something I found funny, and I think the audience enjoyed watching them squirm as well. This was a trait that, as we went forward, would begin to annoy Wama a bit, but for the time being it was all new, so he went along with the joke.

The first set concluded, and we were clapped and cheered as we left the stage. I know it was a home crowd, but I did feel deep down that we had deserved it for our valiant efforts. I had had about four pints in front of me onstage where people had been buying me drinks, which I suspect were purchased with a mixture of appreciation but also the knowledge that the more I drank the more animated and dangerous I would become onstage. I disappeared out into the garden where I chain-smoked as I tried to compose myself for the second half. There were a few others outside and it was fulfilling to see them enjoying banter with each other. There were people giving me really positive comments and I remember vividly that there was a real buzz about the place as I witnessed old friends catching up and merrily chatting away to each other. It was as if the band and the gig had become a catalyst for all of these people to get together. I went back inside and checked in with Tree, Maddie and Chris, and all seemed to be going well on that front.

Break time was over, and I went around the room to gather up all the members of the band and ready them for the battle of part deux. They all appeared to be fairly relaxed, and I felt their attitudes were a lot different compared with before we had started our set.

I hopped back onstage, and the rest of the guys took up their starting positions. Tony counted us in to launch the second half.

Very much like the first half, the room was buzzing, and the audience participation was in full flow. We made shedloads of mistakes, but it didn't matter to me or the audience as I would just laugh and turn it into a joke. The second half went by in a blur due to the amount of adrenaline and Foster's that were swimming around my bloodstream. Eventually we came to our final number, which was 'Brighton March'. I think you know my thoughts on this song. As the opening chords were struck, the place erupted. It helped that there was a large contingent of pissed-up North Standers in the crowd, and as the final note of the final song rang out, the appreciation from the crowd was overwhelming. As the saying goes, 'the crowd cried out for more'. They really were and that gave us a bit of a problem to contend with. The trouble was we didn't know any more songs, so I made the executive decision that we would just repeat a couple of the liveliest songs on the setlist. We did this to more and more cheers, and finally brought this extravaganza to its conclusion.

Tony told me he went to the bar and the first words Pobs said to him were, "I was not fucking expecting that." My voice had almost gone by this stage and, as always, Tony was sitting in a puddle of his own sweat.

The smiles on all of our faces were glowing and without having to say any words to each other we could all tell that, although it had been daunting and hard work, we had loved every single minute of it. Maddie and Chris came up to me to say their goodbyes, which was a good thing as it would get messy from here on in. I remember asking Tree whether she thought it was an alright gig and am pleased to say she responded positively. I talked about the mistakes and was beginning to be a bit overly critical. She then said something that always stuck with me, "The best thing about your band is that it looks like you're having your own party onstage and you have invited everyone to join you."

We may have not been the best of musicians, but when she said that it did resonate with me. I think it's important to enjoy what you do and the act of not taking yourself too seriously can have make your audience feel at ease. At the end of the day, we are all on a night out getting a little escapism from the day-to-day issues we encounter. It is good to give yourself time to do the silly things in life.

The next two hours or so were spent in wild abandon celebrating the fact that none of us had been murdered. We went around and spoke to just about everyone who had come to the gig to support us. Looking around you could witness old friends re-engaging with each other, whilst new friendships were being formed and developed. There was a real sense of community in the air. I know this might sound a bit romanticised, but I genuinely felt this. The rest of the evening is a bit of a haze to tell the truth, but I do know that it carried on long into the night as my sore head the next day would testify to this.

We were off and running now and feeling like an unstoppable force. Onwards and upwards.

FOOTNOTES

POOL TROPHIES – Tree moved down from Derby where she had played for many years in pool teams. She tells me how she represented the county and aspired to represent her country. I turned out to be her bogey player and would normally go home with the Irish dancing trophy.

MUSHY PEAS – Pointless, end of.

DIVORCE PAPERS – It would take me another six years to complete these. Admin is not a strong point of mine.

CHRIS POBJOY (POBS) – Legend. Makes my mid-life crisis seem mild in comparison. Went off around the world to do volunteering work in Vietnam, Borneo, Sumatra and Java, to name a few, where he taught kindergarten kids English, God help them. He also worked in an Orangutan rehabilitation centre. (Sadly, he was beyond the point where they could help him.) After his extensive travels he came home where he volunteered to be a porter at the hospital during the Covid-19 pandemic. He is still there, doing his bit.

NORTH STANDERS – This is a reference to the Goldstone ground which was the old home of Brighton & Hove Albion. You knew where you were in those days, unlike the modern all-seater stadia that you have in the world of football today. If you had young kids or were middle-aged you would locate to the East Stand. If you were well off and were a bit materially minded you sat in the West Stand. If you were visiting as an away fan you would probably be stuck in the South Stand. But if you were there to have a good singsong, meet up with your mates and generally liked to bait the opposition you were a North Stander. Many a rowdy youth was part of this scene, and they loved every minute of it.

BIG FOOTNOTE

I asked Wama to give me some detail on 'Brighton March' and he kindly sent me the following.

'BRIGHTON MARCH' by Wama Marmont

It was a sunny day and I found myself drinking in this strange bar in Islington on the day of the match. I remember thinking that the bar reminded me of a garage for some reason, but it was what I considered to be a proper football bar. It was not like a pub, and I thought it might have been an unlicensed establishment at first, but there were police about and they did not seem to be bothered about it. I liked going to the oppositions' pubs as it always interested me to meet other fans who were passionate about their teams. I never used to wear my colours and I just used to mix in with them. I liked to let it slip that I was an away fan and enjoyed seeing their reactions. Most fans are OK with it. I had a few incidents that were quite hairy, and Sheffield Wednesday and West Ham are a couple that spring to mind that had some nasty undertones.

So, there I was in the Arsenal bar and looking around you could see caricatures of Arsenal players and the manager Arsene Wenger hand-painted on to the wall, and they played a rolling selection of Arsenal songs from different bands. Loads of them, rock, pop, rap, just about any type of music genre. The fans inside were singing along, I really liked it and wished Brighton & Hove Albion could have a pub or bar like this. The Seagulls were going through a terrible spell in their history and could not match Arsenal at anything at this time. We had a few songs made about us, 'Goldstone Rap', 'Old White & Blue', 'Seagulls' and 'Brighton Ska', so I decided to do my own take on it all. I got what I thought was a good heavy beat going that was quite catchy and put my lyrics down.

It got a mixed reaction at first, but soon racked up over 5,000 YouTube views, which I was quite pleased with really. However, it never really took off and the club paid absolutely no interest in it whatsoever. People would say it had loads of swearing in it, but it did not. The first copy we made had one swear word in, and that was a solitary "shit". The song was re-recorded at a later date and that is a much better version, and we removed the solitary swear word.

One strange evening I was accosted in The Montpelier Inn, shortly after I recorded the song, by three heavy looking geezers who said they had heard I had written a politically motivated anti-Catholic song. During the song I shout, "It's no surrender cause we're Brighton & Hove Albion". I convinced them it was not political at all, and the situation passed without an incident thankfully as they were big lads.

Despite the reaction from my Catholic friends the song still was not getting much attention, JC (Joe Colburn lead guitarist) does a great intro of a song called 'Sussex by the Sea' at the beginning in a Brian May style. I always thought that should have got some compliments from Seagulls fans, but I barely heard a thing. I did hear that the song would get played regularly on the coach that Chris Pobjoy used to put on from The Romans in Southwick on their way up to the Amex Stadium. Attila the Stockbroker, who is a professional punk performance poet and lives locally, said it sounded like "somewhere between Eddie & The Hot Rods meets The Fall". He said he liked it and that was good enough for me.

CHAPTER 5 – THE EGO HAS LANDED ON PIGEON STREET

We have now arrived at the back end of 2011, the year that saw a number of tumultuous events all around the world. For a start you had the Arab Spring, which would lead to the start of the civil wars in Syria and Libya. But more importantly as far as I was concerned, Frankie Cocozza had been kicked off of *The X Factor*. At the time, nationally this was considered to be a massive news story, with all of the tabloid newspapers devoting endless column inches to it for weeks on end. As he was a local lad from Brighton, his celebrity status within the city was bordering on that of a Hollywood A-lister. I wasn't to know it at the time, but this earth-shattering event would eventually go on to have a major impact on my future creative life. (All will be revealed a little later. I think this is what they call a teaser.)

It had been a few weeks since the band had successfully completed the first full gig and, buoyed by the feedback and goodwill that we had received, we had dived back into rehearsals with renewed vim and vigour. Our tails were up as we continued on our mission of learning new skills and exploring new material with Alex and G.

So here we were, situated in our third-storey headquarters above the security firm, and on the face of it all would appear to be going along very nicely indeed. The atmosphere within the camp at that stage was best described as harmonious, although unbeknownst to me at the time there were clandestine moves afoot. These could in essence undermine the status quo of the band and might just bring us down, down, deeper and down (see what I did there).

It was Tuesday night and with what was now my new routine I found myself arriving at the practice session with a certain degree of hope and optimism. I was soon joined by Tony, Mark and Clive, and they too seemed in fine fettle. We were gently bantering and chatting about a series of banal and light topics, whilst we set up our instruments and went about the process of tuning up. The door opened and in walked Wama, who gave us a pleasant hello as he placed his guitar case down on to the floor. I then realised that he wasn't alone as following close behind him was his good friend Mark accompanied by a young chap who I recognised from somewhere. The young chap turned out to be Joe, the young guitarist who was one half of the support act from The Romans gig. I began to wonder what they were doing here and assumed that maybe they had just dropped Wama off to rehearsals and had decided to show their faces to say a polite hello to everyone.

Wama seemed a little tentative as he proceeded to introduce Joe to everyone individually. He then went on to explain that the reason Joe had come along was that he thought it would be a good thing if he sat in on the session and maybe even joined in a bit as well. This was certainly the first I had heard about it and I began to wonder if we were trying to set a new world record for getting the most guitarists into the smallest space. I wondered if maybe he played keyboards; I knew he didn't sing so I was alright. Glancing briefly towards Clive, I definitely knew that, from his facial expressions, he clearly had no idea why this invitation had been extended. There was now a very strange atmosphere in the room, and my mind was instantly transported back to when I was asked to come along for the first time. I glanced over in Clive's direction again; he had a look of complete shock about him and must have been wondering what the fuck was going on. At that point déjà vu kicked in and my thoughts again turned to the motives behind this. I mused over how the hell this band had become so ruthless. I seriously believed that a course in the art of diplomacy would not go amiss for some of our members.

When researching the book, I had asked Clive about his memories from the moment I was introduced for the first time at my infamous debut rehearsal session and it was only recently that he told me he had thought, "Thank fuck he is not a guitarist." So here was a remarkably similar scenario being played out in front of us, with him being the leading character in the scene.

Joe and his dad (Mark) took a seat and made themselves comfortable as we got ready to start our practice. There was a discernible lack of any banter going on between us at this point as everyone seemed to be much more committed to avoiding eye contact with any other member. We decided on the song that we would work on first and Tony counted us in. As the opening chords to The Killers song 'When You Were Young' kicked in, my initial thoughts in all truth were, "This is fucking awful." We had played this song at the first teaching showcase gig and, on that occasion, it had gone down pretty well. I remember at the time I thought we had done a good job and judging by the audience's reaction they had concurred. What I had probably forgotten was that on that occasion we were joined onstage by Alex, and he had done all the lovely solo bits as well as anything that you might suggest was on the tricky side. We had played it many times since, but for some reason it never sounded quite right and even though it was bleeding obvious, I could never put my finger on the reason why. As Clive started playing, it still didn't sound as it should, and I expressed not understanding why and that in my opinion the first time we did it was the best. I then went on to say that, as far as I could tell, the more we played it the worse it sounded. As I said, I had completely forgotten we had Alex play with us, and it is only in researching this book that things have fallen into place. I owe Clive and Wama a little apology really, as I was a bit of a git to them regarding this song. You see the more I carried on about us getting worse at playing it the worse it got for them and this would have the result of sapping all the confidence out of the guitar playing of Clive and Wama. This in turn would lead to them fearing the tune and making the performance of it seem like a real struggle for them. It wasn't too long after this that we ditched it from any future setlists.

Back in the practice room and whilst in full flow of murdering The Killers, Joe piped up and said in a slightly patronising way, "You are doing it all wrong." Joe had what can only be described as a look of bored distain about him, and he also, in my expert opinion, appeared to be a tad drunk. He stood up and swaggered over to Wama. He reached out and Wama handed over his guitar. He then proceeded to show us how he thought it should be played and left us in no doubt about exactly how he thought we were murdering the song. There was no denying he was an incredibly good guitarist, in fact probably one of best I had ever heard. At the same time though he exuded a total contempt for our level of musicianship and maybe because he was a little tipsy he was acting like an egotistical dick. We once again attempted the song, this time with Joe orchestrating proceedings. He would stop us all playing at certain points to give Tony tips on playing drums, tell Mark how to play the bass and give me tips on singing. Clive was in the background, watching but not contributing anything and looking like he just wanted the ground to open up and swallow him.

It was at that point I suggested we take a break as I felt things were starting to spiral out of control. I left the room as I needed to go out for a cigarette and collect my thoughts. There was a fire exit that led to a large, flat roof that overlooked the surrounding area. I gestured to Mark (Joe's dad) to join me. Once on the flat roof we looked at each other and laughed. I said, "I think Joe needs to go mate." He agreed and I asked what had brought them along in the first place. He said Wama had mooted a plan about Joe joining and just wanted to see if it was going to work. We both concluded it was not going to work and then went back inside to join the others in the frosty room. Mark said to Joe, "Come on mate we need to let this lot get on with things." We all said pleasant goodbyes and thanked Joe for giving us some tips as he left the room. This was my first proper meeting with Joe Colburn and at the time I thought it would probably be the last, but in reality, it was only the start of our story. I didn't know it at the time, but he would end up being a major influence on me in the coming years and would also become a true mate as well.

With Joe having departed, to say the room felt weird would be a massive understatement. There was a long silence that went on forever. Maybe it was a mixture of shock, embarrassment or hurt feelings, but everyone was quiet, until I said, "What the fuck was that all about?" Wama held his hand up and simply said, "Sorry guys."

He explained it was something that he wanted to try out because he just wanted to keep the band improving. The one thing I was finding out about Wama was that he was always looking for an edge or advantage that would make the whole package better. Most of the time he got this right, but sometimes he got it wrong. If he did fuck up, you had to admit that he always owned up to his mistakes and took it on the chin. He explained that he knew Joe was an amazing lead guitarist and he thought this would be a good thing to push the band forward. By his reckoning Joe would be an asset to both himself and Clive as they were new to this and would benefit by learning from Joe. I do think his intentions were fundamentally good, but I his methods were piss poor in the execution. Clive didn't say much but you could tell he was really hurt, and I was just a bit shocked at quite how sly the whole episode was. I cannot testify as to what Tony and Mark really thought about what occurred that night, but I do believe this was the start of them questioning the ability of Clive as the lead guitarist. I kind of understand this reasoning but do not agree with it. As far as I was concerned, we were all novices and at this stage. Maybe we were beginning to get ahead of ourselves, and we were losing sight of the fun factor.

We finished the practice early that night and the conversations were strained and slightly false. Walking out of that practice I did think maybe this was the beginning of the end for the band as I couldn't see how we could continue with this degree of stab-in-the-back chicanery. This was a good lesson for me into the nuances of band politics and it would be the first lesson of many to come. I reckon Jeremy Kyle could devote a whole series purely to band politics as people would be enthralled to see just how dark it can become.

After finishing this god-awful practice session, I took solace as I made my way to the Harbour View, where I had a couple of pints with Tony and Mark, and obviously the main discussion was all about what had just occurred. I was explaining to them that I found the episode to be a bit weird and reminded them that it was similar to when they had asked me along to rehearsals for the first time. They were of the opinion that it was not quite the same. How they came to that conclusion puzzled me. They were discussing Joe and saying what a great guitarist he was and maybe the time was right to think about having another guitarist play the lead.

In my head I was thinking, "Why the fuck can people not just be happy with what they have?"

Sam was working behind the bar and, once he had served us, he joined in the conversation. He wasn't what you would describe as rushed off his feet. Bereft of any other punters to talk to he had no other option but to join us bunch of saddos and weigh in on the weekly meeting of the mid-life crisis gang. He had led a colourful life and had all the qualifications to join the club. He was asking us about how things were going with the band. We gave him a flavour as to how the gig had been received and he was a bit taken aback when we told him how well it had been attended. I think he was interested in the number of people we had been able to pull along and was now enquiring when and where our next gig was going to be. Maybe he thought he had stumbled across the new Beatles and this could be the start of us doing a residency like you see in casinos such as Caesars Palace in Las Vegas. Maybe this could be the thing needed to bring in the high rollers from out of town.

Although at this stage we didn't have any full gigs lined up, we did have a rather interesting and unexpected support slot in the pipeline. Wama had recently informed us that Atilla the Stockbroker had offered us a slot supporting the pretty well-known punk band Peter and the Test Tube Babies. They were a big deal on the punk scene in the UK and for this to be only our second gig was ridiculous. Not only that but the gig was to be in Dick's Bar, which was the main function room at the Amex Stadium, the new home of Brighton & Hove Albion FC. I was going away on holiday and would be flying back on the day of the gig. I didn't see any problem in doing a cheeky little session to announce myself back into the country. In my mind it reminded me of another Phil when he played the UK and the USA on the same day for Live Aid.

When Sam realised we had no other gigs lined up, he said, "Why don't you play here?" It didn't take too much persuasion, so we took him up on his offer and set a date three weeks on Saturday. He told us we were going to get paid as well, which was a bonus, and I wondered if this qualified us as professional musicians. Thoughts began to turn to what I would spend all my money on.

The following day I went online and after checking the flight details worked out OK, we confirmed the Amex gig, and I flew off on my jolly holidays in the sun with Tree. A week in the Tenerife sunshine didn't stop me from preparing for the upcoming show as I was now a professional, and every opportunity was taken to keep my voice in fine fettle by engaging in several drunken karaoke nights. It had been a good week, but perhaps I had slightly overdone the late nights as on my return flight I began to feel rather unwell. In fact, by the time the plane landed I felt like death and wondered if I was about to pass out. The journey to the show had not been ideal. Firstly, the flight had been delayed. Before the delay, I had figured we would have plenty of time to get to the venue prior to the gig, but it was now touch and go whether we would get there for the start at all. On top of that I was feeling awful, as I had come down with some kind of bug that had drained me of all energy and my temperature was through the roof causing me to sweat buckets. I could only put this illness down to the fact that I had been bitten really nastily by some insect whilst away and had a trail that had been tracking up my arm. I had seen a doctor who had informed me he was going to have to give me an injection. I rolled up my sleeve and waited for the jab; he then informed me that it would be going into my bottom. I remember dropping my trousers and turning around to witness Tree furiously trying to get the camera function on her phone to work. Luckily, she couldn't take the shot in time, and I was saved from having the offending pictures splashed all over *Hello!* magazine. Meanwhile, back in England…

All of this then led to panic attacks as I felt that we were going to let everybody down. The plane landed, we quickly got through customs and baggage reclaim, and hopped into the first available taxi towards Brighton. On the journey I was seriously thinking that I was going to die as I felt that awful, but I pretended to Tree that things weren't so bad as the show must go on. We arrived about five minutes prior to our start time and made our way to join the others who must have been wondering where the hell I was.

The audience was made up of die-hard Test Tube fans and I estimated there to be at least 250 people in the room. I was led to believe there was a little bit of friction with the Test Tubes as they were not entirely happy to have us plugging into their equipment. At the time I thought this was a bit petty, but nowadays with a little bit more experience I can understand their concerns in a way, although personally it has never really bothered me when bands would play with us many years later. Back to the Amex, the time had arrived for us to go onstage, and I was starting to see double. My temperature was raging, and I just wanted to go home to bed. We got through a short set of about 30 minutes and given our skill and experience, had not done too badly. I think, it was fair to say many of the Test Tube fans would probably disagree as we were not exactly the sound that they craved. But, hey there were probably a few people in the room who thought we were the Test Tubes and were wondering what all the fuss was about, It was another lesson learned and Wama was beside himself having played at the home of his beloved BHAFC. I got through it and that is all I can really say about the show. I should've been pleased to have the opportunity to play at such a great venue. I wasn't taking much in and was certainly not soaking up any of the energy that would provide me with everlasting memories to cherish. The truth was I just wanted to go home and hug my pillow under a duvet. It took me many days to get back to normality and by the middle of the week I had just about got my head back in gear to focus on the next gig.

The following weekend we were to play our first gig at the Harbour View. Time passed quickly as we rehearsed in preparation for the big day, and very soon we found ourselves in the venue and beginning to set up. As was our usual habit now we had arrived way too early, but at least this gave us some scope to figure out the space restrictions.

For some reason we chose the wrong end of the pub to play in and this resulted in us having to put Tony and his drumkit in the conservatory at the front of the building. This would prove to be a bit of a problem and looking back our stupidity was quite breath-taking. The pub began to fill up as we approached the advertised start time. Much like the Romans gig we had managed to draw a healthy crowd of friends, relatives, and one or two people we didn't know but who had heard good things about us by word of mouth. We did a quick soundcheck and then came to the realisation that as Tony was in the conservatory and the speakers were in front of him, he couldn't hear a single note we were playing. Not only was it too late to change things around, but we really were that naïve that we didn't even know if it would make any difference.

It was quite clear from the first song that we had a bit of a problem as Tony appeared to be about half a second out from the rest of the band and kept trying to look at the guitarists' hands. He couldn't work out what I was singing as I was facing away from him, and blind panic was now taking over. Tony was wearing his famous sweaty look a lot earlier in the set than expected, and he and Mark did their usual routine of staring and moaning at each other. The song was a complete disaster from start to finish and at the end the audience had a look of stunned confusion. I then came into my own somewhat, as I tried to salvage something positive from the ensuing mess. I chose to engage the crowd head on and began taking the piss out of our own abilities. For some reason, probably a mixture of comedy and pity, we managed to turn the whole audience into loyal supporters, and they could sense that this opening had been a bit of a laugh that they weren't expecting. We then re-positioned some of the amps, and for the rest of the gig I was sidewards on to the audience and Tony, so that he could see my lips moving. The poor sod was bricking it and spent the next two hours drumming in an echo chamber that had the temperature of a greenhouse, all whilst I was taking the piss out of him. I loved it, but I don't think Tony shared my enthusiasm for some reason. It was a thoroughly enjoyable gig for everybody except him and the audience loved it, not just because of the music but also the cabaret that Tony had provided in his own personal torture chamber. Sam had done well at the bar, and we got paid our fee, as well as there being a whip round in the jug. We then decided to give all the money back and donated it to the charity the quiz team had been raising money for. As was our custom after the gig we all hit the bar and I got slaughtered.

Wama and Tony were working hard to get us a few more gigs to look forward to, but the general week-to-week work of the band carried on along its usual path of lessons and practice. Practice could be somewhat monotonous for me at times as it seemed the progress was laboured whilst the instrumentation was being worked on. There was a little bit of diva building up in me as well, as I was getting tetchy at some of the song choices we were working on. Alex introduced us to a song by Aloe Blacc called 'I Need a Dollar'. Over and over again I spent what seemed like an eternity singing along to this soul-destroying dirge. It was considered a cool song and at the time had reached the top of the charts, but in all honesty if I had Aloe's address, I would have gladly sent him any sum of money as long as he burnt the master tapes. I felt I was being a bit short-changed and felt a little aggrieved to think I was paying good money to learn this shit.

Tuesday night practice would be changing for us soon as Alex and G hadn't had their lease renewed and it looked like Rock School was going to be winding up. It was unclear at this stage what the plan would be going forward.

After a particularly fraught session where Tony and Mark were at each other's throats, and Clive was receiving some negative comments, I once again found myself at the bar in the Harbour View contemplating our current position. Like one of those films where the guy walks into the bar and proceeds to pour out his woes to the friendly psychologist barperson, I updated Sam on what we had been doing and told him we would soon be looking for a new place to practise.

He said, "You can use the factory."

At first, I didn't know what he was going on about, so I just replied, "What bloody factory?"

"The one next door."

Sam went on to explain that, yes, he was running the pub, but he was also here looking after the whole site for a friend by the name of Fash, and that included the deserted factory next door, a car wash and a number of businesses on the block that were housed in another building.

He then got hold of some keys and asked me to come with him for a look. I followed Sam a hundred metres or so up the road. He unlocked three locks on a very non-descript door that was sunk a couple of metres into a plain-looking brick wall. He then descended a small set of steps and flicked a switch where a small light lit up above the door. He had a torch in his hands and shone it into the space. I could hardly see the end of the beam as it was directed into the abyss. I couldn't see much but I could tell it was huge. Sam said, "I think we can fit you in." He then suggested I come back the following day when it was light so that I could have a proper look. He switched off the light and we returned to the pub. I was straight on the phone to Tony to tell him that I thought I had found us a small practice facility.

Tony met me outside the pub the following day and seemed a bit confused at the place I had found for us to rehearse. We met Sam at the pub, and he led us up the road and through the door I had entered the previous night. We stepped in and were greeted with a vast sea of nothing. It was 30,000 sq ft of absolutely nothing. A vast expanse with a few concrete pillars that carried on into the distance. We asked if Sam would be OK with us using some space and he said it was fine by him as long as we provided a music night once a month in the pub. There was a purpose-built room in the far corner that we thought would be ideal. It was roughly 20ft wide and 30ft long and the ceiling was a good 20ft high. It was full of junk and Sam said if we cleared it out, we could have it. So, the very next day, Tony and I were down there looking to get it all sorted. The only problem was this room had been closed up for a good decade and the only life in there over the last ten years were the hundreds of pigeons that had been using it as their luxury hotel. They were able to gain access through the broken windows high above us. I cannot truly do justice with words to just how bad the stench was in that room. Just thinking about it now makes me feel queasy, and on that day myself and Tony lasted little more than half an hour in there and had to come out every minute or so wanting to throw our guts up. We saw a couple of rats as well and decided this space was not for us. It was then that Tony said, "How hard could it be to build our own room in the corner by the front door?" And so, with Sam's permission, we began constructing our very own rehearsal studio. The cost of materials was kept low by the fact that we didn't have to buy any expensive soundproofing as the only ones that would be disturbed by our sweet music would be our neighbours the pigeons and rats. Tony and I did the bulk of the construction, with the other guys chipping in to help decorate and add finishing touches. So, within two weeks we had our very own headquarters. It was surreal going down there to rehearse and time spent in physically constructing the room had really given us a great bonding experience, but this was not destined to last.

Sam had done us a great service in providing the space and true to the agreement it was now down to me to organise a music night in the pub once a month. I had never done this sort of thing before and so was unsure how I should approach it to make it not only good fun, but also popular so it would give the pub a decent night's trade. I figured we had to come up with about two hours of music at the very least. My approach was to treat these music nights as an opportunity to try out the new songs we were learning. I also thought it would be a great platform for introducing other acts. I had earmarked the band to do about 45 minutes. Our friends had seen us play recently so it was only fair to introduce them to other acts they had not seen before. This gave me the task of finding others who could join in and show off what they could do.

First up were John H. and Adam, who I knew from the Three Graces pub. John didn't take a lot of persuading as he was, I soon found out, a musical whore. Give him a mic, a guitar and a stage, and you really couldn't keep him from stepping into the spotlight. Young Adam, my thrash metal friend, was a bit of an untapped gem. He could play acoustic guitar brilliantly and had a number of mainstream songs in his repertoire. His covers of 'Tribute' by Tenacious D and 'JCB' by Nizlopi were theatrical in the extreme and something to behold. Tony then asked if his daughter Giselle could do a bit of a set and, as far as I was concerned, the more the merrier. Clive surprised me as he informed me he had an acquaintance called Kevin and they had been mucking about musically, might be forming a band, and would like to come and have a go. Wama volunteered to do a solo set as well, and before you knew it, we had what can loosely be described as a show.

On the first night of our musical jam my most vivid memory is a long line of people going backwards and forwards from the factory studio to the pub carrying various bits of equipment. It really was a team effort and that was the beginning of a musical community forming. Not just performers, but those that had come to listen. Everyone was treated as a part of the tribe, and those music nights would go on to help form so many new friendships and provide a focal point. It gave people the excuse to get out and meet up with each other. This was the start of my understanding what it took to try and promote music nights. In the future I would try to replicate the ethos that all were welcomed and involved in participating in any way they wanted to.

The band got up first and we did a short 20-minute set to get things going. It was a slightly lower key than previous gigs, which was good as it came across as relaxed and fun. John H. was next, and he persuaded Mark and Tony to accompany him on drums and bass whilst he performed some good old rock 'n' roll numbers. John H. is a true performer, and you can tell from every move of his body and soul that he simply loves it. This was conveyed to the audience, and they simply loved his sense of fun. Pretty soon everyone was joining in and singing along. He got me up to sing with him and I was trying to get the lyrics up on my phone as he suggested 'House of the Rising Sun'. We did it – and without boasting and to my complete astonishment, I have to say that it was kind of epic. (Diva alert.)

Tony's daughter went up next to perform a couple of numbers and I remember how nice it was to see Tony looking on all proud and generally enjoying the experience he was having with her that night.

Clive was next with his potential new band. This comprised of a guy called Kevin who played guitar and keys (he also wrote most of the original material), and a guy called Monty on drums, who was a very dapper looking fellow dressed in a waistcoat, Dr Martens and a bowler hat. (He will go on to to be a major player in this story.) That line-up would soon go under the banner of Blind Ammo.

Wama then did his solo set which gave him an opportunity to do some covers he dearly loves, which were a mixture of Bob Dylan, Tom Waits and Leonard Cohen. Once he had finished, we had a break so that if anyone were thinking of killing themselves, they could do so in the privacy of the back garden.

The night was going well, everyone was buzzing, and the bar was doing a very steady trade. We carried on into the second half with all the acts doing a second set and the highlight being a very drunk Monty on drums, who missed hitting his cymbals and ended up on the floor. The evening came to an end for the music at about half-past eleven, but the night carried on for a lot longer. Sam was really happy with how it all went and was asking me if I could organise a night every week. We stuck to the general format of once a month, but I did start to introduce some bands into the pub on a weekly basis. I was at this point watching a few bands at other pubs and getting to know some of the players on the scene – and soon found myself acting as a bit of a go-between and getting them gigs. If I thought about this more seriously at the time, I probably could have made some money in agent booking fees, but I just enjoyed seeing live music and this was my way of making sure that there were venues I could go to in order to get my fix.

My personal life was going well at the time with myself and Tree appearing to do more than just tolerate each other. It was so nice to meet someone who didn't really appear to be impressed with material items or worry about hanging out in some of the places that I took her because they were certainly not what you would describe as hip and happening. Work life was all right as well. I was good at what I did and although the job didn't excite me, I did have the luxury of working with a really great bunch of characters. Another manager, Colin Peachy, and I were thick as thieves and he loved hearing the stories of my crazy rock star life that I would impart to him whilst we were having one of our many thousands of cigarette breaks together. He also knew Serge my Polish friend well and was familiar with the "WHY NOT?" mantra. So much so, I recall a time when Serge was going back to Poland for a holiday to see his family and said that we should go with him. We both said, "WHY NOT?" and Peachy and I, as well as another chap called Gary, found ourselves aboard a plane heading towards Krakow. On the first day Peachy nearly broke his back on a ski slope, we were surrounded by neo-Nazi skinheads in a club, and we were toasting the death of a pet rabbit called 'IT', with a shout of "Nostrovia!". Again, I realise that I have digressed, so back to our tale.

It was at work, though, that music would have another strange impact on my life. It was a Sunday night, and I was running the night shift as the only manager in the building. I was outside having a fag, working out what was still left to do on the shift, when suddenly a colleague ran out and told me something bad had happened at the end of the cereal aisle. I ran in and as I reached the aisle there was a group of colleagues looking agitated. Lying motionless on the floor was a young lad called Gary. Gary was about mid-twenties and was what can only be described as a really pleasant individual, well liked and pretty physically fit. I crouched down and I was joined by a colleague called Taczka (I know lots of nice Poles). Taczka is best described as looking like a new-age travelling, survival enthusiast with a mohawked punk-rocker hairstyle. We looked at each other and realised that Gary was dead. I turned Gary over on to his back and together we started to try to resuscitate him. I was doing the chest compressions and Taczka concentrated on his airways. Someone was calling the ambulance and as it may be a bit of a wait, we set about assisting Gary. Neither of us had any training in this and the only thing that I could remember to help was an advert on TV that had footballer Vinnie Jones doing mouth-to-mouth whilst bopping along to the tune 'Staying Alive' by the Bee Gees. I never imagined it would become part of my repertoire, but I was about to go all Barry Gibb on Gary whilst my punk Pole pal got all kissy, kissy.

As if by some kind of miracle, it actually bloody worked, and Gary started breathing. We placed him in the recovery position and relaxed while we waited for the professionals to arrive, but Gary must have been a fan of the Bee Gees as he decided to die again. The punk Bee Gees do an encore and once again success was achieved, and we replaced Gary into the recovery position. Unfortunately, though we had to do another two encores and then the paramedics arrived to take over. Everyone was in a bit of a daze, and I cleared the onlooking audience back to work to let the paramedics get on with it. They were working on him for what seemed like an age and eventually he was taken away after being placed in an induced coma. Although I was not aware of it at the time, I suppose I was in some sort of shock as I carried on rallying the shift to get the store ready (fucked up priorities).

Over the next few weeks Gary was kept in the induced coma and when he was finally brought back to consciousness he had no discernible brain damage at all, which I am told is something of a minor miracle considering how many times he died. To this day that is probably the most influential musical duo I have performed with, but I hope the punk Bee Gees never have to reform.

This episode had a profound effect on me as I started pondering my own mortality and was considering that life is too short to be found dead at the end of the cereal aisle when there were so many different experiences I had left to try.

Rehearsals continued down in the factory and the music nights at the pub were going well. Our setlist was ever expanding and we had a few small, local gigs in the pipeline. On top of this, Wama had written a new song about his beloved hometown, which he had called 'Dirty Weekend in Brighton'. Inspired by his creativity, I started to wonder if I could also write some material. Looking for something to ignite a spark in you to put words on paper is a very personal process I suppose. For some, I imagine they look at their own life experiences or world events that they are drawn to, to spark the imagination. Others just write meaningless drivel that sounds good with a beat. I decided I would attempt to write songs that had a purpose or story that I could either relate to by experience or have an opinion about. I also vowed not to use the word "baby" as this word in all songs drives me up the fucking wall. For my first attempt I decided I would write a story about my interpretation of something in the news, and this is where Frankie Cocozza comes in. See the next chapter for a big footnote detailing the meaning of this song. The band was moving into a period of heavy activity, with a gig at the Albion pub in Fishersgate, and the George Inn in Portslade successfully completed. Both were well attended and fun and had enhanced our reputation for being a good night out. We had improved bit by bit and managed to look like we were enjoying it, and Wama's new original had been received so positively that we decided we would venture into a recording studio to make the first Dirty Weekend record.

Another piece of exciting news was delivered by Wama as he told us we were on the bill to play at the Robin Hood pub's street party in Brighton on the May Day Bank Holiday. This was a big deal as this event could be really well attended, weather permitting. The Robin Hood is an excellent pub run by a lovely couple called Chris and Anna Dodds. They hold an annual street party that heralds the beginning of summer. It is very much a community-based celebration that supports local bands, and also has a variety of stalls supporting local artists and caterers. It has also raised money for a variety of brilliant charities such as Emmaus (help for the homeless), Spiral (artistic opportunities for people with learning difficulties) and the Carers Centre, to name but a few. The festivities are held outside the pub on the corner of two roads that are shut off for the day. It starts at about midday and carries on into the night. There are around ten acts that provide the entertainment, and these can be a mixture of bands, DJs and every year the amazing 20-plus-member Brazilian drum band Maracatu Cruzeiro do Sul. To get a slot at this event is a rarity and I had a warm glow inside feeling that the reputation we had started to gain as a great band has earnt us this reward. As it turned out, it was Wama being friendly with the landlord that had probably been the deciding factor in our appearance.

This was a big chance for us to extend our reach out into the big city, as so far all of our gigs had been centred out in provincial Portslade. We practised hard over the weeks leading up to the gig and as this was only a 45-minute slot this meant we could select ten crowd-pleasing bangers and really go to town on them. As an added extra, Wama had arranged for some chap to come down and shoot some video footage of our performance. I wasn't sure what this was to be used for, but at this stage it didn't come as a surprise to me anymore when Wama came up with these added titbits. I didn't feel the need to question him and was sure this was all part of some grand plan. I figured, if I really needed to know about it, he would tell me.

We were to be the second band on that day. I remember as I arrived and went down the side street that led to the Robin Hood, how amazed I was to see the number of people that had gathered in a relatively small place. It was decent weather and there was a real buzz in the air. I met up with the other guys and they all seemed to be excited for the day ahead. The stage was in the road, and we were covered by a large gazebo that had been erected to house the equipment and the sound engineer. I don't recall the name of the first band, but I do remember their sound. They were a group of young lads who specialised in droning, trippy, shoegazing songs that probably went down well in a university bar, but I thought they had read the crowd and the event wrong as this was all about having a good time and enjoying the late-spring sunshine. They were given a smattering of generous applause when they finished, and deep down I was pleased we were following them as I knew our tempo and our tunes would easily ratchet up the mood of the crowd.

We all assumed our positions and went straight in with our now usual start of 'Rock and Roll' by Led Zeppelin. The atmosphere in the crowd lifted immediately and we soon had a plethora of people bopping along and singing all the lyrics. Our setlist was unashamedly crowd-pleasing for this very reason. This was probably the first time I had strayed more than a couple of feet away from my music stand. Not only was I actually beginning to retain some of the lyrics, but I was starting to mingle with the audience whilst performing. This was quite a liberating experience and also a lot of fun. We finished our set and the reaction we received was positive. Everyone in the band had got a real buzz from this and now we had the rest of the day to enjoy as well. I am certainly glad we didn't go on after Maracatu Cruzeiro do Sul as we would have been real buzz-killers if we had. Their set started off with a mixture of all ages and genders assembled in rows, all dressed up in colourful and exotic garb. Some of them had small drums, some of them had large drums. Some of them had rattles, and some of them clackers. The beat started slowly with a solitary drum, which was slowly joined by one more and then one more, and so on and so on. Within the next couple of minutes, the orchestration had built up to resemble something akin to Mardi Gras in Rio de Janeiro. The beats, the colours, the dancing and the audience participation resulted in the next 45 minutes being a magical fiesta for the senses. It was the perfect music for the location, weather, event and audience. We had been lucky; I cannot remember who went on after them, but they must have been terrified and cursing as they watched this masterclass in action. I recall I was watching them with Tree, and she became so excited she felt the urge to get up with them and Samba dance (still no evidence of Irish dancing to be had). We stayed all day and had a great time, and of all the bands we saw that day they were the most fun. There was one other band that deserve a mention, but for different reasons.

Later on in the day the weather took a turn for the worse. The wind was really getting up and the rain was starting to set in. The bands outside were under a gazebo, but the audience didn't have any cover and so naturally people were either finding refuge inside the pub or else they were going home as there just wasn't enough room inside. It was about eight o'clock and the last of the advertised bands were about to start their set. They were four members of an outfit called the Brighton Beach Boys. This was a scaled down version of the whole band, which could sometimes feature around nine musicians of outstanding quality. As their name suggests they did a number of covers of Beach Boys songs but were very well known for putting on shows featuring a variety of artists from the Beatles to Bowie, for example. The rain outside was pissing down and the wind was blowing a real hoolie as they battled through the numbers one at a time. The only audience they had was me in the doorway smoking a cigarette and Wama stood beside me, just soaking up their professionalism. I recall watching the drummer closely and marvelling at his talent, tenacity and sense of fun for what he was doing. I was contemplating whether he was a genius or just a complete nut job and one day I would find out that he was simply a mixture of the two. This performance had a profound effect upon Wama who was awe inspired that even in such rotten conditions they still not only did their job, but they did it to the absolute best of their ability. This I am sure resulted in a step change in Wama's approach to anything that he would contribute to the band. They finished their set to the rapturous applause of the two of us and we all went back inside the pub. The evening was finished off with drinks, laughter and a camp chap playing the piano whilst the assembled crowd sang show tunes.

FOOTNOTES

HARBOUR VIEW – The pub in Portslade that was to become our headquarters. No longer there as it has been pulled down. Once Sam and Penny (lovely couple) left the place the new owners oversaw a dubious period, which resulted with the police revoking the licence. The adjoining factory is now the home to a large underground gym as well as a venue called the Circle. Owned by local businessman Fash Ghiaci who is renowned for the setting up of a worthwhile charity called the Supported Living Programme that helps many individuals move on with their lives.

ATTILA THE STOCKBROKER – Punk poet who had a close connection with Brighton & Hove Albion in helping them through some tough years. Organiser of some great local festivals. Not a fan of Margaret Thatcher.

MARACATU CRUZEIRO DO SUL – Brazilian Samba band. Tree was so won over by their performance that she found out about them and went to join them. She went to about three rehearsals where she was allowed to shake a tin with some beads in them before she got bored and gave up.

BEACH BOY DRUMMER – Goes by the name of Theseus Gerard. One of the founder members of STOMP. All-round musical maestro who has been known to have his diva moments, but in the main is one of the most generous supporters of those who give a shit about music and do their best; 50 per cent genius/50 per cent nuts.

THE ROBIN HOOD – Superb non-profit pub right on the border of Brighton & Hove run by a lovely couple by the names of Anne and Chris. All the staff are lovely as well. Highly recommended, but a bit too nice for the likes of me, ha-ha.

BIG FOOTNOTE
(WORDS SUPPLIED BY WAMA)

'DIRTY WEEKEND IN BRIGHTON' SONG – Our signature song 'Dirty Weekend in Brighton' came about because of my love for poetry and lyrics. My brother Michael Marmont who was 12 years older than me, (but has now sadly left this world) was a huge Bob Dylan, John Lennon and Neil Young fan and that had a big influence on me. He would bang on about Dylan's lyrics, you know the ones, they are endless. "How many roads must a man walk down, before you can call him a man", "the times they are a-changin'" and many others. They say to get the best lyrics you have to have lived in that situation. For example, being low and out of love with your partner, hence blues songs are about low points in your life. I have had my ups and downs like anyone but, overall, I thought I had generally been lucky in life. The lowest point was my mum dying when I was 14. There is never a good time to go, but, hey, come on Mum, your teen life is hard enough without leaving me to get through it alone. Dad did what he thought was his best, but he found it hard of course, so he would get drunk every night down the Portland pub. Me, well I got involved in loads of bad-ish things that I was not proud of. Luck came my way when I met my Gill who was to become my wife. She took on the task to love me and we are still happily married to this day. So, where I am taking this is how this impacted the way I wrote the lyrics.

I like to always write about Brighton. You see I have no reason to have the blues (touch wood) over relationships or life in general. The track 'Dirty Weekend in Brighton' (check out the excellent video) is about the town's seedy image, which I found so interesting. It opens with a scene I pinched from the old black-and-white film 'Brighton Rock'. The lead character Pinkie is in a record recording booth. It is a dark, rainy scene near the Palace Pier, and he is making a recording for Rose the girl he is besotted with. Actor Richard Attenborough says in a soft mystic voice, "You asked me to make a recording of my voice, well here it is, what you wanted me to say is…" at this point the line goes dead and Rose thinks he's about to say, "I love you." She doesn't hear what he actually says, "But I hate you, you little slut." The song then kicks in with a verse about Graham Greene the writer of the book the film was based on creating Pinkie. The other verses are about locations and events involving the town of Brighton. Things I came across from about the time I was 17. I mention the charismatic Pelirocco Hotel in Regency Square. I was fortunate enough to become friends with Mick Robinson and Jayne Slater who set it up and then with Mark Gibson who is still running it. I then go on to mention the infamous Curtain Club, The Queen of Clubs, that was a club in the corner of Bedford Square, The Lindon Club down Waterloo Street, owned by the Minter boxing family (Alan Minter went on to be the undisputed champion of the world) and the Zipadeedoodah Bar, which was Gary Worley's very 'in-place bar'. This was the first place I knew to ever pour shots, they were called 'Testicoolz Test Tube Cocktails' and 'Slambango', which you slammed on the bar before downing it. All these bars were late-night or afternoon-drinking establishments long before the licensing hours changed to all hours. As I write this, others come to mind. Brighton at this time was polluted with dingy, seedy backstreet clubs that I found fascinating and dangerous. I liked Brighton's image and I felt part of it even if it was only from the sidelines. This was my tribute to the town I loved and writing about things I had experienced was how I would go forward. For example, my best mate was a very 'lovable rogue' (some would disagree) who was raised by an underworld family near Hove station. The next song I was to write was about him. It is called 'Drugs & Sin'. The story of that song may appear later if Phil lets me.

CHAPTER 6 – NEPTUNE LANDING AND ISSUES WITH RE-ENTRY

There is a pub in Hove called the Neptune Inn. It is hard to quite describe just what this place means to me, but also how it has been the catalyst for some of my happiest memories. To most people this place is just a pub, but for me it is different, as this place has been like a musical university to me. It has been my own personal playground as well as the place where I would get the chance to meet some of the most talented and beautiful individuals you could have the good fortune to encounter. I had been someone who would venture in every now and then, but you could certainly not describe me as a regular. Wama, on the other hand, had been frequenting the place for a few years and was something of a well-known face around the bar.

The Neptune is situated on the seafront road in Hove, just one mile west of Brighton. It is a small and unassuming place at first glance when you look at it from the street outside. You would hardly even notice it was there as you stroll along the pavement out the front. Even amongst the people who live in the area many locals who don't know of its existence. It is, however, very well known to those who belong to two particular groups: musicians and lovers of live music. This is not a bar, bistro or even a night spot. This is a proper pub and a celebrated live music venue. No a la carte menu to be found here, unless you count crisps, pork scratchings or pickled eggs deserving of a Michelin star.

It is currently owned by a great supporter of the arts and an all-round super individual by the name of Jan. In 1999 she and her partner Alan took over and inherited what can be best described as a small local pub that had clientele who mainly liked sports and had a slight interest in music, with the odd sporadic gig performed. As soon as they took over, Jan and Alan set about building up the music side of the business, and with the help of a guy called Cliff White – who had some connections within the local music scene – they began to increase the frequency of the gigs. At first this focused on Friday nights and was heavily centred around blues music. This was then complemented with a Sunday afternoon session, which was predominantly jazz based.

Word spread and the audiences began to build steadily. New bands were introduced and, with the help of alliances with pubs like the Raneleigh in Brighton, it meant bands from both sides of town were able to have shared audiences from which both establishments benefited.

It was during this period that the clientele was slowly weaning itself off its sports addiction and was being moulded into something that would soon become much more accepting to new experiences. This, in turn, was to herald a sea change in the general atmosphere that was now being generated. It was slowly but surely turning into one of the few pubs that was bucking the trend of being invaded by Sky Sports and it didn't take long for the underlying core of the place to be converted to music, poetry, ale and the art of conversation. No one really noticed that the TV in the pub was hardly ever on, even for so-called big events. It is amazing how you can be hypnotised by the screen in pubs even if they are showing any old shit with the volume right down.

In around 2010 the day-to-day management of the pub was taken over by a lady called Mary and her very dear friend Roger. Jan was still the owner and was still very much involved in the place, but Mary and Roger would oversee the running of the place. They had previously been involved in another pub, the Portland Rock Bar. Because of this association they had a lot of musical connections and as such the frequency of the gigs increased with the introduction of Saturday nights as well as an open mic.

It wasn't unknown to have the odd famous face from the music industry in the place and no one really paid much attention to these people. It was always accepted that they were just like the rest of us and deserved their privacy, if that was what they wished. No one was really considered to be more special than anyone else in the bar and it created a healthy atmosphere to chill out in.

Music had now become the mainstay of the pub, which not only attracted people who liked to listen, but it also became a focal point for performers as well. There were lots of bands doing lots of gigs all around town, and because the Neptune was open until two in the morning it became a place where musicians would congregate once they had finished off their gigs in the other pubs. You would be at the bar, listening to different bands discussing how they had performed that night, and the place became something of a social club and a centre for learning as well.

The bar itself has decor that looks familiar to many traditional London taverns, with an emphasis on good beer and good company. It attracts a melting pot of locals and at the bar you can witness a millionaire having a conversation with a homeless person, or an ageing mod chatting away to a refined older lady. All types are welcomed, with the only rules being to behave with a level of common decency and to not be too much of a twat. In the main this worked well as it is exceedingly rare to see any disturbances in there that would warrant any more than a passing glance. The majority of the punters know each other, but not in a recognisably cliquey way. Strangers are made welcome, and a large number of new visitors come along to support the music nights and watch the bands play. There is normally a fair number of people who follow a particular band, whether that be as friends or relatives.

As you walk through the door you are greeted to the sight of a pub that is long and narrow. To the right is a sizeable wooden bar set out in the traditional way. Many real ale hand pumps are in view as the place is a recognised CAMRA destination with many positive write-ups in the trade press. All the walls are adorned with hundreds of framed black-and-white photographs of the great and the good from musical history, and you can spend ages enjoying the depictions of some classic moments caught by the lens. Jan was given most of these images when she and Alan took over. They were collected by famous photographer

Fin Costello, and they had found the ideal home on the walls of the Neptune. As you approach the rear of the pub you will come across an extremely small raised wooden stage. The size of said stage is probably adequate to house a three-piece band although I once played on it with six others (very cosy). It is funny to think that the late, great guitarist Gary Moore had performed on it. He had lived just up the road and would pop in from time to time. David Gilmour of Pink Floyd fame also lived close by and had been spotted on a couple of occasions, but I am not sure he was considered good enough for the Neptune stage (I'm joking, Dave). Literally thousands of musicians must have played on this stage over the years and the variety of acts is quite mesmerising. The Neptune has live music several times a week. Monday night is open mic night – and this is a good chance for new musicians to have the opportunity to jam alongside seasoned pros. It has been run in recent years by Theseus, the musical genius I mentioned in the previous chapter. He comperes proceedings and generally starts off the night by playing guitar as well as using a looper pedal to help set up some drumbeats. Often, he might be accompanied by Chris Hookway on bass and Ginny Bourne playing some sweet harmonica. They are pretty much the house band on a Mondays and happily accompany solo performers if they so wish. This can be great for a newbie performer, as it gives them a completely different feel to what they have perhaps been used to. The quality of the music night is excellent, but what sets it apart in my mind is that it is truly welcoming and supportive. There are performers that are not so gifted, but they are given encouragement at all levels. The audience is educated enough to know that it takes a certain amount of bravery to share your art and take part, and they are thankful for anyone who has the guts to put themselves in the firing line. Nobody is overly critical, and they all realise that not everybody can be the next Bowie or Dylan.

Friday nights are predominately handed over to the rock and blues crowd. This is probably the busiest night of the week, and you really are packed in like sardines. I am not a great fan of the blues. I can listen to about four songs before I start getting the feeling that I have heard it all before. You cannot question the quality of musicianship, but quite simply it is not my bag. I have had some great nights in the Neptune on a Friday night, but if you could pick out one night where cliques could form, then Friday is it. There seems to be a generation of blues players in the scene that give off an air of superiority. A lot of them can be critical and in an underhand way. When I watch them perform, I feel a bit sorry for them, but at the same time short-changed as they appear to me to be just going through the motions. They regard themselves as superior beasts and barely acknowledge the audience. I regard them as being up-their-own-arse dickheads who do not have the balls to try something new and different. None of them seem to write any of their own material. Surely it cannot be that hard to write about misery, death or divorce. I think myself and Wama would agree that we admire the skills but are left cold with the show.

Saturday music nights in contrast are the reverse. The music is a bit more varied and fun. I suspect this was influenced by Mary and Roger, as they have transferred some of the Portland Rock Bar vibe into proceedings. Saturday night is more party night and I suppose it is classed in some circles to be musically inferior but, to my mind, some of the stuff I see on a Saturday is of an excellent standard. One of my favourites that stands out is a band called Mad Badger (more on them later).

Saturday bands in general are covers bands, but the genre can vary wildly from week to week. There are the odd turkeys that get booked, but this is bound to happen when you are trying out something new. If you are not much good you simply don't get asked back, but at least you are given a chance. We have played the Neptune many times over the years, and Mary and Roger have said we are definitely a Saturday night band.

The Sunday afternoon session is simply divine. It is a bit more laid back, and this is reflected in most of the bands that play this spot, but sometimes absolute gems will appear that can take your breath away. I remember seeing a band called The Captain's Beard and the day will always stay with me. They were a four piece all dressed up as pirates in full makeup, who performed two hours of hard-hitting punky sea shanties. Another Sunday highlight are personal favourites of mine – The Fabulous Red Diesel. I remember the first time I saw them: as they were setting up, I was thinking that they looked interesting, but I wasn't expecting much. There was a lady dressed in bright colours with long purple dreadlocks; a black drummer who had a Rastafarian look about him; a very tall and slim transgender double bass player with long, flowing blonde hair tied into the biggest ponytail I had ever seen; and a shortish bearded guitarist who resembled an eco-activist. The guitarist also had a selection of brass instruments in front of him. I turned around to Jan who was sitting in her usual spot and said that this could be bloody awful. All she said back to me was, "Just you wait."

They were only about one minute into their set, and I intuitively knew that I was about to witness something incredibly special indeed. It was an absolute masterclass in musicianship and entertainment. Most of it was their own original material, which was masterfully orchestrated. One jaw-dropping moment was when the double bass player produced a tuba and had a duel with the guitarist who was now playing a trumpet. You would seriously pay very good money to see this skill and here I was 4ft away drinking a beer and watching it for free. It is difficult to describe their sound. I have seen a poster where they describe themselves as a "jazz/funk quartet with echoes of funkadelic and The Meters, cherry topped with retro jazz vocals". Think Barbara Streisand crossed with Janis Joplin over a jazz/funk/disco sound, and you are probably close enough. Sunday afternoons in the Neptune are the perfect way to finish a weekend and long may it stay that way.

So, there you have a snapshot of the Neptune and I hope I have been able to convey what the place means not only to me but many others.

Wama played his first gig at the Neptune before the Dirty Weekend ever existed. He was talked into teaming up with Alan the owner, a masterful musician called Stuart Parkes and a Neptune regular called Sandy Riley. This supergroup was formed by accident and went by the name of The C Niles. I am led to believe they formed from a regular Monday afternoon herbal cigarette gathering around someone's house where they would strum a guitar and talk complete bollocks. They spent some time practising a little set together and when they eventually got around to unleashing this on to an unsuspecting world, they were given the accolade of being the worst band of all time. They would mainly do covers by the likes of Cohen and Dylan, but Alan had written an original about his own relationship with cancer treatment. This song was called 'Take it One Prick at a Time'. This was a really upbeat pub singalong song believe it or not. Wama was undeterred by how bad they were, and this is where he caught the music bug.

In all honesty someone could write a book solely about the Neptune as the number of stories and characters are infinite. Who knows, if this becomes a bestseller, I might be able to afford to spend a year researching it? The Neptune means the world to me – and now for the story of the first time we played there.

As with previous gigs, it was Wama who informed us that we had our first gig at the Neptune. By this point, I was no longer naïve enough to think that we had got this on our musical merits, and I was fairly sure that Wama had either begged or blackmailed Mary or Roger. We would be playing on a Saturday night so at least the blues brigade wouldn't be up in arms and the crowd were a bit more forgiving. We were certainly not taking for granted that we would be well supported, and it is hard to fully explain how much playing at the Neptune meant to us. There were lots of bands wanting to play the place and I dare say that there were many other bands that considered us underserving of our slot. On the flip side I must point out there are just as many supportive musicians out there as well and many came to watch us as they knew it was a big deal. Fresh from our relative success of the street party, we certainly didn't rest on our laurels. We were pretty determined to be as good as we could be for our Neptune debut. The catalogue of songs we could perform had grown to a respectable number, meaning we might even be able to do an encore without any repeats. I would like to say we weren't taking for granted that we would get an encore, but let us not kid ourselves, all bands do one whether they are asked to or not. For the next two weeks we practised like demons and found ourselves spending a lot of time together. We were getting tighter as a band, but the extra time together also saw some obvious signs of tetchiness as well. Tony and Mark were still doing their love/hate/get-a-room routine with each other and they were perhaps a bit too quick and snappy at discussing guitar parts with Clive. I was head down learning lyrics and Wama was practising relentlessly at home as well, plus his head had also gone into promoter mode and he was trying every trick in the book to persuade punters to come to the gig.

The day of the gig arrived and – as was usual now – Wama wanted to get to the venue about two and a half hours before we were due to start. We arrived and Roger behind the bar said to me, "I hear this band tonight are shit." I agreed and said, "I hear the barman is a complete knobhead." Pleasantries over, we started to set up. As per usual, I didn't have an awful lot to do, so I decided to sit at the bar and have a drink whilst I read through some lyrics. For some reason this was perhaps the most nervous I had felt before a gig. I wasn't sure if it was because we were playing the Neptune, or because we had started to create a little buzz and I knew it would be mobbed tonight with a lot of people coming to see what all the fuss was about. I figured the best way to deal with this was to drink, and drink heavily.

Wama was at the back of the stage with his trusty hammer and was nailing up banners to form a backdrop. Not only did we have the one with the band name, but there were two new additions. One was modelled on the kind of saucy seaside postcards that were popular in the 1960s and 70s. It was of a very buxom woman wearing thick cherry-red lipstick. She had exceptionally long flowing black hair that gave her a mysterious enchantress like look, and her miniskirt stopped just above her frilly knicker line. If this was considered a bit risqué, it had nothing on the 4ft by 2ft piece of porn that joined her on the other side. The young lady on this banner had long blonde hair tied back in a ponytail, she was also wearing glasses that were balanced on the end of her perfect nose. She was kneeling on the floor and was naked apart from a black suspender belt and fishnet stockings. She was bound by ropes that lifted up her pert naked breasts and continued around her body where both her wrists were tied together. Some thought this was just pure filth and porn, I thought it was genius and some weeks later was so pleased when Wama presented it to me printed on a T-shirt he had had made up. This banner would upset a few people, but on a later occasion was to cause quite a lot of trouble. This will rear its head again in a later chapter.

We went through the painstaking routine of the drumkit setup, with Tony once again being anal on the position of every piece, Clive annoying the shit out of everyone by playing random notes in no discernible order, Mark gurning at his amp, Wama redecorating the pub and me getting pissed. The pub was pretty empty at that point and I was beginning to worry that we were about to play the quietist night ever known at the Neptune. This worry was unfounded, as within the space of ten minutes in came a load of people from my work, as well as quite a few family members and friends of the band. More and more were pouring in and by the time we were due to begin the place was packed. I gathered the guys together from all corners of the pub and told them we had better get ready to start. They all appeared to be really nervous, and I was confused as I didn't feel that way at all. This was due in no small part to the fact that I had been consuming copious amounts of alcohol since we arrived. There was a method to this madness though. The rest of the guys weren't allowed to drink before a gig as we had seen the effects it could have on someone playing an instrument. On one of our music nights down the Harbour View, I remember Wama had had quite a lot to drink and when it came to playing guitar it was an absolute car crash. Me, on the other hand, being the singer found it quite beneficial to be half-pissed when I was getting up to perform. It helped to release inhibitions and I found that my level of piss-taking with the audience reached levels of excellence that I would have found hard to attain otherwise.

All the guys got into position and checked over their amps. I made sure my lyric book was in the right order and I made doubly sure that my mobile phone was on hand as we had learnt a few new songs and I had downloaded the lyrics on to the phone as I didn't have time to write them down on paper.

I took the mic and welcomed everyone to the show. We went straight in with our now familiar start of Led Zeppelin followed by Bowie. The assembled crowd were right into it from the very beginning. The level of support we received was amazing. Admittedly, the majority were very much for us on a personal level, but we were playing OK and I think the level of fun we projected did transfer over well. I would have my usual drunken banter in between songs and my taking the piss out of the other band members was at its usual high level. I actually relished pointing out our mistakes to the crowd, which I found out in later years was not fully appreciated by the chaps. As I spotted individuals I knew in the crowd, I would chat to them on the mic in between the songs and take the piss out of them as well, but this was done in a loving way of sorts.

One example was when we about to do one song I pointed out my brother Kevin at the back and went into a long monologue about him and generally tried to embarrass him. I then dedicated the next song to him as we launched into 'Creep' by Radiohead. As we moved into the chorus, I had the crowd directing the words directly at him, which filled me with pure joy. As the old saying goes, 'Revenge is a dish best served cold' and he was as cool as the proverbial cucumber. The next song required me to use my phone for the lyrics and so I had it positioned on the music stand close enough to read from it. We started the song with all going well when all of a sudden, the lyrics disappeared and all I could see on my screen was an incoming call from Kev. I looked up to see him with his phone held in one hand to his ear whilst his other hand was raised with one solitary middle finger raised in happy defiance. The smile on his face was one of pure satisfaction. I was in a brief moment of panic and a flash feeling of sweat consumed me instantly. In this millisecond I learnt an immensely powerful technique that I would use many times over the coming years. That technique was to make up my own lyrics and sing any old shit that pops into my head. As long as it goes in time with the melody a large proportion of the audience would be none the wiser. You just have to bluff it out in the most confident way you can, and the beauty of a semi-drunk audience is they either do not care or they do not realise.

This reminds me of a time at a gig when we did 'Hotel California' by The Eagles and I sang the third verse where the second should be. As we were about to go into the third verse, I realised this and then went on to make up my own words with the last two lines being, "I sang the third verse when I should have sung the second, can you please forgive me," then straight into the chorus, "Welcome to the Hotel California" (try it in your head). Not one person noticed or mentioned it, they just all joined in with the chorus.

Back at the Neptune gig, we had about six or seven songs that I had to read from my phone and Kev (bastard) sent the word round so that every time I sang a song with the phone, I had loads of incoming calls.

The gig was going great and now we had the opportunity to add a bit of class. We were fortunate in that we had met a lot of supremely talented musicians in a short space of time and one of these gifts to the music scene came in the form of Ruth Egau who was known to everyone as Ruby. We had met Ruby as she was a good friend of Alex the guitar teacher and she was the lead singer of the South Coast Soul Revue, which they were both in. The term 'pocket rocket' has been used over the years to describe many performers, but in her case it is fully merited. Her voice is excellence personified and the way she can deliver the story behind a song really does burrow into your soul. On top of all this she is one of the most fun-loving and generous individuals you could wish to meet. We had persuaded her to come up and do a few numbers with us and the result was truly magical. It added a whole different aspect to the gig and without wanting to be detrimental to my fellow band mates it was the first time I had been on a stage with such quality. The only word that can describe the whole experience is quite a simple one, and that word is 'FUN'.

The rest of the gig went by in a bit of a drunken blur at some kind of hyper-speed. We were having a party onstage and the crowd seemed to be joining in. Mind you, you cannot please everyone, as I vividly remember spotting an older super-talented bass player from a band I had seen many times over the years standing there with a critical look on his face looking slightly disgusted. You could tell he was thinking, "Who the fuck are this bunch of upstarts?" I would later overhear him making disparaging remarks about us, but it didn't bother me much at that moment as I was on a high and, to my mind, he was just a precious twat. The final song finished, and the audience were cheering and clapping loudly as they shouted out for an encore. This was not a false encore, they actually really wanted one.

We had been working on some new covers and had just the song for the occasion as we launched into 'Pretty Vacant' by the Sex Pistols. I am fairly sure I hadn't seen many pub bands do this and certainly not down the Neptune, the home of blues and jazz.

The place went mental – and I went mental as well as I channelled my inner Johnny Rotten, which to be fair was not that much of a challenge for me at that point. It all came to a glittering and violent end, and we all just looked at each other with the biggest grins on our faces. We got paid and had money in the jug that went around as well. We gave it all back to the pub as they had been raising money for the excellent Martlets charity. The after-gig session was crazy, and it was so good to catch up with all of my friends and work colleagues. Roger behind the bar gave me the lovely feedback, "You weren't as shit as I thought you were going to be." Believe me this was high praise.

This was the first time we were to play the Neptune and it was the only time with this line-up of the band. This was the high point as things were about to go on to take a different course for all of us.

FOOTNOTES

FIN COSTELLO – In a career spanning 40 years, he has worked with some of the most influential names in the music business, including Aerosmith, Ozzy Osbourne, The Police, Thin Lizzy, Deep Purple, Kiss, The Rolling Stones and Jimi Hendrix. In 1981 Fin's photograph of Duran Duran featured on the front cover of the band's debut self-titled album.

THESEUS GERARD – He was one of the founder members of the world-renowned theatrical dance company STOMP. He is a sublime percussionist, singer-songwriter, dancer and, more importantly to my mind, a teacher and friend to those who want to embrace music in the right spirit.

PORTLAND ROCK BAR – Before it was the Rock Bar it was just the plain old Portland. I spent a misguided youth in this establishment, which had a reputation for being rough and uncouth. This was the place where I would cross paths for the first time with Wama. We were in different circles, and I think he regarded me as an annoying little shit, whereas I regarded him as a complete bellend. Fairly sure some would contest that we haven't changed much.

STUART PARKES – All-round good guy with a penchant for exotic headwear and bright shirts. More importantly, a brilliant bass player who has been around so long that he actually played on the same bill as Little Stevie Wonder.

MAD BADGER – One of the most entertaining bands you will ever have the pleasure to share an evening with. The two stalwarts of the band are Noel and Andy. One great memory of them was when they did a charity event at the infant school that Noel's son went to. To watch them onstage with loads of toddlers dancing around their legs and a child on Noel's shoulders whilst they sang 'Turning Japanese' by the Vapours, which is allegedly a song about an inmate masturbating in his prison cell, will stay with me forever.

ANDY THE DANDY – A recurring theme with the band was the artwork for the posters and this is the man we have to thank. A very dapperly dressed man, who not only was a brilliant graphic artist but is also a DJ of enormous talent. Can be seen regularly doing a set at the

Paris House in Brighton. My eternal gratitude to one of our most generous of supporters.

'POST-GIG PINT' – As explained in this chapter, the Neptune was a meeting place for bands after they had done their shows around town. I was lucky enough to persuade a talented chap by the name of Jim Best to allow me to use a poem that he has written that sums this up so beautifully. Jim is a multi-instrumentalist and fronts superb band The Cracklin' Griffins (well worth catching them live).

'POST-GIG PINT' by Jim Best

The band blasts its final chord
And the crowd may_ or not_ applaud
But the same thought happens, on this, and many a night
'Get the speakers in the van_
In twenty minutes if we can
And we'll Nep it, for a post gig pint'

The boys stuffed in the back
Jabbering away about the craic
Dissecting the songs gone wrong_ and those gone right
All eyes are on the clock
Will we need to stop?
Will we make the Nep, for a post gig pint?

We've come from the coast, the town, the sticks

Worthing, Lewes_ further afield_ Kent, Essex!

Is it too far to get back in time tonight?

'The crowd went nuts'_ 'they were bored'

'There was bugger all there'_ 'it was packed'_ 'they roared!'

We certainly need that post gig pint

With time getting close

We start to think, who'll be our host?

If it's Mary_ she'll see we're alright

But if it's Sharon_ and it's ten to two

She'll have some words to say_ a few!

And we may not get that post gig pint!

Once Roger was the familiar face

When we walked into the place

'You been playing in Molly's tonight?'

We'd ask about the next dark ale, and how the band played

Never really blown away, he'd say 'they were alright'

And Charlie would have a lemonade topped pint

And the finished band might crack_

A speaker in your back

As they take their gear past you, into the night

And you ask them 'how'd it go?'
And they say 'great!' or 'cool' or 'slow'
And you swap stories with your post gig pint

And Jan might be there, in the corner on her chair
But she'll wisely go, before last orders ring tonight
And Carol might ease the volume up for a song_
If Rod Stewart happens to come on
As you sip that post gig pint

Rock, Metal, Jazz and Blues
Any genre you could choose
All rushed back from personal stardom this night
Whether amateur, part-time, or pro
They've all given it a go
And hanker for that post gig pint

But a year to stop the sounds_ and the applause
And seal shut the pubs doors
Music on computers, our only sight
And we miss the tunes and chat
A culture gone! Just like that
And we long for a post gig pint

But the bands will return once more_

And gingerly try the door

Hoping that those lights are still on bright

And they'll heartily unwind

With whoever's there inside

And they'll get to have that post gig pint!

ONE Prick @ A TIME - ALAN's CANCER SONG.

E7   A7   E7   A7
I ASKED IN THE PAST - HOW LONG DOES IT LAST
B7   A7   E7
U TAKE IT ONE PRICK AT A TIME......
                          E7   A7
THERE'S SHRUGS AND THERE'S DRUGS & MY WIFE'S PERFECT JUGS
BUT YOU TAKE IT ONE PRICK AT A TIME
                    A7   E7

Chorus
    E7   A7   E7   A7
    YOU TAKE IT - YOU TAKE IT - U DON'T WISH TO BREAK IT
    B7   A7   E7
    U TAKE IT ONE PRICK AT A TIME

    E7   A7   A7
IT SEEMS TO TAKE AGES - U TAKE IT IN STAGES
U TAKE IT ONE PRICK AT A TIME
    B7   A7   E7

    E7   A7   E7   A7
U SIT AND YOU WAIT - U STAND BY THE GATE
U TAKE IT ONE PRICK AT A TIME
    B7   A7   E7
    E7   A7   E7   Prick
    YOU TAKE IT - YOU TAKE IT......... WISH A7-B7 A7 E7
                                            TAKE

    E7   A7   E7   A7
YOUR BOLLOXS GET BATTERED - YOUR SCROTUM GETS SHATTERED
YOUR CONFIDENCE IS LACKING - YOUR MATES GIVE YOU BACKING
    BUT YOU TAKE IT ONE PRICK AT A TIME
            B7   A7   E7
                                                Prick
    E7   A7   E7 WISH   A7-B7 A7 E7
BUT YOU TAKE IT - YOU TAKE IT.........   TAKE

    E7   A7   E7   A7
& WITH LUV ALL AROUND YOU - WITH FRIENDS THAT SURROND YOU
QUITE   B7   A7   E7
            YOU TAKE ONE PRICK AT A TIME

LOUD   E7   A7   E7 DON'T WISH TO BREAK IT
BUT YOU TAKE IT - YOU TAKE IT.U.   A7
    B7   Prick AT A TIME x 2 or 3
    U TAKE IT ONE   E7
                    A7

BIG FOOTNOTE 'ONE PRICK AT A TIME' – These are the lyrics to Alan's original composition about his cancer treatment. It was performed with gusto and happiness.

CHAPTER 7 – GROWN MEN FIGHTING IN THE PLAYGROUND

This is not the jolliest or the most fun-filled chapter in the book, but it is a particularly important one. After our debut at the Neptune, I was incredibly happy with how things had gone, and I began to think of us a proper band. Don't think for a minute I was getting ahead of myself and thinking we were world-beaters or even good enough to be considered above-average musicians. I was, however, confident that we knew how to put on a show, and we were able to deliver something that the audience definitely felt part of. Certainly, other bands were much tighter and had some supremely polished players, but I felt we had a fun factor that many lacked. I also felt we made sure the audience were not taken for granted and we never came across in such a way that some could accuse us of with being arrogant.

We returned to our usual routine of rehearsals and had a number of small gigs on the horizon for us to get our teeth into. I felt that now we were gigging maybe once a month, I was looking forward to having something to continually work towards. I especially liked that we would try to learn a number of new covers for each gig – breaking the monotony of singing the same tunes over and over again. The upcoming shows were actually at venues where I was confident we had been booked on our own merits and not just because Wama knew the owners.

As it happened, word was now beginning to get around that not only were we not a musical car crash waiting to happen, but we also had the ability to draw a bit of a crowd that would follow us. The fact that a band could draw a crowd definitely helped to get gigs. Overheads are high when you run a pub and putting a band on is not something you do just to be kind. You do it to offer something different that will ultimately bring people in, who will then drink you dry of beers and spirits and have such a good time that they tell all their friends about what a great pub they went to. It has to be financially worthwhile for all, and it is not unreasonable that some bar owners' despair when a band doesn't make the effort to promote the night as much as they probably should. Money paid to bands is always a contentious issue and I was always in favour of a reasonable flat fee plus a jug going around the crowd to put cash in if they felt so inclined.

If you booked us you were not only guaranteed a good turnout, but the added bonus that people who supported us did like a good drink. Whether that was because we brought out their fun side or they needed to be drunk to listen to us is open for debate. We also had a secret weapon – our own Don King who went by the name of Wama. He would go to any lengths to get our gigs noticed. It wouldn't be beyond him to take out ads in local magazines and he would leave flyers in every pub and café in the surrounding area. I am sure he disguised many pub crawls to Gill as just going out to do some promoting.

It may sound like everything was all rosy in the garden, but unfortunately rehearsals were beginning to take a bit of a dark turn. Over a short period of time some splits and factions were beginning to form. This could be described best by breaking it down. Mark and Tony were the seething, festering superior rhythm section; Clive and Wama were the under-fire trainee guitar section; and I was a kind of drunk Switzerland.

There was no doubt that at this stage Tony and Mark were the more accomplished musicians, as they had put in a lot of graft. They had started learning their instruments earlier than the others, and they also probably had a bit more time to take things seriously. Maybe they were at a point in their lives that meant that they could devote more of their spare time to practice. They would even spend extra time practising together on their own in order to get their parts as tight as possible. Wama and Clive were real newbies. They were no less dedicated, but their circumstances were probably a lot different. Also, I am not saying that one instrument is easier or harder to learn than another, but in the case of learning lead guitar like Clive had to, I would guess that that takes more time. I was in my own little bubble and was pretty oblivious to the pressures of having to practise at all. As far as I was concerned, I just took a song and sang the words. I was so lazy that I didn't even bother to memorise the words, I just sang them from my lyric book or phone as I needed to.

I It was now apparent that patience was being strained and some of the comments exchanged between the other members were not particularly encouraging'. I wasn't attending every practice because of work commitments, but I became aware of one particular session that overheated and the comments became too personal. This wasn't a healthy situation in which to create sweet music.

At the time I certainly didn't see why it mattered if things were taking longer to improve. As far as I was concerned, we weren't changing the world, and everyone needed to chill out a bit. I thought it was petty and that things would sort themselves out in the end. Years later I probably changed my opinion somewhat, as I found that I too could get frustrated if things didn't improve at the rate I wanted them to. I don't know if this is a natural reaction to just getting better at what you do, or if you start believing your own hype and develop diva-like tendencies.

So, as you see the current climate was not great, but we did have some good things ahead of us in the immediate future. The first of these was my first venture into a recording studio to record a song that Wama had written. I was definitely the novice here as the other chaps had done this once before when they had recorded the Morning Glory song 'Brighton March'. Leading up to the session I remember how excited I had felt and had pictures in my mind of the mega groups just larking around, getting inspired and then putting down some solid-gold shit. I imagined we would be working in a haze of jazz cigarettes and Jack Daniel's bottles.

Maybe there might be the odd celebrity or supermodel popping in to see what sessions were going on that day.

We all met at a designated spot on the corner of New Church and Sackville Road in Hove. We were recording at the aptly named Church Road Studios, which is situated in the basement of a large building that years ago used to be a Barclays bank. The basement area is where the vaults used to be and with the thickness of the walls it is the perfect place to make copious amounts of noise. I was introduced to a cool-looking dude who went by the name of Paul Pascoe. He was our sound engineer and producer, and he certainly appeared to look like the sort of character I had pictured in my imagined scenario. That is where the similarity ends between my expectation and the reality. The guys had used Paul on the previous record and so were slightly familiar with how these things work.

We were led into a room where the guys started getting their instruments out to tune and start the setup. The general chatter was quite cheerful and light, which made for a refreshing change. Paul was scurrying around and began to set up a variety of different mics for the amps and the drumkit. This, to my mind, was taking an eternity and so far, not one bottle of Jack nor a supermodel were to be seen.

Once all the mics were in place, we went about getting all the levels correct. All instruments were checked and double checked, and the mics were examined one at a time. Believe me when I tell you this is not as exciting as it sounds, so I made my way outside to have a fag and swig on some Lucozade in order to lubricate my vocal cords. I popped back inside to see that nothing seemed to have occurred in my absence and decided to go back out for another cigarette. Some more twiddling and tuning, and apparently we were ready for our first take. We went through the song called "Dirty Weekend in Brighton" written by Wama– I thought it was surprisingly good and that it was in the can. I was then told we weren't actually recording, and we needed to go through the song several times to get loose and release our inner mojo. Over and over again we did it, and my mojo was bored shitless. Finally, we were given the green light to actually record something. We did several takes before retiring into the inner sanctum of Paul's control room. We lounged on comfy sofas and pretended we all knew what we were doing. Paul sat at a mighty console that wouldn't have looked out of place on the *Starship Enterprise*. Thousands of knobs and dials all interconnected by a spaghetti junction of different coloured cables. He then instructed us all in turn to get back into the recording room one at a time as we individually re-recorded certain parts or added more stuff. The other guys acted really enthusiastically about the whole experience, and I began to wonder whether I was missing something. I found the whole process tedious and soul-destroying, and I can honestly say to this day I will never understand how anyone can enjoy the recording process. I am not knocking anyone and if this sort of thing gets you off then good luck to you. I have known guitarists who would spend a whole day just going through their parts on a track and they have loved every single second of the task. I just get off on the live experience as, to me, that is something pure and spontaneous, and I like the fact that it cannot be replicated the same way twice.

Rough recordings of the track were finished and eventually we were able to listen to what we had prior to the mixing and mastering, which would take place at a later date. It was pretty reasonable, I thought, but we would have to wait a while for the finished article. We thanked Paul for his work, and I for one couldn't wait to get the hell out of there in the hope that we would never want to record again.

A few days passed and Wama messaged me to say we had the track back. On top of that, we also had a video to go with it. I was intrigued to hear how the track would be compared with the rough cut I had heard, and, at the same time, I was confident it would come out well. I was also really confused as, for the life of me, I certainly couldn't remember anything being said about a video and I was certain I couldn't have been so drunk that I didn't remember being filmed. He also told me it had been released and was now on YouTube ready to view. I was filled with dread as I knew Wama could be slightly impulsive, and I would have appreciated a little bit of time in quality control before we pushed the release button. It was fairly late at night, and I stopped off in the Three Graces pub for a late-night beer so I could steady myself before witnessing what we had unleashed on to the internet. I found it on YouTube, sat down on my own in the corner and pressed play. The opening bars to the song pushed through and comes imagery and stills that depict our hometown. Scenes from the iconic film *Brighton Rock* are entwined amongst pictures of rioting mods and rockers. All of a sudden, I appear and am singing with the band in black-and-white footage that had been shot at a street party in town months ago. This footage is used throughout the video, mixed in with images of historic landmarks and some of the more colourful local characters. There is a high percentage of sleazy and sexual content, and the overriding impression is that you are witnessing the beating pulse of a city bursting into to life in the best traditions of Sodom and Gomorrah. Three minutes and 48 seconds later I sat back and took a large gulp of my beer. I couldn't believe what I had seen and heard. It was actually good. Really fucking good. It had exceeded any expectations that I could possibly have had. I sat there on my own in a stunned silence for a while. I texted my brother Kev and told him to go on to YouTube and tell me what he thought. He soon came back and asked me about how we did the video and said what a great track it was. It was probably the first time it had occurred to me that we were a serious band. This was an original composition and this track Wama had written inspired me to start writing material as well. I should add that the previous song 'Brighton March' didn't touch the same nerve. The whole recording and video process had been a success, and now it was on to the next thing.

A couple of local gigs followed, and it was all OK. I decided to take a leaf out of Wama's book regarding onstage accessorising. Wama at the time had a very colourful jacket that was covered in iconic imagery in the form of colourful patches. I asked him where he had purchased such an item and he told me about a weird boutique in the North Laine area of Brighton. This area is very trendy and popular with the arty-farty types as well as the student set. I decided I too wanted something like this as it would show that I was down with the kids. I was seeing my daughter that weekend and thought what could be better than having a little daddy-and-daughter time, whilst we gaily spent the day amongst the hip and trendy folk doing retail therapy. I took Maddie to a few shops that she liked and then ushered her towards the swanky boutique Wama had told me about. We went in and Maddie naturally asked me why I would want to come to such a shop. I told her about Wama's jacket and how I too wanted one for a bit of stage craft. I explained that you apparently take a jacket from the rail and for a price they would then sew on various patches that you chose to give you an individual look. Maddie was quite fascinated that her old dad was out there leading the frontline in emerging new fashions. She then said she was looking forward to helping me and would be picking out the patches. You might think this was a beautiful bonding moment, but I knew I was in trouble as my coat of many colours was about to take shape. The back was to be a large target with the emblem from *The Kids Are Alright* album by The Who, so we were off to a good start. The right-hand side on the front was a Union Jack and just above this was something called 'TZ THE ACADEMY TACTIC ZONE'. I had no idea what this was. On the left side was a big patch with geckos wearing sunglasses. Just below was an alien in the lotus position sitting below a peace sign. Below that was a giant skull sitting above a giant red cross made from two zips. My daughter was pleased with her work and asked me if I liked it. I should have said that I thought she must be on drugs or something, but instead I just put it on and smiled.

When I showed Wama the coat of many colours that I intended to wear at the next gig, he was very complimentary to my face but deep down I suspect he was not happy, as now he had competition in the looking-like-a-twat stakes. Looking back, it was like we were seven-year-old girls playing dress-up.

Around this time, we had another gig back at the Romans, where it had all started for us. Chris Pobjoy was leaving the pub and would be going headfirst into mid-life crisis mode (good for him), and so he was having a bit of a do which would last most of the day. We played an hour set and it went down well. It was a good crowd, and all were in a great party mood. A couple of other bands played and they went down a storm. There were some good musicians on show that day. In the main, most of them were good guys, but there was one particular prima donna who was a bit of an arsehole – in my opinion, that is his problem not mine. We would come across him a few times over the years and he has never really gone up in my estimation. In fact, he went further down. I will not name him, but if he reads this book he will recognise himself, so for now let us just call him X-Man. It is not uncommon to come across people like this in musical circles and he was just one member of what I used to refer to as the 'Brighton Music Mafia'.

Things with Dirty Weekend were ticking along nicely and there were a few interesting developments in my personal life. I was working at Asda still. Gary – the young chap who had had the heart episode at work – was out of his induced coma and was doing fine. I had grown a bit fed up with the upper management of the firm as I felt they didn't properly address the concerns I had about what had happened. On the spur of the moment, I decided that life was too short and I didn't want to be found dead at the end of the cereal aisle, so I handed in my notice after spending 25 years working in the retail sector. I had no idea what I would do for work and there was absolutely no point as far as I was concerned in going into something that was even remotely similar to what I had been doing all these years. I had no plan at all and was not completely sure what my particular skillsets had me marked out for. What I did know was that I wanted to go in a completely different direction and all I had to do was figure out exactly what that was to be. Colin Peachey, my best friend from Asda had a wife called Sue whom I had known for many years. She worked in adult social care at the time and informed me that the company she worked for were always on the lookout for individuals to join their list of bank staff who worked with adults who had learning difficulties. Equipped with my "WHY NOT?" mantra I surmised that this might be the complete reverse of what I had been used to and, as such, could give me the drastic change I was seeking. I also foolishly thought it couldn't be that difficult, surely. How wrong I was. Without going into too much detail I will sum it up as such. You have days that are so good you cannot buy the joy that you experience. On the flip side you have days that are so challenging you cannot describe how bad they are. I was a complete novice and, looking back, the training was pretty shoddy. I was just thrown into situations that I had certainly not been equipped for. But I did alright, due to the fact that I had a kind of gung-ho attitude and no fear of situations I would encounter. Unexpectedly, what was a big help to me at the time was that the majority of service users I worked with had a love of music. It amazes me to this day that the power of music can overcome many obstacles. It is an international language that can bring an understanding between people who may not be on the same wavelength. A lot of the guys I was working with had certain limitations with things such as speech, hearing problems, autism, Asperger's, Down's syndrome and others. It can take time to get to know an individual and for that person to be able to trust you. You have to remember you are encroaching on their personal life. When you find that both parties have a love of music, I swear to you barriers are sent crashing down in record time and life becomes not only easier but a damn sight more enjoyable. One particular chap I had been assisting was the lead singer in a band called Heavy Load. They were a five piece that included three members with learning difficulties. He used to love stories of my band and I used to love listening to his experiences. He was a lot more punk than me, and he lived up to the stereotype of the bad boy of rock. There were some people who didn't approve of the way he led his life, but I knew from spending a lot of time with him that he loved the whole situation. So here I was in a new line of work and basically making it up as I went along. Things were going strong in my new relationship with the Riverdance champion and, all in all, life was sweet.

* * *

The next gig was to be at the Three Graces pub in Hove. Again, it was very well attended and lots of fun was had by all. I thought we played very well and were getting better and better with every live show we did. The only thing that marks this gig out from any of the others was the fact that it was to be our last – although we didn't know that at the time. There were no glaringly obvious signs that things were to come to an abrupt halt. I can only put this down to the fact that I was maybe not paying close enough attention or was dismissive of things I deemed not that big a deal. My mindset might have been influenced by the fact that on a daily basis at work I was spending my time with people who had real-life issues to contend with and as such I tended not to sweat over stuff I considered to be trivial in comparison.

There was no doubt that tension had been building up in Mark and Tony, and this was being directed mainly towards Clive, but also a bit towards Wama as well. I will never know the complete truth behind this, but I suspect Mark and Tony had been told that they were on a higher musical plane. They were soaking this up a bit too seriously and losing sight of what we had started out to achieve, a fun time with mates. The actual night of the split was not something I was there for. I was working an evening shift on our usual practice night. As I understand it, Mark and Tony were already down at the factory rehearsal room when Clive and Wama walked in. Allegedly, Tony said they needed to have a chat and then went on to tell the guys that he wasn't happy with the way things were going. He wasn't enjoying being in the band and for that reason he thought they should go their separate ways. Wama then said something like, "Fuck this then," packed away his guitar and left. Clive stood in silence for a while, and then he too packed up his stuff and left the room without saying a word. So, that was the end, and at that point I was unaware.

The following day, I received a message from Tony asking me to give him a ring. Not long after, Wama called to ask me if I could possibly meet him for lunch in the next day or so. This was weird in itself as I can assure you that Wama and I are not the types who 'do lunch'. I rang Tony and he told me what had gone on and asked to meet up for a beer. I met Tony and tried to sort the issues out, but it was evident that this route was pointless. He then went on to tell me that he and Mark certainly didn't want to give up the music and that they were going to form another band. They had been given the name of a new lead guitarist that might be interested as well. He asked me my thoughts and if perhaps I might still want to carry on and be the singer. I said I would have a think about it as I was totally undecided what to do. Don't get me wrong,

I did fancy saying yes straight away. I have always quite enjoyed the experience and Tony had become a good friend as well.

The following day at midday I found myself sitting at a table in the Stoneham pub with Wama. This place used to be called the Portland and I chuckled inside, visualising myself and Wama from the old days in this place. We would certainly never have been sitting together at lunchtime enjoying frothy lattes.

We got the small talk out of the way and he came out with, "Look, Phil, I know you are a close mate of Tony's, but I would kick myself if I didn't ask you what you are going to do about the band."

I asked what he meant, and he went on to explain that he had chatted to Clive and they didn't want to pack it all in. He then asked if I would consider still singing with the band. At this stage I felt like a whore and I would be lying if I said I didn't like it.

Now, at that point, it is fair to say Tony was probably the one that I was the friendliest with. Wama I liked much more than when we first started, but my decision was based, in truth, on what I felt about Clive at the time. I really liked him. I found him to be such a genuine human being and although he will kill me for saying this, he was akin to a favourite puppy. I told Wama that I would stay, but also informed him that I would be singing in the other band as well. He agreed and said he was pleasantly surprised. Some might think I was taking a cowardly decision by not picking one over the other, but the bottom line was I didn't have an axe to grind with anyone and I liked them all. Wama then let me in on his plan. He thought young Joe Colburn could join us to play some bass and Joe's friend might be interested in doing the drums. We finished our coffee, shook hands and went our separate ways.

I then got in touch with Tony and informed him I would be staying in Dirty Weekend, but I was quite happy to be in his new band as well. He agreed and from that moment I was the lead singer of two bands.

FOOTNOTES

PAUL PASCOE – Paul has been a producer, engineer, teacher, songwriter and performer for over 25 years. His work with local bands and young musicians starting out is inspiring. One of music's good guys who is also involved with Northbrook College in Sussex and Super8Sync, a music agency that provides services for film and TV.

NORTH LAINE – Not to be confused with The Lanes. This is my favourite part of town. A large variety of wacky shops and boutiques. Great pubs and the location of the Komedia Comedy Club and the world-famous music shop GAK. It is like a mini Camden Town.

VIDEO FOR 'DIRTY WEEKEND IN BRIGHTON' – The video was put together by a chap called Simon Oliver who ended up working for the BBC on a range of documentaries. Quite how we got hold of him remains a mystery to this day.

BRIGHTON MUSIC MAFIA – A collection of arseholes who seem to think that they are the scene and any newcomers should be looked down upon. This group does not just contain musicians, but also venues, promoters and music colleges. They seem to have forgotten that music is for sharing and also for encouraging people to participate for the right reasons. Luckily, they are counter-balanced by some truly astonishing and caring musicians who do not have their heads up their own arses.

BIG FOOTNOTE

HEAVY LOAD – Heavy Load were an English punk rock band, described by *The Sunday Times* in 2009 as "possibly the most genuinely punk band touring today". Active from 1996–2012 the band members were Simon Barker (vocals), Jimmy Nichols (bass), Paul Richards (guitar), Michael White (drums) and Mick Williams (guitar). Its members met at Southdown Housing, a non-profit assisted-living community for people with mental health issues and learning difficulties and were a mix of service users and staff. The band composed the theme for the BAFTA-nominated film *Cast Offs* and this is documented in the film *Heavy Load* (a must-see). The band were also the founders of the charity Stay Up Late, a campaign seeking to improve the social lives of people with learning difficulties by calling for more flexible staff hours. Stay Up Late is a national charity promoting full and active social lives for people with learning difficulties.

Heavy Load split in September 2012 with a final gig in London's Trafalgar Square as part of the Paralympic festivities. Simon Barker died suddenly on 10th August 2017. I will always remember him fondly.

CHAPTER 8 – DOWN WITH THE KIDS

So, through no fault of my own, I had now managed to double my workload in my fledgling music career. I would soon be practising two nights a week – on Tuesdays I would practise with Dirty Weekend, whilst on Thursdays it would be Fingered By Aliens (an unfortunate band name I think you will agree). Quite how we got that name escapes me to be honest, but you have to admit, it is not easily forgotten. What I do know is that when we would do gigs in the future, you would see our name advertised outside of pubs on chalkboards displaying the simple abbreviation of 'F.B.A.s'. It was considered too rude for the general public apparently. The F.B.A.s just so happened to be the name of a quiz team at the Harbour View pub, which actually stood for The Fat Bastards' Association. We even had a big bass drumskin made up specially to depict the character of an alien standing facing frontwards raising the long middle fingers of both hands. It was quite a sight to behold, and it always made me laugh when we played family-friendly events and all the little kiddies wanted to have their picture taken alongside it.

So, two separate practice nights would mean that when we were ready this would lead to two lots of gigs. The Aliens' line-up was Tony and Mark from the old band, another chap called Stuart who played lead guitar and my old friend Mr Rock 'n' Roll himself, John Hickey.

Stuart had been a pupil of Alex's and there was no doubt he was a very accomplished lead guitarist. He was a similar age to us and did some work in the financial sector. He was a kind of accountant by day and a rock god by night, within the confines of his own garage. Remarkably similar to Clark Kent and Superman. This was his first foray into a band although you wouldn't have guessed that as he fitted in straight away. All appeared good and you could tell by the way Mark and Tony nodded and gurned at each other that they were happy bunnies. John H. played rhythm guitar and the natural bonhomie that he brought to proceedings made it a polished and fun environment. I could do a separate story about the Aliens, but this is supposed to be about Dirty Weekend so let us concentrate on one band at a time. Wama in particular might not be too happy if I spend too much time talking about the virtues of what he always called "that other band".

So, the first Tuesday night of Dirty Weekend's brave new dawn was upon us. I arrived at the same time as Clive, and we gave each other a warm welcome. We were soon joined by Wama, Joe Colburn and another young chap who was introduced to us as Creeda. This was a name I had never come across before and if you were asked to pick out a Creeda from a line-up you would definitely choose this guy straight away. He was 21 and so a similar age to Joe. As a consequence, we now found the average age of the band members had gone from 47 to 29, which I thought was a much more respectable number. I was feeling at least ten years younger already as I started up a conversation with the new young hipster, Creeda. He was very well spoken, had a trendy amount of sculptured facial hair and was as funny as fuck. He was so laid back and cool, and really looked the part. "Let us just hope he can drum," I thought. Once all the customary pleasantries had been executed, the time had come for us to get down to some serious work.

Wama then went about suggesting how we should just have a bit of a jam and work through a few simple songs to get a feel for what we were doing.

Clive said, "Why is Joe playing bass?"

We pointed out the bleeding obvious – that we didn't have a bass player.

Clive shocked us and said, "I play bass."

I looked at Wama in befuddlement and Wama looked at me, his face just as surprised as mine. Clive suggested that he play bass as it would be such a waste having a guitarist like Joe and not using him to his full potential. I thought back to the time when we first met Joe at the practice where it looked like he was brought in to replace Clive, and I found it funny how we now had this bloodless coup laid out before us. So, now that we all knew what we were going to play, it was time to see if this beast could fly.

Joe and Creeda had known each other for a few years. They had obviously mucked about with each other musically in the past and knew how to read one another. Joe was here with us because of his affiliation with Wama, and Joe had then persuaded his mate Creeda to come along. I didn't understand why this young, cool, handsome hipster would want to do this, and my only conclusion was that he had to be a shit drummer. We decided to start with our usual opening song of 'Rock and Roll' by Led Zeppelin and from the very first second, I was totally gobsmacked. In this version Creeda started off with a short intro section, which is true to the recording (we had never done that version before) and then when Joe came in with the powerful guitar riff I was blown away and was mouthing "What the fuck?" to myself. We carried on with the track and near the end there was a drum and guitar battle going on in front of us. I just stood back admiring and soaking up the masterclass from these two little shits. The song finished and I caught the eye of Wama and Clive, we all gave each other a knowing smile of happiness. I recall that in my head I was questioning just how long these two were going to be hanging out with us three comparative pensioners, as it was obvious they could play just about anything. We moved on to the next song, which was quickly followed by another and then another, and with relative ease by the end of the practice we had achieved more than I could have ever felt possible. To sum it up, I would say it was two hours of a quality I had not experienced before with a freshness that then permeated into the fun side of our personas. It was relaxed. It was spontaneous. It was educational. Above all, it was a bloody good laugh. I came out of that session on a real high as I had a feeling that we would be able to not only keep the band going but would also be able to make it a lot better. I did wonder what the kids had thought about things, and Joe and Creeda had given me the impression that they had enjoyed the experience. You couldn't have smacked the smile off Wama's face and Clive turning out to be a secret bass player was the icing on the cake. I am not sure what the future would have been if we had kept Joe on bass and Clive on lead, but my hunch is that it would not have been of a similar calibre. (Sorry Clive.)

Tree reminded me of a memory she had of when she came down to visit us on our second rehearsal night.

She told me that as we had a quick break in between songs she went up to Clive and said, "I didn't know you could play bass guitar, Clive."

His whispered response to her was, "Neither did I."

It actually turns out that Clive had gone to a bookshop two days before our first rehearsal with Joe and Creeda and purchased a copy of *Bass Guitar for Dummies*.

Before we move forward in the story, I think it would be helpful to give you a little insight into our two new members as, you may have guessed, they will be major recurring characters in this tale. As explained in an earlier chapter, Joe was known to Wama as he was the son of long-standing family friends, Mark and Mandy. Having played guitar from the moment he could walk; he went on to study at the music college BIMM in Brighton. He had mucked about in a few bands with friends and then went on to do mini tours with an up-and-coming singer called Larissa Eddie. He also did a number of YouTube videos with a young girl who would go on to have some success – Fleur East of *The X Factor* and *I'm a Celebrity... Get Me Out of Here* fame. The videos went under the banner of 'Fleur Fridays' and would consist of Joe playing acoustic guitar whilst Fleur was singing in her kitchen. He then had the opportunity to accompany Larissa as she was chosen as the support act on the upcoming Peter Andre tour, and after that they embarked on a tour supporting Lionel Richie. Joe would send us photos of some of the huge stages he was playing on, and it was funny when he would come back to us and play the music nights we were still doing in the Harbour View. Alongside Larissa he played some great venues up and down the country, with the highlight being the Royal Albert Hall. This was a young man who lived and breathed guitar, and it looked like he was on the verge of being able to do the thing he most loved and earn a living out of it. We were incredibly lucky to have him, and I think we were good for him at that point as he seemed to relish playing the stuff that we did. It was an opportunity for him to be full-on lead guitar rock god and I would guess it was a lot more fun than some of the mundane stuff he was required to do with others.

Creeda in his younger years had studied music at ACM in Guildford. He was now down in Brighton scratching a living by doing bar work whilst pursuing his goal of advancing a career in music. He was mainly playing with others that were into a funky/jazzy type of groove. He did some playing with a well-known band called Yumi and the Weather and is currently part of the setup of a band very much on the verge of success called Kudu Blue. They have been tipped by some illustrious peeps in the business and are regularly featured as ones to watch by Radio 1.

Without going into too much detail I know first-hand just how hard it is to catch a break in the music business and even if you were lucky enough to gain some success it is surprising how poorly paid it is. Creeda is also an excellent drum teacher, and his style is one of imparting how much fun drums and life can be. There is a great video you can find on YouTube called 'M4 Drummer', where you will find him playing his kit on the deserted side of the M4 motorway that had been shut for some reason. One memory I have of him in the early days of practice was that he always seemed to be eating and I think he had a thing for bananas, which he would eat even during the song. While researching this book he told me he had got to know Joe as their dads were friends, and that he and Joe actually formed a band together when they were younger. The band was called the F.F.M., which apparently stands for the Foot Fucking Masters. This was because of some connection to the film *Pulp Fiction* and a foot massage scene. (And to think I thought 'Fingered By Aliens' was a crap name.)

So, back to the practice room. We had these two new guys and I had assumed it was going to take some time to get them up to speed with learning the 30-odd covers we did. I envisaged that a gig was a good couple of months away at the very least. Fast-forward a couple of hours and they had already mastered about a third of the material. Not only was this completely unexpected, but it was also something that neither me, Wama or Clive were used to. For me it was my first experience of working with a musician as opposed to a band member. The pace was quicker, clearer and much more fun for me, as I wasn't spending ages just sitting on the side-lines whilst the players were learning the nuances of their parts. Creeda being on drums naturally had to have a good working relationship with the bass player. Now, remember Clive was a newbie at this, but the way he and Creeda gelled was beautiful to watch. Clive would ask questions and Creeda was more than happy to oblige with help and together they really did work together to form a solid base for the band. Watching the body language between them was a joy. They joked, they laughed, and Clive was growing in confidence. With each session the bromance was building. I don't think we could have got a better drummer, especially for Clive, as Creeda was a truly gifted teacher and a very giving human being. I have asked Creeda about his impressions of the band when he joined, and he told me his overriding feeling was one of fun. He was used to being in bands where it was all about subtle grooves and where the drummer was not really put forward to showcase their solo talents. With us he got the chance to completely rock out and we were also incredibly open to him having centre stage to whore out his talents. He reckons the whole Dirty Weekend experience helped him with future projects as we gave him a structure to work towards and the regular gigging made him a better performer. It does amuse me that a bunch of middle-aged non-musos gave this genius lessons in how to perform. He also told me that when he walked into a 30,000sq ft empty factory and found that we had built our own studio, he was initially under the impression that we were a serious outfit indeed. (Sucker.)

At the next practice, Wama announced we had our first gig with the new line-up, and it was to be at the Neptune. I was happy about this as I couldn't think of anywhere better. It would be the perfect launching pad for us. Creeda wasn't aware of the Neptune, and I did wonder if it would provide the same buzz for him as it held for me. Practice carried on at a very rapid pace and the progress appeared effortless. During a break I disclosed to the guys that I had written an original song and wondered if we might have a quick look at it to see if it was worth progressing. It was the first song I had written. I had the melody and chord structure worked out already as I had started to play a bit of acoustic guitar to a basic level in the privacy of my bedroom. I was certainly not at the stage for my chord strumming to be inflicted on an unsuspecting world. The song was called 'Frankie' and it was my take on what had happened to Frankie Cocozza of *The X Factor* and *Celebrity Big Brother* fame. I began to sing and play the basic chords and all of a sudden Creeda came in with an accompanying beat. Joe then started to riff over the top, and soon Clive and Wama were getting their heads around the chord changes. We continued working on it for the rest of the session and as I walked out of there I was amazed at the result. It sounded like a proper song and my sense of pride was through the roof.

A couple more practices and not only did we have enough material for the gig, but my song 'Frankie' had gone from strength to strength, and, to my mind it wouldn't seem out of place in our set. The gig at the Neptune was fast approaching and there was definitely an air of quiet optimism in the band. No issues were evident apart from trying to tell Joe to turn his amp down to 11 as the boy does like the sound of his own guitar. I felt we were now ready for Dirty Weekend part two.

The day of the gig arrived and Wama went one step further by setting up the stage and backdrops at the pub in the afternoon. Clive and I gave him a hand to get all the gear down there early, and Roger welcomed me from behind the bar by saying, "Here, I see that shit band are back again tonight." I replied, "Yeah, but I hear they got worse." Wama then hung up his wall porn and after putting his hammer away into his girlie satchel, he pulled from the bag the first official Dirty Weekend fanzine. It consisted of a front cover and three pages of writing. The front cover was a picture of our now favourite trussed-up naked bondage woman. And in the top right-hand corner was a logo he has had created, depicting a suitcase with a sun hat and a bra hanging off of either side. The suitcase was adorned with stickers of far-off places that someone had ventured to. Underneath the logo was some info telling you how to find us on Facebook and to give us a click on the 'like' button. It was news to me that we had entered the digital age and I decided these things were best left to Wama. Page two had a column by someone called 'Eddie Torial' (Wama), who went on to say how disappointing it was to lose Tony and Mark, and to welcome Joe and Creeda.

There was a piece written about the hooligan song ('Brighton March'), a cartoon of a couple in bed reading books on sexual positions, and a plea to find anyone who would like to look after our social media for fun (because we couldn't pay them).

Page three had a pointless story regarding word play with chocolate bars, a list of upcoming gigs and instructions on how you could buy advertising in the fanzine with prices ranging from £100 to just buying us a drink.

Page four was a puzzle page, which had an anagram game and a quiz. I was hoping that people wouldn't start filling in this page whilst we were playing. The quiz was based on questions to do with music, but question ten puzzled me. It was, "Which religious ceremony comes from the Greek word 'to dip'." This confused the fuck out of me as I was doing the quiz half-pissed at the bar whilst the others were setting up.

He spread these fanzines all around the place and admitted to me that he had been going into Brighton during the week and leaving them in loads of random places. That gave me a small cause for concern as the cover wasn't something you would like to see in a nursery or playground, for example. The look of the fanzine wasn't particularly polished. It had much more of a juvenile or anarchic look, which I reckon made it more appealing and underground.

So, I was at the bar reading with Roger and consuming my many pints of bravado juice as the others set up. I noticed that Creeda took about a quarter of the time to get things ready as Tony used to, which was impressive, but this led to Clive having extra time doing his annoying noodling shit. The only difference was that he was now doing it with a bass guitar, and I couldn't work out if this was more or less of an annoyance than the usual six-string apparatus. Joe was strutting around and giving it the full-on 'I am a rock star' vibe as he chatted to a variety of guys he knew, pint in hand and entertaining various souls with his bloody Robert De Niro impersonation he had mastered. We did a quick soundcheck that lasted all of 20 seconds, before I then ran outside to chain-smoke and sink a few more pints. There were a few others outside and they were quizzing me on how I thought it would go and did I think it would be much different from the last time. I gave nothing away and thought it best to keep the anticipation going and for them to make their own unbiased judgement.

The place was absolutely rammed with our usual friends and loved ones as well as others who were curious to see just what the new line-up would offer. It was nearly showtime and I flicked through my lyric book on the stand. Wama looked on in disgust and muttered something about learning lyrics and getting rid of that shitty stand. I ignored him and checked with the guys that we were already to go. I gave Creeda the sign that we were ready and he launched into the short drum solo of Led Zep. Joe crashed in with the riffs, and we were off and running. Looking out into the crowd for the first few minutes I intuitively knew that all would be good. I saw that everyone could tell we had improved, with the quality of the guitar by Joe and the excellence of Creeda on drums.

These two had also forced Wama and Clive to naturally raise their game and the whole sound was solid. I think Clive and Wama had their own personal points to prove, not just to others but to themselves as well. Personally, I wasn't too fussed as I felt I was in good form as the rest of the band had given me the confidence to just perform. I also didn't have to think of ways in which to get the crowd on our side for mistakes we might have made. Joe was a dream for me as well as he didn't just play guitar, but he gave a performance and was something to look at, which in turn would take some of the emphasis off me as the so-called frontman.

The Neptune felt like it was rocking and then we played a song that would showcase the difference in quality. We did a rendition of 'Hey Joe' the famous Hendrix song. Since the introduction of our youth team, we didn't have to stick to a completely rigid structure and could now go a little off-script and have mid-song jams or extended solos. We agreed in practice that we would use this as a showcase for both Joe and Creeda to show everyone that we had that little bit extra. There was a drop-down section where Creeda went into a drum solo that went everywhere in timing, touch, technique and ferocity. This was followed by Joe doing similar things on lead guitar and then merged into an epic battle with all of us building to a crescendo. We finished the song, and the reaction was massive. To be fair, I was thinking at the time we had delivered something of quality, and we were no longer a beginner pub band.

One other personal notable highlight of that gig was our first public performance of the song I had written called 'Frankie'. I started by asking if there was anyone in the audience who was related to Mr Cocozza and luckily no one replied they were. I then went on to say what the song was about and informed them that it was either a tale of a young man who was used and abused by the cruel industry of celebrity, or a tale of someone who quite simply was a knobhead. We then launched into the song and the reaction we got at the end was mega. I had random people coming up to me telling me how good it was, and their praise gave me the belief to carry on with the songwriting and see what else I could come up with. I knew that Wama was close to completing another original and I also had some ideas for my next effort. I did think that what might set us apart from some other bands was the ability and the drive to produce our own material. It can be tricky slipping in your own stuff, but this wasn't so hard to do at the Neptune as the crowd there was always appreciative of new original material. They might not necessarily like it, but they did recognise the effort and artistry that went into it.

After two banging hours the gig came to an end. We did a long-asked-for encore and then basically got pissed into the early hours of the morning. We raised £208 for the Martlets charity as well. Roger gave me the fine accolade of, "How did you get those young'uns to play with you old fuckers?" and Wama told me that he had said to Duffy from Primal Scream (who was in the audience), "Thank god we didn't play any of your stuff" and the reply he received was, "Why not? You would have probably done it better."

It is hard to explain what this meant to Wama. He knew there was a large group of people who thought his bands were a bit of a joke and that there were loads of musicians who wouldn't fully accept us. We weren't supposed to be playing in their playground, but that night went a long way in showing people what we were about and what we were capable of. I think deep down he had a mixture of pride, relief and a large amount of "take that" and "fuck you".

FOOTNOTES

BIMM – This stands for British Institute of Modern Music. The B used to be for Brighton, but this college has expanded and evolved over the years. I have to be honest and say that I am not a fan as I think that the sheer volume of students that they have makes it feel like a factory. My opinion would be that creativity is diluted and replaced by the need to process the numbers through to feed the business model. I fear that a lot of these youngsters are living with expectations of a future career that doesn't exist. As I said, just my opinion, and if your time at BIMM has worked out for you then I am pleased for you. One of the founders was a chap called Damian Keyes who now runs an operation called the DK Academy of Music. He has developed a large following and produces many videos detailing the business side of the music industry. Some things he says do have a few detractors, but my take is that he is just being upfront and honest as to how things work in the real world.

PETER ANDRE – Some Australian bloke who married Katie Price. I have heard that he is rather pleasant.

DUFFY – Keyboard player with Primal Scream. I have had it on good authority that he has excellent taste in music.

LIONEL RICHIE – Support act for the Joe Colburn tour.

THE MARLETS – Martlets is a local charity that provides terminally ill people in Brighton & Hove, and surrounding areas, with the absolute best care and support. Their expert team helps patients live life to the full during the precious time they have left. Martlets opened in 1997. The staff and services were formed from the merger of three separate charities: Coppercliff Hospice, Tarner and MacMillan Day Hospice. Across the hospice services, more than 25,000 local people have been supported and cared for since 1997.

BIG FOOTNOTE

'FRANKIE' – I cannot lie, when I first wrote this song it was because I thought the guy was a complete bellend. As I added more and more verses my mind was somewhat changed as I explored the roles played by people around him that should have known better. When you consider his age at the time and the amount of media attention that was focused on him it was quite obvious to me that he was a victim of some poisonous individuals who were peddling this pathetic cult of celebrity. The main culprits to me were the TV execs chasing their ratings, newspaper editors chasing readership, but most of all the general public for fuelling this shit by loving a good old public execution.

I remember at the time sending Frankie a message on Facebook asking him if he would like to record the song but was not surprised that I received no reply. I have stated in the chapter that I used to ask if there were any members of Frankie's family in the audience before I then went into a monologue about whether he was a twat or a victim. I would like to place on record that I believe he was a victim. Here are the lyrics so that you can make up your own mind.

'FRANKIE'

Oh my God I am through round one,
And all I had to do was show them my bum.
Certainly, can't sing, certainly can't dance,
They think I'm kind of cheeky which gives me a chance.

Oh my God I'm through round two,
My rock-star swagger has carried me through.
Haven't heard that phrase in 10 years or so,
Now everybody uses it, the ones in the know.

Chorus

And if only you could see.
What is the real, the real me?

And if only, you would not believe

What the papers write, they write about me.

Get me to the final I'm a rock 'n' roll god,

Got to act really laddie and fun,

Be seen on the town, with a right bunch of clowns,

To make the front page of *The Sun*.

Stay up all night with the help of some drugs,

And bed some strangers I've met.

See them sell their story for their moment of glory,

And I haven't got a record deal yet.

Chorus

Local radio backs local lad

I'm the best bloody story that they've ever had.

Everyone agrees that I will go far.

Everyone agrees that I am a star.

My ears start to burn as the press start to turn

At the first little sign of a scandal.

And I soon realise that the ultimate prize

Is getting quite tricky to handle.

Chorus

Cracks begin to appear in my rock-star veneer,

When they work out, I'm a bit of a bum.

Phone numbers I collect, show girls no respect,

I hope you're still proud of me Mum.

To my ultimate shame I'm kicked out of the game,

People think will I never recover.

I say watch this space when you next see my face,

I will be on the famous *Big Brother*.

Chorus

CHAPTER 9 – HANGING OUT WITH BIG DICK

So, at this stage, all is good in the life of the new and, some would say, improved Dirty Weekend. For the purposes of this book, we will move on at a different pace, as by now you do not need to go through the routines of the practices and all of the gigs, as much of it is similar to what I have written beforehand. The practice sessions would carry on with Joe blasting us all out as he was only interested in hearing himself; Creeda eating copious amounts of bananas and other random foods out of Tupperware; Wama attempting to look organised and professional with his ever-growing guitar pedal collection; and Clive grinning inanely whilst revelling in his bromance with Creeda.

We rarely went through the rigmarole of practising the songs that we already knew, as we would be continuously concentrating on doing new stuff that you wouldn't normally see done by a pub band. The best times spent practising, in my opinion, were when we were working on our own material, as I found this process much more creative and fulfilling. There was something about the evolution of a song going from a simple idea into a fully-fledged musical piece that I found fascinating.

As for the gigs, the setup was much as you have already heard and would follow the same, familiar pattern. So, as we progress, I will pick out little snippets that were fun memories and some other parts that will provide a bit of relevance to what was going on. When it comes to an event that has more importance, I will dedicate more time and detail to give you a fuller picture.

So here I was, practising and playing with both bands and enjoying each one for completely different reasons. Both bands did dissimilar sets and, although I sang for both, the sound of each band was unique in its own way. Unfortunately, there was still an element of bad feeling lingering in the air between the members, but as there was little chance of meeting each other on a social basis, I figured this wouldn't be an issue.

We had just done our second gig at the Albion pub in Fishersgate. It had gone down well with the locals, which is no mean feat as this place can be a bit of a graveyard for some bands. The place itself is a little rough and ready, but in the main the people are genuine, and they will let you know whether you have pissed them off or not. They like a good drink as well, and after a short time they become our perfect crowd as they are loud, boisterous and up for fun. You get the feeling that you can have a good amount of banter with them, but you also need to know where to draw the line. If you push your luck too much you might run the risk of wounding someone's feelings and this in turn could lead to you getting your head kicked in. Wama and I have been brought up on this kind of place, but I reckon it was a bit of a shock to our well-spoken hipster drummer who was more familiar playing in front of carrot crunchers up Muesli Mountain.

Wama then gave us some big news that he was finding hard to contain. He had a big grin across his face, and it looked like he might wet himself with glee.

He then said, "We're playing the Amex in Dick's bar."

Now I know you may be thinking that we had already played there so what was the big deal? Well, the big deal was that it would be just us, playing for two hours. Also, this would be on a match day, and it just so happened to be the last home game of the season. This I assumed meant that the bar would be at full capacity with slightly inebriated and joyous fans. We had this opportunity thanks to a connection at the club by the name of Richard. For some reason he had developed a soft spot for Wama, which made me think that he was obviously missing something in his life.

* * *

The day of the match arrived, and Brighton were playing Wolves. At this late stage of the season Brighton had already secured promotion and Wolves needed to get a result to avoid relegation, so we knew the home fans would be in a celebratory mood and up for a party. We had all been given tickets for the game as well, so the plan was to get up there early, set everything up in the large bar area and then enjoy the match before the gig.

The instruments were all in place and the only thing left was for Wama to set up the backdrop and to distribute whatever other paraphernalia he had for the day. As I have said before, the place is large, and Dick's Bar is not just a bar but part of a large stadium complex. It is accessible to all, and as such BHA FC have taken their responsibility of providing an arena that is family friendly and tolerant to all very seriously indeed.

We all went off to watch the match, of which the only notable thing to report was the funny sight at the final whistle. The result meant Wolves were relegated and as it was the last game of the season it was customary for the players to go over to the section where their fans were to thank them for their support over the last season. Wolves player Jamie O'Hara went over to the travelling fans, took his shirt off and threw it into the crowd as a nice memento perhaps for a young fan. The funny thing that happened was seeing the shirt come hurtling back at him from the crowd as no one wanted it.

The match came to an end, and we made our way back to the bar. Wama noticed something was missing as he realised that most of his banners were no longer there. Also, the hundreds of copies of the new fanzine that he had distributed were nowhere to be seen. Wama approached the bar manager, a lovely lady called Debbie, and asked her if she knew anything about it. She then informed him that the police had been in and removed all the items due to a number of complaints that had been received. By all accounts there were quite a few kids in the room, and mums and dads were getting lots of questions as to why the naked lady had been tied up. I completely understood their concerns and thought that the reasoning in removing the banners was not only fair but also completely logical. She then informed him that the fanzines had also been taken away and that the police would be in touch with us to discuss the material. I was somewhat confused and asked Wama if he had any idea what this was all about. He produced a copy of the fanzine from his satchel and handed it to me to have a look at.

The front cover had a picture of the naked bondage lady, so I could see the obvious concerns there. I turned to page two, which had a really nice update about the band and what a privilege it was to be playing at the home of the football club. There was also a nice thank you to Richard Hebbard for organising it and to the right of this was a small cartoon of a naked man on his knees being whipped by a dominatrix, so obviously that was an issue. Page three contained some photos of the band at one of our previous gigs, so at least that was safe enough. I then turned to page four and instantly realised that the club and the police were perhaps not being unreasonable after all.

The back page of this fanzine was pretty graphic to say the least. It was a cartoon that took up half of the page and it consisted of two young Crystal Palace fans being bent over a table whilst they were being taken from behind by two burly Brighton supporters. There was a small detail that gets overlooked a lot, and that was that the shirts the Brighton fans were wearing were being sponsored by Brighton & Hove Knobs.com, as opposed to Jobs.com who were the sponsors at that time. I said to Wama that maybe he had gone a bit too far with his stage dressing this time and his reply was a very earnest, "That's the problem today, no fucking sense of humour."

Now we had the small matter of a gig to perform. I was feeling a bit weird and to this day the only one who knows what was going on with me was Joe. When the others read this, it will be a bit of a surprise to them. There were ten minutes to go until we started, and the bar was packed. There was a lot of noise around the room and although you couldn't make out individual conversations you could hear a loud buzz as everyone was in exceedingly high spirits. We once again had the pleasure of having our good friend Ruby perform with us and as I have pointed out previously her singing and stage presence is summed up in one word, and that word is 'class'. I suddenly had a strange feeling come over me and it was a feeling I had known before. I recognised the signs and knew I was in trouble. I had over the previous few years suffered from panic attacks. This is not down to a lack of confidence or fear that we were about to perform, and it is not down to what some may call stage fright. For the majority of people who have never known what a panic attack consists of I will try to explain to you the feelings that took over me. Quite frankly, you would never be able to understand how or why it manifests. In quite simple terms this is what it was for me: I thought I was going to die. Your heart beats in a weird rhythm, you start struggling for breath, you get hot, you think irrationally, you want to be somewhere else on your own to curl up in a ball and try to ride it out. Joe had noticed I was not my usual self as I was quiet, drinking copious amounts of water and sweating profusely. I told him I thought I was going to pass out and I didn't know why. I then thought about how I had been through this before and convinced myself that it was a panic attack, but the difference this time was that I couldn't just lie down for a couple of hours out of sight of everyone.

I remember doing the first song and singing the lyrics, but all the while having a separate conversation in my own head telling myself to just get through it, just fucking get through it.

It felt like the longest two hours of my life, but somehow we had made it through to the end. The gig had been great, and we had acquitted ourselves well. The crowd loved it, the rest of the band loved it, but all I wanted to do was to get home and try not to die. This was now the second time I had played Dick's Bar and both occasions had been awful for me. One highlight of the gig as far as the band were concerned was when we played 'Brighton March' song at the end and had the whole room bellowing out, "Seagulls, Seagulls" (BHA's nickname).

We were then joined onstage by chairman of the club Dick Knight, a very imposing and flamboyant character who thanked all the supporters for a wonderful year. He then thanked us, before adding that he did not think he could play our stuff to his grandchildren. The gig finally came to an end. The party carried on, but not for me, as I made an excuse and said I had to meet up with someone in town. Instead, I went straight home where I decided I would ride out the attack, which had not fully worn off. I am sure if ever I was afforded the opportunity to play the Amex again, I wouldn't commit to it. In my mind it could easily trigger another attack, which I know sounds ridiculous, but not everything to do with the mind can be easily explained. That is the thing with panic attacks, as irrational behaviour can be set off by something totally inane.

* * *

With the Amex gig now behind us, I inwardly celebrated the fact that we had escaped a custodial sentence. We had some nice feedback as Debbie from behind the bar told us that they had taken the most money ever in a session, which was nice to know. It was now time to move into the studio to record Wama's new original song 'Drugs & Sin', which is a very personal tale about one of his old friends. As you will know by now, the whole recording process leaves me cold, as it is, to my mind, one of the most boring things I have ever done. I was more prepared this time, though, and no longer had dreams of supermodels or endless bottles of Jack Daniel's littering the room, so there is no way it could be any worse than it had been the last time.

How wrong I was, because I didn't account for the fact that we now had Joe and Creeda, who for some reason thought recording was like having a multiple orgasm. They couldn't think of anything better than spending time doing take after bloody take perfecting a particular note that sounded like a noise a woodlouse would make if it farted (slight exaggeration). We were in there for what seemed like weeks, and I couldn't get my head around their giddy schoolgirl enjoyment. This enthusiasm spread as even Clive and Wama were getting off on the technical bollocks that was being spoken by the scratchy bearded musos.

I spent most of the session outside smoking and wondering if the pub would still be open by the time we finished this torture session.

We recorded my song 'Frankie' not too long after this and I was wondering if I would feel different about the process because it was my song and not Wama's. Maybe because I would have a bigger input and would be more protective over my creation, my whole take on the recording process would change. The answer to this was a resounding no, as it made no difference to me if it was my song or not. I will state here and now that recording is dull, dull, dull, and is best left to those who like sitting in a dimly lit room twiddling an assortment of knobs for hours on end in the hope of eventually reaching the climax. Give me live gigs any day.

* * *

Moving on, we played a gig at the Albion in Hove, and this is where two important elements were introduced. The first of these was that Wama built his very own portable stage. When we played in most pubs we were normally ushered to an area of the room which was ours for the night. It was basically the carpeted area in the corner. We had been spoilt at some of the places we played that had their own raised stage area, but most were not like this, so Wama had constructed a stage that had about seven pieces made from an assortment of chipboard and wood that were different lengths and widths. It looked like it had been hacked together by someone who was obviously not a carpenter, but it did a job. It raised us by about ten inches, and this can make a nice little difference when you perform. When you put it together it was a strange shape because of all the pieces being various sizes, and at this first gig we had a hole in the middle that all of us had a go at falling down throughout the performance.

The second important add-on was the introduction of the newest band member and the first groupie we'd ever had. She was about 5ft tall and had long flowing blonde hair. She wore fishnet stockings and had a constant look of excited surprise upon her face. As well as that, she never wore any clothes on her top half. Her name was Maisie Trollope, and she was made of latex. I first met her when I tapped Wama on the shoulder and he turned around with her dangling out of his mouth. Once she had 'come up for air', he introduced us and from that moment on she was in the band onstage with us. Mind you, she was a fickle bitch as she would often disappear mid-song and would be dancing in the arms of some random in the crowd. She went on to have her own Facebook page and would often post comments about our gigs. From time to time though the rock-star life would leave her feeling a bit deflated and she would disappear for a few weeks to pull herself together. These breaks seemed to work though as she would return looking like a new woman. On one occasion she came back six inches taller and had brown hair. The Albion gig was a bit of a riot, and I was wondering if Maisie had a sister that might want to join.

We had done a few more new covers as well. One that sticks in my mind was 'Delilah', but we were doing the Alex Harvey version and not the

Tom Jones one. I had reservations about doing this song as I thought it was a piece of shit, but Wama was very persuasive and assured me that it was an inspired choice. We did it and the crowd seemed to really love it. As it finished to wild applause, I remember thinking, "I was right, that was a piece of shit."

* * *

August was fast approaching, and the town would be taken over for the weekend by the upcoming Gay Pride event. Pride generated an atmosphere that was fun and exciting, with a plethora of events taking place that we wanted to be part of. The trouble was it was hard to get involved as all the main areas of entertainment had been planned well in advance and there was no room to get anything put together that would be part of the main throng. So, in true Dirty Weekend style, we found a pub that didn't do music and had absolutely no affiliation to Pride and just did our own thing. The pub was called the Royal Standard and it was located just down from the train station on the main thoroughfare that led down towards the seafront. It was small with a tiny performance area crammed into the back corner. We were all dressed in very colourful garb and had been in town quite early in the day soaking up the carnival atmosphere and as such were pretty inebriated ourselves. The front of the building had these large, magnificent ornate windows, and we opened all the doors so anyone passing could see us. There were a lot of people milling around town but not many were venturing into the pub. We then started playing and the noise bellowed out to the road and could be heard from a long way away in all directions. Suddenly the place was starting to fill and what transpired over the next few hours was a full-on party with everyone dancing on tables and joining in with every song. This was the first time we met a couple who were to become lifelong friends, Jimmy and Daiga. Jimmy was tall and slim, with hair that stuck up to make him look about 6ft 4in. He was involved with bands in the local punk scene and went by the name of Jimmy Slag. Daiga was his partner and was striking in her appearance. She was a long blonde-haired Latvian who was extremely tall and leggy. She was dressed like a hippy from Woodstock and had rings of daisies in her hair. She loved to dance and didn't stop from the first to the last minute. She was up onstage with us and to many others it would appear that she was part of the band, which was fine with us as she just added to the whole look and feel of the day. This was our first stab at doing something for Pride and it was the beginning of our love affair with it. Bigger and better things were to come, which you will hear about later.

* * *

We followed this up with a small gig at a pub called the Blue Lagoon in Hove, which was notable for me because of three things. The first one was that Wama in his never-ending search for the show to move to new heights had purchased a smoke machine in order to add that extra level of stage craft. I say smoke machine, but in reality, it resembled one of those things you rent to help you strip off wallpaper, only with a bit more oomph. It was switched on and put into position and would be controlled by me having a handheld trigger button that was attached by a long lead into the device. We had what was now usual for us, a decent sized crowd. A mixture of the usual suspects, locals and curious newcomers. A good boisterous start to the gig and now was the time to add a little smoke to give us that mysterious yet professional look we had been missing. I pressed the button and in the space of about 30 seconds I could no longer see the microphone positioned six inches away from my nose. It was like doing a gig in a sauna on a foggy autumn morning during the worst smog of the Victorian era in old London Town. The bar staff opened all the windows and doors and asked us to refrain from using our new device. They feared all the smoke alarms were about to be tripped in the entire building which was also a ten-bedroom B&B. The smoke gradually dispersed and once again I could begin to make out the silhouettes of the audience. We never did use that machine again.

The second thing of note from this gig was our first meeting with a stranger by the name of Richard Wood. He was not a local and actually resided in the Surrey area. He had been down for the weekend visiting friends in Brighton. He told me that when he was out and about in town, he had picked up one of our fanzines and noticed we were playing that night. He decided to book a taxi and along with a friend he travelled to the other side of town to come and see something he thought might be a bit different. We had a brief chat and thanked him for coming all the way to see us. We didn't know at the time, but not only had we made a lifelong fan of the band, but we had also just met our unofficial band photographer. (He didn't know this either.)

The third thing of note is tinged with a bit of sadness, but I like to view it as a thing of joy. A good friend of ours had recently passed away after a truly short illness. His name was Rod Cameron, predominantly known to Wama and I as he was the lead guitarist from a local band called School for Scandal who we followed when we were younger. He played in many bands over the years, but one in particular he played with for a long time until he was sadly taken away was Dolly Dagger. It is hard to impart to you just how good this guy was at his craft. He made guitar playing look effortless and it was a joy to be so close to see him perform. He really looked the part onstage and away from the spotlight he came across as the most mild-mannered bloke you would ever meet. One memory I have is from when I was first starting to play guitar. Tree had organised for Rod to give me some lessons. It was the equivalent of Mozart giving a lesson to a baboon. I felt honoured that he was so patient with me, and I was lucky that I got to sing with him when he would turn up at the Three Graces open mic on a Monday night and accompany me. So, at the gig at the Blue Lagoon, we covered one of his originals called 'Picture a Rainbow', which was one of his favourites.

* * *

We were drawing near to the end of our first year with the new line-up and had certainly done quite a mixture of different things. On a personal level I had also been doing gigs with the other band, as well as attending some open mic nights and playing some of my beginner guitar to gain some experience. I did most of this in the company of Johnny H. in the Three Graces, as he liked me to accompany him on vocals.

John H. asked me one day to go to a music night that a good friend of his was putting together to raise a few funds for a local charity and I went along willingly to support him. He introduced me to a chap by the name of Jon Orrell who was a bit of a singer, harmonica player, guitar player and compere supreme, and was involved with a local charity by the name of "Whoopsadaisy" which supports children with disabilities. This would lead me to arrange a meeting of the two bands on one bill. And so, the next chapter is dedicated to Whoopsadaisy.

FOOTNOTES

MUESLI MOUNTAIN – Area of Brighton officially known as Hanover, where a high proportion of students reside. Known for a high density of vegans and beardy types putting the world to rights without actually doing anything. Lots of pubs which cater for lots of "right on" events.

ROYAL STANDARD – Pub just down from Brighton Station. It was never known for live music, but we would use it to stage some random events over the next couple of years. Was to become a regular haunt for the more colourful of the Brighton football fans and was eventually shut down in dubious circumstances.

JIMMY SLAG – He may look like a poster boy for the master race, but this man is a great mainstay of the local punk scene. In a variety of bands such as Pig City Angels and Penny Blood he puts his money where his mouth is and has promoted many events that support the local music scene. His other half is the lovely Daiga, and I can only assume that because Jim looks Latvian this is what must have attracted him to her. (It is certainly not his singing.)

RUBY – AKA Ruth Egau. A beautiful person with a voice that can have you out of your clothes in under ten seconds. Ruby is one of the main components of the South Coast Soul Revue and the simply sublime Frank Greene Band, which she started with Danny Holt. This group specialises in harmonies and was brought about when Danny started a choir group called Harmonessence. It encouraged individuals to join a choir and to enjoy the sheer pleasure that music and singing can give you. The arrangements that they come up with are truly pieces of fine art.

SUSSEX POLICE – Wama had to attend an interview at the police station to be questioned about the fanzines at the Amex gig. He was taken into a room and interviewed by two police officers. He was informed that he had not broken any laws, but the club were keen to try and tone down any hostilities between Brighton and Crystal Palace fans. I believe in all honesty that the police officers actually found it all quite amusing.

DICK KNIGHT – Harry Richard Knight is a businessman and former chairman of Brighton & Hove Albion F.C. He held the post from 1997 to 2009. A lifelong fan, he took control having led the fan pressure to oust the previous board following their sale of the club's Goldstone Ground to property developers. Knight remains life president of Brighton & Hove Albion and chairman of the club's charitable wing Albion in the Community. Dick's Bar, a pub inside the new stadium, is named after him.

BIG FOOTNOTE

RICHARD WOOD – I have introduced you to our unofficial photographer in the chapter, but it would be remiss of me to not expand on what this man did for us. He is a superb photographer and some of the images of the band that he has captured over the years are stunning and, on reflection, would probably have cost us a fortune if it were not for his generosity. He was a great supporter of the band and along with his friend Paul Denton they introduced us to the joy of inflatable instruments and multi-coloured wigs. This is where the importance of the band comes into its own by being a focal point for meeting strangers that are to become friends.

I contacted Richard to get his recollections of our first meeting and he was kind enough to send me the following.

"The first memory for me was being completely bored one night in Brighton and in search of live music. There wasn't much going on, then I found a listing for Dirty Weekend at a nondescript pub somewhere near

Hove. Thinking it was better than nothing, I jumped in a cab to came and check out what was going on. It turned out to be a fantastic shout, and great to see a band with personality and charisma playing a great selection of covers mixed with original songs. It set you apart from other cover bands who didn't play anything original, and the songwriting was fantastic.

"Getting in contact with you after the gig I found you were playing in Kemptown at the Latest Music Bar. So, thought I should bring along some mates and my camera to capture this event. Little did I know that this would be the start of being our unofficial photographer.

"Since then, I photographed the band in action at many events and pubs, the most notable being the weekend festival gig in Hove Park Tavern where the man, the legend, Disco Pete made an appearance; the Old Market in Hove, which was an absolute epic blast and a real showcase of what the band could do; and last but not least, twice on the Brighton Pride float, which is another story altogether.

"Mixed with that were countless other pub gigs. What I really appreciate is that the original songs Dirty Weekend wrote were just outstanding. I still play the songs regularly and they are sheer quality."

CHAPTER 10 – WHOOPSADAISY

At this time, I was not only a member of Dirty Weekend, but was also in the other band Fingered By Aliens. One of my fellow Aliens is my good friend John Hickey (John H.), and you may recall that I have told you that he and I would more often than not attend an open mic night at the Three Graces pub on a Monday night.

On one of these nights, he told me that a good friend of his was putting on an evening of music to support a local charity he was involved in, and he suggested we do a little set together. I agreed to it and so a few weeks later found myself performing a six-song set with John at a lovely event that supported a local charity that goes by the name of Whoopsadaisy. The night was run and organised by John H.'s friend who is a larger-than-life character called Jon Orrell. Jon is a bit of a muso himself and plays guitar, sings a lovely low baritone and plays a good harmonica as well. He thanked me for coming along and we had a chat about the charity.

He informed me they were a friendly local charity with their base in Preston Park supporting children with disabilities as well as their families. It was founded by a lady called Nina Holland who discovered the power of a somewhat new therapy called 'conductive education', which she had come across when her own son Christopher was diagnosed with cerebral palsy.

I found the conversation with Jon illuminating and the people at the event lovely, and so began an association with the charity. This association started mainly with the Alien band. We would get gigs and most of the time the fees we received would go into a pot for the charity. We also used to take a collection pot from the charity with us that was shaped as a teddy bear. During the gigs some of the audience members would put a bit of change in it and on average we would collect an extra £20 to £30. I would now like to give you an example of how my opinion towards individuals was influenced due to this small plastic bear.

We had a gig on one particular night in a pub in a nearby town. It was the first time I had ever been to this place and from the moment we walked in we knew it was a very 'local' pub, and I had the impression any strangers coming in probably didn't get the warmest of welcomes. We introduced ourselves to the landlady standing behind the bar, and she and her staff were welcoming and lovely. They appeared really pleased to see us and directed us to where we would perform. We went through the usual setup routine and the pub began to fill up. The background noise was loud, and it felt to me to be quite aggressive. The locals were certainly going through the drinks at quite a pace. As an outsider, it looked like everyone was arguing, but by all accounts this was how they usually talked to each other. I was setting up my music stand when I was approached by a woman who appeared to be in her late 60s.

She spoke in a gruff Scottish accent and her first question was, "Who thought of that fucking name?", as she pointed at the picture on our bass drum.

This was then followed up with a series of other questions such as, "What music do you play? Do you do any Elvis? Why the fuck don't you do any fucking Elvis?" and "What the fuck is wrong with fucking Elvis?"

She wasn't happy and looked like she wanted to kill me.

We were then approached by a youngish lad who just said, "Come on, Nan, let them get on with it."

She had one more question to ask me before she went and she stared me in the eyes and said, "What the fuck is that bear for?"

I explained we supported a local charity and saved the fee up and then we did a little collection. The young lad again said, "Come on, Nan," and he led her away.

We started the gig, and the locals were into it from the very first moment. The crowd were very boisterous, completely pissed and there were little arguments going on all around, plus lots of mad drunken dancing. A number of the patrons were falling over, and the landscape in front of us resembled something you might see in a film about the Wild West. In general, all were having a blowout and it looked like it was more out of control than it probably was.

We finished the gig, did an encore that went down a storm and then came to the absolute end. The old Scottish lady appeared and demanded that we do some more. I politely told her we did not know any more. She looked at the bear, picked it up and said, "You do four more songs, and I will go around with the bear."

She looked like she meant business and so I told the guys we were going to repeat four more songs. My Scottish lady disappeared into the crowd and my first thoughts were that we would never see the bear again. We did our second encore and by the time we had finished the crowd were pretty paralytic and I was not far off either.

My Scottish friend reappeared and said, "You lot were pretty fucking good, here's the bear."

She handed my collection pot back and I placed it on the stage. I went to the bar and was chatting to the manageress who paid us our fee. She thanked me for a great night and gave me a drink. On the bar was a poster explaining the plight of a young local girl. The regulars were raising money for her to buy an advanced wheelchair that she needed. I gave the manageress some money to go towards it and asked how it was going with the collection. She told me that they were nearly at the target. She then went on to explain that they may all seem like a right rough bunch, but that was just the way they came across and that they were some of the most decent people she had ever met. We packed up our stuff while having nice chats with locals and were asked to come back.

When we met for our next practice, I opened up the bear to retrieve the £20 or £30 that we would usually get and was amazed when I counted over £300. This was an important lesson to me about how I had judged certain people before I knew them. Since then, with the work that I did and with future events that I would put on, I can honestly say that I have found the people with the least amount of disposable income turn out to be the most generous with their time and money.

* * *

Having had the experience of meeting some of those behind the charity I wondered how hard it would be to put on some kind of event. The primary motive was to raise some money and awareness, but also it seemed to be the chance to have a bloody good time. Hence, I came up with the first Whoopsadaisy Day. I started by approaching the pub over the road from my home (the Three Graces) and said I would like to use the premises for a one-day mini festival. Nathan, the landlord, was all in favour of it, but he had to get permission from the pub company Drink in Brighton, which owned the place. I suggested that if the pub company could donate an amount of money to the charity pot then I would go about getting a number of bands to perform on the day. This to my mind would be good for the pub and also be good PR for the company. At the time, a minimum fee for one band was roughly £150, so I figured that for an evening event lasting roughly four hours with 4 bands they could make a fair contribution. I wasn't looking for 4 x £150, but I did feel maybe £300 minimum was acceptable. I didn't put anything in writing and relied on them to do the right thing. Nathan came back to me a couple of days later and told me he had been given the go-ahead so now was the time to see if I could get the bands.

The first two bands were quite easy to book, seeing as I was in both of them. This would be the first time both bands were in the same room as each other and although there could potentially be some tensions, I considered enough time had passed for any ill feelings to have dissipated. After all, we were adults. I also figured that with the event being for charity there was less chance of anyone being a dick in public. I did feel, however, that it would look like I was some kind of prima donna fronting both bands on the day, so I persuaded the Aliens it would be better to get a guest singer in for this show. Thankfully, my mate Adam (from the band King Leviathan) stepped up to the plate. The absolute truth is that even then I saw Dirty Weekend as my number-one band, but I didn't want to admit it for fear of upsetting anyone.

I had started to form connections with some local bands and approached the ones I knew as being fundamentally good guys and not precious musical arseholes. The original idea was to get about four bands and provide a long evening of entertainment, but because the guys I approached were so nice and grounded I ended up with ten bands and it was now going to be an all-day event. Although this was my first foray into promoting, I knew that logistics and communication were the key. I suppose my years in management at Asda did have some use after all. I kept it pretty simple and was just honest about what bands could and couldn't do. I had a running order worked out and the importance of this being stuck to was clearly laid out. There is nothing worse when you have a band that decide to run over their time by five to ten minutes just because they are on fire. To me they are just selfish twats who show no respect to the next band, and I would gladly just pull the plug if I had a band play like that on one of my nights. Luckily, this problem didn't arise as the bands I put on weren't selfish and they seemed to appreciate my upfront honesty.

I had provided pretty much all of the equipment and we did a proper soundcheck for the first band. After that it was just line checks so that we could do a plug-in-and-play show, which kept the flow going. It meant we didn't have to go through the god-awful ritual of every band changing over tonnes of equipment and then subjecting everyone to the familiar pattern of "one, two, one, two, one, two, check, check". Don't get me wrong, the sound quality is obviously important, but believe me if you give too much leeway, it can be chaos. Especially with lead guitarists as they have some inbuilt gene that makes them act like a different species. They feel that the world is here only to bask in their majestic excellence and have absolutely no idea just how delusional they are.

Wama and Clive had turned up really early to help prepare the room. We had brought our stage with us, and all the equipment needed for the backline. Wama had also produced a special fanzine for the day, which had a page detailing what the charity was about and gave a history on how it was formed. Also in the fanzine was a list of all the acts that were to perform that day, with a description about them as well. (I will individually acknowledge all the acts in the footnotes of this chapter.) The fanzine also contained the usual assortment of politically incorrect pictures and cartoons, which I am not sure a charity aiding disabled children would really want to be associated with. There was also a plug telling people to check out the new video for our original song called 'Drugs & Sin'.

So, the stage was set, and it was still only midday. We were due to start the proceedings at two o'clock and I was getting a little nervous wondering if anyone would actually turn up for this considering the early start time. Also, it was 8th December so not a nice warm summer's day where you would gladly spend the whole day listening to bands and getting slowly battered. Joe and Creeda arrived on time, which was handy. We were going to be the first band on, so it would be good to get a proper soundcheck done before anyone turned up. Joe had been dropped off by his father Mark who was about to give us the first display of a skill that we would tolerate for the next few years. For some reason Mark believed that he had some sort of hidden talent for sound engineering. He would stand in front of the band about 20ft away with his arms folded and would listen to us, then he would look at Joe and tell him to turn up. He would listen for another 20 seconds and then tell Joe to turn up again. He would repeat this process a few more times before he would give the thumbs up like some kind of Roman emperor at the colosseum. We finished the soundcheck and as I walked off stage, I would go over to Joe's amp and turn it down to its original setting. Mark was happy though as I think it made him feel part of the band, similar to a road manager or something. We kept this pretence going for years, and you would find Mark going through the same procedure time and time again. In fact, I remember at one gig he apologised for not being there for the soundcheck, as if we would be at a loss without him.

My fears of no one turning up were dispelled by one o'clock as the place was already half-full and there was a real buzz starting to build. After worrying it would be cold, it was actually a nice sunny day so there were a lot of bodies using the outdoor space as well. It was rare to see the pub buzzing at this time of day and this in turn was making passers-by pop in to see what was occurring. Two such passers-by were a couple called Dave and Floss Croissant who told me they had seen a poster for the event and having just moved back into the area decided to have a nose to see what was going on. I didn't know this at the time, but they were to become two of my closest friends and I would go on to do lots of weird musical shit with Dave in the future.

The format of the day was quite simple. I would compere, a band would play a 45-minute set, and then a bucket would go around and we would collect money for the charity. The line-up had a bit of everything from full on rock and blues bands, to solo folk performers doing original material.

So, we were first up and although the place wasn't full it was still a fairly good-sized crowd and when we had finished our slot the numbers were definitely going in the right direction. We were received well, and I had a fairly good feeling that at the very least it was going to be a fun day. On the plus side as well, Wama and Clive were being cordial with Tony and Mark, and as this was the first time all of them had been in the same room since the original band split, I was quite happy with the outcome. It was a bit like the Christmas Day story when the Allies and the Germans had a ceasefire followed by a game of football.

Fingered By Aliens were next, and it did seem a little strange to me that I was not singing with them – but to be fair Adam did a more than adequate job of fronting the band. They even managed to get Jon Orrell up with them to jam along and he was quite the performer.

As the day went on, the busier it became, and because the pub was so small it was a godsend that the weather had allowed for the excess of bodies to spill into the outside areas. The mood was lovely, and it carried on late into the night with all the bands playing a massive part in making the day flow so well. It was one of those occasions when on a personal level I was pleased it was all over, but by the same token I didn't want it to end either. I was told that the bar had taken a record amount of money for a single day and in fact it was close to a full week's takings. My only disappointment was that I felt the pub company didn't make a very generous contribution to the charity. It was roughly the fee for one band. Considering the amount of trade that had come in and the fact that the whole thing was set up by me and a few helpers, I felt they could contributed more. We raised £1,200 in the bucket collection, which I thought was amazing, but in hindsight I wish I had thought about other ways of getting more money in – from sponsors perhaps and definitely the pub company Drink in Brighton (they have rebranded now, but I am sure you can google to find out who they are).

So, we had this money to give to the charity and Jon invited me to attend the Whoopsadaisy children's Christmas party. Tony and I turned up at their small headquarters in Preston Park where we met the kids and their families. Jon played the part of Father Christmas and there was a buzz of excitement that eagerly anticipated his arrival. I think it may help set the scene if I let you know my thoughts regarding Christmas. In a nutshell, I hate it. For me personally it has become the worst time of the year, to such an extent that I have developed what could be described as a phobia of it. It really does make me feel unwell, as well as anxious, and makes me probably one of the most miserable arseholes you could ever have the misfortune to meet at the so-called most wonderful time of the year. But this day actually reignited a little beacon of hope for me. As I watched Jon walk in wearing full Father Christmas regalia, I saw every young face in that room light up. He sat down on a chair in the middle of the room surrounded by a large circle of kids. In his booming voice he welcomed everyone and told them tales about his reindeer and the busy time he had in front of him. He had a large sack beside him and began to reach in and pick out some gifts. He read the label and announced a boy's name. He asked if the boy was there and with that a hand went up. The little boy shouted, "I'm here!"

Jon then said, "I have a gift here for you, so you had better come and get it."

The boy was helped to his feet and was standing behind what can only be described as a small wooden Zimmer frame. The boy was approximately 12ft away and slowly began to shuffle towards Jon. It seemed to take an age for him to make any progress and I wondered why Jon didn't just stand up and give it to him. Jon didn't budge one inch and the boy edged ever closer until finally he took the gift from the hand of Father Christmas. The effort etched on the boy's face throughout this short journey was apparent and this look was transformed into one of sheer joy once he had the moment of achievement. I was then informed by one of the parents that this time last year this boy couldn't stand. The gift ceremony continued as, one by one, each child was made to feel loved and, above all, normal. I can honestly say that this to me was the true spirit of what you might class as the joy of Christmas and that even I began to think maybe there was a role for this kind of nonsense in people's lives. Tony and I went on to present the money that the band had raised and were thanked for what we had done. We spent a little more time there having a chat and a cup of tea, before saying our goodbyes and leaving the building. We both looked at each other and had stupid grins and tears in our eyes as we couldn't believe what we had witnessed. We both agreed we would carry on raising money for the charities. We also agreed that we had nothing to complain about in our own lives.

FOOTNOTES

WHOOPSADAISY – "Do not ask what I can do to help, but rather what the child can do to help themselves." This is a quote from Dr Andras Peto, the founder of conductive education.

This is what made Nina Holland set up the charity Whoopsadaisy. Her son Christopher was diagnosed with cerebral palsy, and she went on to provide a service that would assist children and their families in dealing with the challenges of physical disabilities and motor disorders. The aim was to develop a child's independence and confidence by building upon their existing abilities and skills.

JON ORRELL – Structural engineer, businessman, deep sea diver, rugby player, harmonica player, guitar player, charity director, Father Christmas, singer, you name it, this man does it. The world needs more Jon Orrells.

'DRUGS & SIN' – This is an original song written by Wama about a friend he had grown up with. The lyrics of which tell a story that resembles something from a colourful and macabre gangster movie but are in fact based on the real life of this character. The song contains violence, drug abuse, death and arson, so just the thing to associate with a children's charity. The accompanying video was not about the story but was instead a collection of images that included nuns snorting cocaine, images of icons who had died of overdoses, a table of death statistics from drugs in Brighton and some bloke twirling a fire baton on the beach that was sped up for no apparent reason whatsoever.

BIG FOOTNOTE

BANDS FOR WHOOPSADAISY ALL-DAYER

THE SMOKESTACKS – Fantastic young Blues four piece. I used to work with the lead singer Kev assisting adults with learning difficulties. As you know by now, I was not a fan of the blues, but this lot kept me awake for more than my usual three songs quota.

EDD MANN – A simply exquisite voice backed by a skill on acoustic guitar that could charm the stitching from your Y-fronts. Had the kind of long flowing silky hair that L'Oréal could make a feature film about.

CHRIS MARSH – Performs an array of upbeat percussive acoustic riffs complemented by a rocky based vocal quality. His performance is like watching a piece of art take shape in front of your eyes. Skateboarder extraordinaire and hopeless romantic.

DIRTY SCAVENGER – AKA Jo Maultby. She began busking on the streets of Guildford when she was just 15, and after becoming homeless quickly learnt to use her musical skills as tools for survival. Her life on the road meant sleeping in vans, treehouses, car parks and tents.

Powerful vocal ability and a unique guitar style. Original songs written based on her own experiences that delve into the darker side of life. I remember hearing one particular song and my first thought was, "You do not mess with this bitch." (She is lovely really.)

UNCLE ARTHUR – At the time they described themselves as The Kinks meets Talking Heads. The first time I saw them I adored them, so much so that I then went on to manage them. (Poor sods.)

THE STUNTMEN – Awesome rock 'n' roll three piece with mainstays Adriene Hervey (guitar/vocals) and Mike Harwood (double bass). Joined on drums by either Stuart Green or Theseus Gerard. Adriene does solo stuff that will seep into your soul. Mike has hands like shovels that make the double bass look like a ukulele. Highly sought after for high-class events, but still have time to tolerate me when I call upon them to help me out on various projects. Two literal giants that make Hagrid look puny. Mike was self-taught and came to the music scene late in life like me and we have banter about which one of us is the worst musician. May I place on record that it is without a doubt him.

MAD BADGER – I have mentioned them previously, but they are worth a mention again as they are the complete reverse of up-your-own-arse musicians. It takes a lot of hard work to look like you do not know what you are doing, but as anyone that has seen them can testify, they know exactly what they are doing.

CHAPTER 11 – MUSIC HAS NO BARRIERS

We are going to take a very quick break from our story now as I wanted to include a chapter about the motivation behind some of the things we did as a band throughout the years. So, as a standalone piece, here is a quick look into what music did for me and the way I have seen it helping others. We, like a lot of bands, have done our fair share of charity gigs and have helped to raise money for various causes. We have supported the Shoreham Air fund, The Martlets Hospice, Whoopsadaisy and also been involved with a number of street parties that have been more community-based.

Having been involved with running a local music platform called Brighton Unsigned, I was approached by a lot of people to help out at certain events and in the main was always willing to help where I could. Musicians, and bands in general, are by nature very generous with their time and this is sometimes taken for granted by some of the bigger organisations. One particular bugbear of mine was when a big concern was putting on an event and was charging good money for it. This, in itself, was not an issue, but, for some reason, not everyone involved would be getting paid for their time and services. Those who did security, those who supplied and erected fences, those who had food concessions, stage suppliers, toilet suppliers, basically everyone who worked to put an event together. The only ones that didn't get any payment, as far as I could tell, were the ones providing the music and entertainment. Small local charity events are one thing and I understand that giving your services for free is completely up to the individual. But I can think of a couple of big events that are held annually on Hove Lawns where the musicians are treated like second-class citizens. I myself was guilty of this when I ran the music stage at the Foodies Festival. The amount of money being generated by this event was staggering, but the amount spent on the bands was nil as they knew they would have a large number of acts willing to do it for the dreaded currency called 'EXPOSURE'.

In a way, musicians have been complicit in the devaluing of their own product and I understand that audiences' attitudes have changed. I wish others could see the value of music in the way that I do, but I do realise that I see things through rose-tinted glasses when it comes to the benefits of music. I would like to give you one or two examples now and hope that it might give you a different viewpoint into how you perceive the power of music.

I have a friend called Lin Hastings. She is the lead singer of a fun local band called Dolly Doom and the Toucan Shuffle. I would supply the band with equipment when they did some gigs and after one of these she asked if I might be able to help out at an upcoming event that she was participating in called the Heartventure Halloween Ball. It turned out that Heartventure is an organisation describing itself as a friendship agency for adults with learning difficulties who meet and socialise with like-minded people in a safe environment. It was set up by Carol and

Barry Wakeford, and Diane Sharkey. Carol and Barry have a son called Daniel who had gained himself a certain amount of celebrity status being one of the lead individuals on a Channel 4 TV programme called *The Undateables*. They saw that their son was one of the many adults with learning difficulties struggling with the barriers which stifled their chances to have a social life. So, they set about providing a platform where these guys and girls could get together and enjoy the simple pleasures that a lot of us take for granted. They organised discos, karaoke nights, a dating platform, and occasionally a big event such as a summer ball or the Halloween party. As I was working at the time with similar adults, it was something I was eager to help with. The idea was that there would be a number of bands playing, a fancy-dress competition and a disco to finish off the night. My role for would be to supply the instruments, and then be stage manager and sound engineer for the evening.

I arrived early and began to set up the gear. Very soon a variety of people arrived who were members of the various bands. There were to be four bands and each one included a number of adults with learning difficulties. They were a mixture of guys who had either made their own way there or had been accompanied by a selection of family members or support workers. One such band was called Zombie Crash and they were an extremely hard-hitting four piece. I met a chap called Ryan and was talking him through the amps they would be using and was telling him that he probably had a better idea than me as to how they worked. They were getting set up and as I walked off stage a young support worker asked me if everything was going alright. I replied that it was all good and that the support worker Ryan seemed to have everything under control – and knew more than me, which I found to be a relief. She then informed me that she was actually Ryan's support worker and that the whole band were adults with learning difficulties. I felt confused at first, but then realised that I had my own misconceptions and that I had made assumptions that were wide of the mark.

Another band that played were fronted by two of the punkiest rappers I had ever heard. They were followed by a solo singer crooning some classic love songs, who in turn was followed by The Daniel Wakeford Experience – who was doing a nationwide tour on the back of his *The Undateables* fame. Dolly Doom and the Toucan Shuffle finished off the live entertainment. A notable mention must go to the DJ Chris Love who put on a sterling set and kept the whole room buzzing and alive.

One weird thing that did happen was that for most of the night the room was completely packed with revellers dressed in the most amazing costumes, letting their hair down and enjoying the experience as if they were clubbing with their mates. But as soon as it started to reach nine o'clock the room thinned out by roughly a third. At first I didn't understand the mass exodus as the event had at least another two hours to go, but then I realised a large proportion of the crowd had been accompanied by support workers as many of these guys lived in assisted-living accommodation. This basically meant that when the workers' shifts were coming to an end, that was the end of your night and you had to go home whether you wanted to or not. I tried to imagine how I would feel if whilst in the middle of a night out that I was enjoying with my friends, somebody told me to go home to bed. It wasn't the fault of the support workers, but unfortunately this is just the way things are.

The night gave me many things to consider, but the overriding thing I took away was that music was a great leveller and one of the best ways of communicating with each other. I have rarely seen a crowd so appreciative of the bands playing, and so uninhibited to let themselves go and soak up the atmosphere. What was really cool was the fact that there was no one there pretending to be cool. They were straight into the music from the very first tune, and even I got infected by the mood and danced like a complete twat with not a care in the world.

* * *

Another example I could give is the time I was doing support work for some guys. I used to spend a Tuesday and sometimes the odd Thursday with a chap who lived with his family, and it was part of my duties to support him in the community for the day. For data protection we shall call this chap 'K'. There were a number of things that he liked to do, and my role was to support him to be able to partake in these activities to his full potential. He had been doing the same thing for years and I wondered if maybe he might like to try something a bit different. I knew that he liked music, as when I picked him up we would sing along in the car to the radio. He knew I was in a band, and he would ask me lots of questions about it. I had the rehearsal studios at the time, and I wondered if he might like to go down to have a look. He was keen and so 30 minutes later we were in the studio and as soon as he saw the drumkit I knew we were on to a winner. He sat behind the kit, I handed him some drumsticks and he smashed the shit out of them. He looked like he was having the time of his life, whilst making the biggest racket you had ever heard. I sat down on a stool opposite and had a guitar plugged in as well as two microphones, one for me and one for him. K loved the microphone and took great delight in doing lots of impressions and the next hour was slightly chaotic to be honest.

There were a few others who used the studios during the day, and they were wondering what the noise was all about coming out of our room. We stopped for a cup of tea, and K met the other guys and we all chatted about music. We went back to our room to play some more, and now that the initial euphoria had worn off we found ourselves actually playing together and just jamming. K was now concentrating and was playing softer and was taking the time to figure out how the beat was going. I played some familiar well-known songs, and K was finding his own beat and was also now joining in with the choruses. We were laughing and bantering with each other, and the next few hours went by in a flash. It was not the greatest music in terms of quality, but it was some of the best music I had ever made in terms of enjoyment. The day ended and I dropped him back home.

The following Thursday I turned up at his house to pick him up. I rang the bell and K answered, all ready to go with his rucksack on his back. I said, "Hi, matey, what do you fancy doing?"
He then reached into his rucksack and pulled out his own set of drumsticks and said, "Music man."

* * *

I supported a girl, who I'll call 'P', who had Down's syndrome. She loved music and her dad, who is a lovely man, would buy lots of music-related stuff for her. She liked the fact that I was in a band and on many occasions I would play some guitar to her whilst she would accompany me by using a tambourine. We would have a lot of fun with this, and I would spend a lot of time trying to work out some basic beats to go with some songs. We were going through 'Jumping' Jack Flash' by the Rolling Stones and she was not getting it. This made her frustrated, but she refused to give up. This went on for some time until eventually something just clicked, and she had it. The sheer joy of achievement on her face was overwhelming. The following day we were down at the studio, and she was now sat behind the drumkit, repeating the beat on the snare drum as I played guitar and sang. I set up a mic for her and pretty soon we were both belting out the chorus to 'Country Roads' by John Denver.
She asked me if she could perform with the band, and I said I would try to work on something. She had a birthday coming up and her dad asked if I could help organise a party. We found a venue and I asked Wama if

he would mind if the band played for free. Straight away he said of course and so we did the gig with two mics set up together, with P as an honorary Dirty Weekend member. It was a great gig and lots of her friends were there to witness her debut as a rock star. The Stuntmen also performed that night for free as they were always the kind of guys who would help if they knew that the love of music was being shared.

It was experiences such as these that made me appreciate my love of music. Whenever I came across some individuals who acted like divas, I would use these times to remind myself that there were plenty of people who also did the right things for the right reasons.

Anyway, let's get back to the main story.

CHAPTER 12 – STAGE INVASION

Welcome to 2014. The year that gave us ISIS declaring an Islamic caliphate, Ebola in Africa rearing its ugly head, the Scots nation voting to stay as part of the UK, and Pharrell Williams annoying the shit out of everyone by singing to us about how happy he was. But without doubt, the most important piece of news was that Dirty Weekend and Fingered By Aliens were about to become homeless.

We were told that our beautiful 30,000sq ft factory had been given the green light for redevelopment and we needed to look for alternative accommodation. It was going to be turned into a massive underground gym, as well as several studios for dance and exercise classes. A large venue was also going to be built, which would have a big stage, state-of-the-art lighting and sound, as well as a large bar area to cater for a capacity of around 500. I wasn't sure how our friends the pigeons and the rats were going to take the news, but they were big boys now and could look after themselves.

It was a shame, but we'd had a good run down there and will always be grateful to Sam and Penny for helping us out when we needed them. Both bands have had a real laugh down in the factory and we would leave with many happy memories and a small handful of sad ones.

So, the search was on to find a place to rehearse, and we pondered on what our options were. There were a few perfectly good rehearsals studios in the immediate area, but we had been spoilt by having our own exclusive home. One night after finishing a practice session with the Aliens, Tony told me of some new units being built on a nearby industrial estate, so we decided to go and have a quick look. We drove into the industrial estate on a cold, dark and dank night. We were the only souls around, and it was eerie and quiet. Looming in front of us was a massive structure of steel that in the next month would be turned into six units. Each unit was around 1,000sq ft floorspace and was approximately 30ft in height. I wasn't really sure if, firstly, we could afford it and, secondly what the hell we would do with all of that space? Tony came up with the idea of sectioning a third of it off to build a room and to rent the remaining space to someone like a builder for storage. After a week of discussions between the two of us we made the mad decision to go ahead. Before long we had signed our first three-year lease and it was agreed that we would build our own studio to house both bands.

* * *

On the band front, Dirty Weekend's first gig of the year was coming up and Wama had decided to start things off with a bang. He had personally hired the Latest Music Bar in Brighton and, as this came at a cost because of its professional setup, we were about to do our first gig where we were charging an entrance fee. This brought with it a certain amount of pressure as the current climate in the music world meant it was extremely hard to get the public to pay to watch live shows by local bands. This was driven, in the main, by the fact that unfortunately, music has been devalued to the point that an audience expects everything for free. They are quite happy to pay a fiver for a fancy coffee that lasts 15 minutes, but for some reason feel cheated paying the equivalent amount for a whole evening's entertainment.

Wama would have a few new additions for this gig as well, as he wanted the night to feel like a real show. For starters, we had secured a support act, our good friend Chris Marsh and his friend Ed Mann. Both had performed for me at the Whoopsadaisy event. They are quality, and we were lucky to have them. We also had a guest drummer for the night as Creeda had a pre-booked event that had been organised months previously, where he was to play poncey music to poncey people at some hipster happening in town. We were lucky to secure the services of Abby White, who worked behind the bar of the Three Graces and also happens to be the partner of our friend Adam. She was even younger than Creeda and consequently this brought the average age of the band down to a new record of 36 years. She had studied at BIMM and had recently formed an experimental band with an excellent young guitarist called Hayden Ashdown. The band they formed together went under the name of Friar's Lantern and the project was a mixture of atmospheric music backed up by stunning visuals.

In the weeks that led up to the show, Abby joined us for some rehearsals and had to learn a whole set very quickly, and it is to her credit that she just got on with it and didn't moan.

The next addition to the show was that Wama had secured a compere for the evening who would not only host proceedings, but for some reason that escapes me, would also do a ten-minute stand-up comedy routine as well. He went under the stage name Papa Dodge and was the spitting image of Roger, the barman from the Neptune. "Hold on a minute, it IS fucking Roger from the Neptune!" Quite when he started his comedy act was a complete mystery to me as I certainly didn't recall him mentioning this before. Also, I had been at the bar many times when Roger had told me jokes and I certainly wouldn't put him in the Eddie Murphy category. I cast my mind back to remember if he ever told me a joke that I had considered to be even slightly amusing, and I can only really remember one and it is most definitely not repeatable.

So, there we had the human additions to the show, and they were to be joined by a new piece of stage furniture. Wama had built me my very own pulpit. My own personal lectern, which I could stand behind looking like preacher delivering the sermon to the masses. It had been designed in such a way that I could hide my lyric book as Wama had said to me many times previously that he thought my usual setup looked too unprofessional. I did worry a little that it was a bit dark, as the wood surrounding the top cast a shadow that meant I couldn't actually read any lyrics. But worry ye not, as Wama had installed two little lights (one red, one blue) that illuminated the book at the touch of a button. The whole of the outside of the pulpit was adorned with newspaper clippings of scandals in the world of music and the level of detail that he had put into this was to be admired. On the flip side, the level of effort and detail he was putting into this gig was beginning to make me worry whether he was missing something in his life as it was consuming his every waking hour.

Once again, Wama had produced a fanzine for the evening where on one page there was a detailed history on the life of Ben Sherman, and on the opposite page was a cartoon story of two robots having a shag. Anyone reading this would be hard pushed to fathom the rhyme and reason as to what influences his editorial decision-making. His mind works in weird and wonderful ways, and I for one am glad about that.

We drew ever nearer to the advertised starting time and the main house lights began to dim. Spotlights were directed towards a mic stand on the stage and the evening got under way with Papa Dodge welcoming everyone to the show. He then proceeded to tell a couple of completely inappropriate jokes, before introducing the support act. The place was packed and was a sell-out, but I was dubious as to whether we sold a lot of the tickets as Wama tended to just give them away. We had a lot of friends there, including my brother Kev, who had come along with Janet who was one of the original and loyal supporters. They had a kind of Ross and Rachel from Friends thing going on. Will they, won't they? (Spoiler alert, they didn't.) It was also pleasing to see Dave, Floss, Jim and Daiga who were new to the group there as well.

Chris and Ed did an amazing set to get the music part of the evening under way, and the room was really buzzing. They finished their final number to generous applause from a happy audience, and Papa Dodge came on to thank them and to announce a short interval.

The drinks were flowing and, in my case, probably a bit too well, as I was feeling particularly merry. Papa Dodge came back onstage and surveyed the room as he was about to start his act. I was standing with my arms around Tree's waist as we gazed upon this comedy genius who was ready to unleash two-barrel loads of comedic gunshot in all directions. I could not for the life of me remember the exact nature of the jokes, but I do recall that they were completely inappropriate for this audience and the silence that greeted every punchline was deafening. Unperturbed, our intrepid jester carried on regardless and the sight of the stunned room was one of the funniest things I have ever experienced. Tree felt the same and we were both crying with laughter, so much that every muscle in our bellies ached. It would appear that we were the only ones who felt this way. Certain comedy that is 'right on' and doesn't offend anyone goes down well with a Brighton crowd and less sophisticated, offensive comedy is a lot harder to sell. Brighton folk do tend to live in a bit of a bubble, and although a lot of good can come from this, there is also a tendency to be a little too precious and to take yourself too seriously.

I'm sure if poor old Papa Dodge had been doing this routine in a club up north, they would have thought he was OK. Papa Dodge finished his routine and there was a ripple of applause that smacked of pity. I went up to Roger, slapped him on the back and told him that it was one of the funniest things I had ever witnessed. He appeared pleased with this and from that moment onwards I addressed him as "the worst comedian in the world" and he would respond by addressing me as "the worst singer I have ever heard".

Papa Dodge then introduced us to the stage and what transpired for the next two hours was one of the most fun gigs we had ever done. We were spoilt really as we had a proper stage with professional sound and lighting, an enthusiastic crowd and a good feeling running through all of our bodies. I was merry as hell; everyone was in a party mood and Abby, our guest drummer, let loose like Animal from the muppets and smashed the living shit out of the kit. We played a new original number that night for the first time. It was written by Wama and was called 'Ben Sherman'. As the fashion icon had been born in Brighton, this fitted in with Wama's love of writing about his hometown. We were also fortunate to have our now unofficial photographer Richard turn up and he took a collection of images which were just reeking of class as they captured the mood of the night. Once again, the party lasted long into the night, and it did feel at times like I was being transported back in time to when I was a teenager out on the piss. So, another fun gig had come and gone, and now it was time to get back to building the new home for the bands.

We had signed a lease on a property that was far too big for what we required it to do, and now construction was to start on our state-of-the-art facility. But where do you start looking to gain the knowledge you need in order to do it all in the correct manner? YouTube of course. We found an obscure video detailing how to make rooms soundproof and the materials that should be used. Armed with this we made a mock-up box that measured approximately 2ft on each side with a small amount of the required materials. We then placed this box over a mini speaker to see how it absorbed the sound and figured that it was doing the job required. We then just surmised that if we did exactly the same again, but this time to a scale that was a hell of a lot bigger, then that was that. And, consequently after spending a little time and a shit load of money that neither of us could really afford, we ended up with a completed room that turned out to be far better than we could ever have hoped for. We had also spent a tonne of money on steelwork with the foresight that we might one day want to add an upstairs, many years into the future. Quite what we thought was going to be upstairs is anyone's guess as we certainly had no clue. We had this massive empty space on the ground floor that was originally intended to be rented out to a builder for storage, but instead we built another two practice rooms, one which we named 'Hendrix' and the other we named 'Bonham'. I admit that I am biased but believe me when I say that the way the rooms and the decorations turned out, were to my mind, pretty classy. I had been in many other practice facilities, and they were not in the same league as the rooms we had created by mistake. What had started out as a search to find a place to rehearse had now turned into some daft construction project, which neither of us knew what the outcome was to be. The new home for the band was now complete, and it was nice to know that we could come and go as we pleased, but we did need to finance this place so we decided we would take bookings for other bands as well. We didn't really push it too much as we were happy at this stage to cover the running costs and neither of us had the time to make a big commercial success of this business. Also, it was reassuring to know that the few bands we did have down would become regulars, and as such a little community was forming that was not going to wreck the place.

* * *

The band had an interesting couple of gigs coming up that I like to call the mini 'heaven and hell tour'. First up, we had been roped into playing at a community event at St Helens Church in nearby Hangleton. It was a three-day event which had a folk and comedy night on the Friday. On Saturday at three o'clock there was a teatime concert with the Hangleton Youth Band, and in the evening, there was Rock Night at which we would be playing with two other bands called Spacehopperz and Beetroot. The cost of the ticket was £12, and this included a two-course supper apparently. I cannot recall what the event was in aid of, but I assume they were raising money for some good cause, and I am quite sure we performed for free.

The audience was an eclectic mix and wouldn't really be considered our typical crowd. The majority were members of the church and were obviously here in support of this civic event. I remember as we set up that myself, Joe and Creeda were having quite a laugh as it was like setting up in a nice village hall that wouldn't have looked out of place in a Miss Marple story. The age range of the audience was from one to 100 and they were all sat around large fold-out tables that you find at village fetes. There was a rather long buffet table at the back of the room that had the usual party food you find at such functions. There was a hatch into the kitchen where you could purchase a small can of lager or, if you preferred, could have a wine poured into disposable white plastic cups. We were to be the last band on and so had some time to kill. A few of our close friends (the usual suspects) had come along with us and we spent the time slowly getting a bit tipsy whilst we watched the first two acts. My memory of the bands is a bit fuzzy, but my feeling is that they were nice people who played very appropriate music to fit the event. I think their setup was probably quite tame and the material they did was warm and wholesome.

It was time for us to unleash hell now, and if my memory is correct Creeda, Clive and Wama were up on a narrow stage, and myself and Joe were positioned on the floor in front of them. We were a lot louder than the previous two bands, and there was a mixture of delight and disgust in equal measure coming from the audience. I think we completely polarised opinion as some thought we were the best thing to happen to lift the event, whilst others probably thought we were sent up by Satan himself to test their faith. Joe and I were pretty pissed. I was in full Johnny Rotten mode and Joe was doing his damned best to replicate Slash from Guns N' Roses. I guess the highlight for me was singing our original song 'Drugs & Sin', which is a story littered with violence and telling the tale of cocaine, MDMA and heroine abuse. At times I felt like some sort of gospel preacher handing out the sermon to the assembled congregation. We walked away from that gig with a few new converts and I would imagine a price placed upon our heads, and this then led on to the next leg of the 'heaven and hell tour' as we were about to play our first ever festival.

* * *

This festival went under the name of the FFS Rally. I'm not sure what the FFS stood for but I know what it should have stood for (make your own guess). It was a biker rally that was held in an exceptionally large field in the middle of the Sussex countryside. It was a three-day event, and we would be playing in the early afternoon on the Saturday. It was organised by a group calling themselves the Nordic Brotherhood and I had visions of something along the lines of when the Rolling Stones played at Hyde Park. It should be pointed out at this stage that I am not having a go at the organisers of this event. As I was to find out, the work that goes into trying to put something like this together is hard, and the support you get back can at times be soul destroying. All successful events started somewhere, and it relies on those brave souls willing to give things a go and to take a chance. Some things will work, and some things will fail, but the ethos these individuals have for trying to achieve something good comes from a place of love.

As was the case with most of our gigs, this had been lined up by Wama, and so excited was he to be playing this event that he decided that he would go up the night before in his van and transport all of the equipment with him. This would also give him the opportunity to soak up the atmosphere and a chance to get the lay of the land. To keep him company would be his ever faithful and much-loved dog Jake. So, he and his faithful sidekick set off on the open road for a weekend of music and hedonism. On arrival, it soon became clear that this event would not be challenging Glastonbury anytime soon, in fact it would be hard pushed to challenge the St Helen's Church Hall festivities. Driving into the field he could spot a few tents in the very furthest corner, and he headed towards them. He got out of the van and with his faithful hound by his side, they explored all that the event had to offer. About a minute later, once they had done that, he sat in his van, opened a beer and wondered how the fuck he was going to explain this to us when we arrived the next day. The weather was somewhat inclement, and he spent the night in the back of the van shivering alongside his trusted companion. No one knows for sure what Jake was thinking at the time, but we can safely assume that he was reconsidering this "man's best friend" bullshit.

The following day the rest of us arrived. It had taken us some time as we were looking out for a large, tented village. After a couple of errors in navigation, we found a local who directed us down an obscure dirt road that led to the main gate of the field. In the distance, we could just about make out some activity in the far corner and drove towards it, giddy with anticipation. We spotted Wama and Jake who welcomed us. Wama appeared slightly deflated (Jake was not a barrel of laughs either) and he looked extremely tired. We realised that this was not what we had envisaged, but it didn't matter as it was a sunny day we were all in good spirits. When Wama told us about his wild night, we all pissed ourselves laughing.

Looking around it became clear that there were not many bodies here, but all major events had to start small and we were just pleased to have been invited. There was a small collection of tents dotted around where some had slept the night before, a couple of concession marquees selling bacon butties, biker clothing and some Viking shit, as well as a beer tent that adjoined the performance gazebo.

The performance area was not big – my best guess would be 25ft by 40ft. At a push, I reckon you could get a capacity of maybe 150 standing. The sound would be piped outside as well so the reach of the music would be fairly substantial. The stage itself was about six inches in height and in the centre of the tent was the sound desk, which was being operated by a robust, mature American lady with long, flowing red hair. She was dressed in a fashion that you would associate with the Californian hippy movement from the 1970s. She was pleasant enough, but she was also blunt and took no prisoners, and I took an instant liking towards her. We were the second band on and were going to follow a group called Mickey Hart and the Heartbreakers. They were a rock 'n' roll outfit that had a loyal following of lindy hop dancers who go to all their gigs. They started their set and their band of dancers leapt into action immediately to do their routines of line dancing and jiving. The arena looked full enough as they obviously took up a lot of room doing their thing, but when you took them out of the equation and also subtracted our little gang, you began to realise that there was nobody else there. They finished their set and, as always, had provided a polished and fun performance on this beautiful sunny day. They packed up their gear and left the tent followed by the small army of lindy hop enthusiasts.

All that was left in the tent was the band, the American sound engineer, and Tree and David who had joined us for this adventure. We did a soundcheck and were a few minutes away from playing as we waited to see the hordes start pouring into the tent. But, alas, no hordes were coming and so we made a start. The whole thing was surreal, and at first I was annoyed and embarrassed as we played our hearts out to no one in particular, but I soon got a grip and started to enjoy the scenario we found ourselves in. During songs we were all catching each other's eyes and laughing at how shit it all was, and I was reminded of the Papa Dodge moment. Things are sometimes so bad that they are good. Two particular highlights spring to mind. The first was, as we finished a song, that one of the event organisers came up and said he needed the mic to make an announcement. He then berated his fellow festival goers as they had only had one entry into some sort of bike competition and was telling those out in the field to show some bloody support. The second highlight was as we were halfway through a song, David got up and went to the bar and Tree went to the loo. This left us with just the American sound engineer who was doing some knitting.

We finished the gig to no applause, collected our stuff, and sat at some tables drinking beer in the sun and laughing. We all piled back into our cars, headed for the coast and ended up at the Albion in Fishersgate, where we did another gig that evening for a friend's birthday. It was mobbed. We got shitfaced and all agreed it was one of the best days we had ever had.

* * *

It was about this time that I had now become incredibly good friends with Dave Croissant, as he seemed to be a kindred spirit who had a similar attitude to me when it came to trying out new and stupid things. One day he told me local music magazine *Brighton Unsigned* was in the process of being wound up as the original creators had decided they didn't want to carry on with it anymore. They used to produce a free magazine that you would see around the bars in town. On top of this, they were known for putting on some music events as well. We both agreed it was a bit of a shame as they really did add something to the musical landscape and were a good independent voice that tended to champion the best side of the local scene. Dave suggested that maybe we should take it on as he felt the creators would surely want to see their project carry on in some kind of format. I was obviously very new to the local music scene and wasn't sure how the game was played, so with this complete lack of knowledge and experience we both agreed it was a fantastic idea. We contacted the original creators and, with their blessing, we were now one of the main players in the local music scene (or so we thought). I was to be the public face with the musicians and Dave was the technical mastermind behind the scenes (God help us). We had no clue what we were going to do at this stage and decided we would just learn as we went along, but both agreed we would try and have as much fun with it as we could.

The first thing we did was organise another Whoopsadaisy day under the branding of *Brighton Unsigned*. This would get us some experience dealing with other bands and also give us some hands-on experience of organising a live event. I'm not ashamed to admit the bulk of the acts were friends. It was easy to work with people you could rely on, but there were also a number of new bands on the bill. We moved the venue from the Three Graces up to the Hove Park Tavern, as I hadn't been happy about the lack of support shown by the previous pub management company. Most things were organised a few weeks in advance, with all the bands in place and the general plan for the day pretty much nailed down.

Two weeks before the event was to take place, I found myself in Brighton on a lovely sunny Sunday. Tree and I were heading down to one of our favourite events of the year, the Brunswick Festival. It is a real feel-good event that raises money and highlights issues encountered by the homeless community, with loads of weird and wacky stalls and a couple of outdoor bars. The main reason we were here was they have live music from midday until seven o'clock on each day of the weekend. We had a friend who was playing a set and so it was a good excuse to go along and support them. In truth we liked all the bands and were quite happy to while away the whole day watching all the acts. At the front of the stage we spotted the local legend that is Disco Pete. I shall do a big footnote about this man at the end of the chapter to give you a better idea of who he is, but for now I will give a short description of this particular character. Pete was an elderly gentleman who you would see at a large variety of music events in the town. He dressed in outfits that smacked of colour and fun and would stand there doing various rave dance moves along with the beat. He was eccentric, perhaps completely bonkers, but above all he was fun and exactly what the town of Brighton is all about. If you went to an event and Disco Pete was there, then you knew you were in the right place.

The day was winding down and I walked up to Pete and spoke to him for the first time in my life. He was extremely pleasant and very softly spoken. I thanked him for his entertainment and mentioned that I was putting on a charity gig in a couple of weeks and, if he was in the area and could pop his head in, he would be very welcome. We said our goodbyes and, in all honesty, I wasn't sure he had taken any of the conversation in as he did appear a bit frail and not completely with it.

Anyway, two weeks later whilst putting the finishing touches to the gig at the Hove Park Tavern due to start two hours later, in walked Disco Pete in his full colourful regalia. I was shocked he had turned up and he looked confused. I said hello and explained that we wouldn't be starting until two o'clock. He looked at me and he said, "OK, fine," and then sat down at a table.

Some band members started to amble into the pub as well as some punters who had arrived early. They all did a doubletake when they saw Disco Pete sitting at the table minding his own business. We were approaching the start and I was lucky enough to have persuaded my friend Theseus to co-compere proceedings. This not only took a bit of the pressure off me but enhanced the day as the guy is just so natural in these surroundings. Dirty Weekend were the first to play and I felt sheer delight as the first chord was struck and suddenly Disco Pete sprang into action. The memory of watching him in front of me doing his strangely hypnotic rave moves to every song will stay with me forever.

Disco Pete was there for the full ten hours of music and did his stuff to every band. Once the music had stopped, he walked up to me, shook me by the hand and said, "I'm off then, see you later," and like Keyser Söze, he was gone.

* * *

On the back of Whoopsadaisy 2, myself and Dave found ourselves managing two bands. One was called The Lanes and the other was Uncle Arthur. We decided we needed to put down a marker as to how we were going to move things forward. So, we decided we might as well start fairly big and go about planning a night to showcase the new talent we had found and tie it in with raising some more money for the charity. The plan was to have a large venue with a professional setup, with a line-up of four bands. This meant, in my own self-serving way, I could squeeze Dirty Weekend on to the bill. So, we had us, The Lanes, Uncle Arthur and our good friends Mad Badger lined up for a night where we would charge an entrance fee and hopefully raise money whilst having a lot of fun as well.

The search for a location wasn't that easy as most of the recognised music venues seem to run some sort of self-interest cartel and are not really welcoming to newcomers. One that stands out for having the right ethos is a place called The Old Market. This is a fantastic arts building on the border of Brighton & Hove, and I thought it would be the ideal venue for us. It has a capacity of around 500 and is used for a wide variety of events such as comedy, theatre, dance, exhibitions and music gigs. Initially I thought we might have some trouble booking the place as they are used to dealing with recognised promoters. I have found it is hard to break through some barriers when it comes to working with creative directors or owners of the more recognised venues. I must put on record that the Old Market is one of the easiest and most accommodating locations I have ever dealt with. They seem to have such a good attitude in supporting live events of all different types and it is almost like they are custodians as opposed to guardians of the beloved building. I talked through what I aimed to do with the show, we set a date and it was all systems go.

I went through the rough plans I had for the night and was pleasantly surprised as the staff at the venue talked through it with me and came up with lots of pointers and ideas I hadn't considered. I liked the way they got involved to make it work as well as possible, and I was left with the impression they were not just taking a booking fee and washing their hands of it. This showed me that they had a lot of pride in what they do and are genuinely there to support the creatives. This would be by far the biggest stage that we had ever played on and potentially our biggest audience. We might have the space for them, but we still needed to get people in and the idea of playing to 50 people in a space that holds 500 is daunting. I would rather play to a crowd of 20 in a venue that holds 21. When I told the band what we were going to do, I could sense the guys were filled with a feeling of anticipation and a little bit of fear. It wasn't really the performance that worried me but the realisation that I had to stage manage this, and also get people to part with their money and come along.

We got some posters made up and started distributing them around town. I had a slot on a local radio station talking about the event and charity. I had also blagged myself a segment on a local TV station where I talked about the local music scene. I blatantly plugged my own event and at the same time managed to persuade them to film some stuff about The Lanes and Uncle Arthur on a future date.

The big day arrived, and Dave and I made our way to the venue. It was late afternoon, and there were many hours before the start of the show although there were plenty of things for us to do. We were welcomed by the creative director, who led us backstage through myriad corridors before we were shown to our dressing room. We had never had a dressing room before and weren't really sure what to do in there. We were like kids, making out we were some kind of megastars and acting out what we presumed rock stars did in dressing rooms. After about a minute we were bored, and the four walls and light-up mirrors didn't seem like that big of a deal. Members of the other bands turned up and were equally impressed that they too had their own dressing rooms. The atmosphere changed when there were more of us, and suddenly the banter and camaraderie between all backstage was excellent and the childish excitement was tangible. As time passed, I began to feel I was the only one who wasn't really soaking up the adrenaline of fun. My adrenaline was instead fuelling a little bit of fear. Outwardly, I was showing all the right signs of loving every minute of it, but inside I was full of self-doubt and worry as I had no idea how many punters would be turning up.

It was time for soundchecks and one by one each band went through the process of making sure all was in place to achieve the best mix possible. This was one of the few soundchecks that I actually enjoyed and I could only put that down to the size of the stage, the quality of the sound and lighting, and the professionalism of the stage staff that made it fun. With our soundcheck out of the way we made our way through the backstage door to the pub directly over the road. We still had a couple of hours to kill, and this time in the pub with the other bands gave us a chance to chill out and to relax with a couple of beers. Wama popped over and approached me, as he could see I was looking a little nervous. He told me there was nothing I could influence now and so I might as well just enjoy it. He then informed me he had been out the front and that there were people queueing and he was confident all would be good.

The start was upon us and it was my job to get up onstage to welcome everyone to the evening and to get the first band on. Up first was Mad Badger and, to my mind, they had the hardest job of the night as the audience was at its most sober and needed warming up. I needn't have worried, though, as Noel the lead singer was an old hand at this and nothing fazed him at all. In the soundcheck he had asked for several XR leads that he could join together in order to make his mic lead as long as possible. I welcomed everyone and estimated in my head that there were roughly 200 people in the room as I could see plenty of spaces in front of me. I introduced the Badgers and they commenced with Noel instantly jumping off the stage and using every inch of the room to explore and sing. He did a truly masterful job of involving as many audience members as he could, and more people were spilling into the auditorium from the bar area. By the time the Badgers had finished being mad, the room numbers had swelled to between 350 to 400, and the buzz they created had set the tone for a great night ahead.

Uncle Arthur followed next and performed a set of musical brilliance. They really were exceptionally good musicians, and they were fronted by a chap called Ross who put everything into the execution of the songs. He was a real showman, and the audience were lucky to be watching a piece of theatre unfold in front of them. They managed to not only keep the crowd with them but also to ratchet up the levels of excitement by another few notches. The end of their set was greeted with wild applause and by the looks on their faces you sensed they had enjoyed the experience as much as the audience.

We were up next and after seeing the previous two bands I was hoping we wouldn't be seen as the weak link. Looking out into the crowd it was hard to pick out individual faces due to the stage lighting that was being projected straight towards us, and the fact that the place was packed and all the bodies just meshed into one big blur. Just off the front of the stage at the left, right and centre were three individuals with video cameras. It turned out Wama had hired them to come down and film some of the performance as he wanted to use the footage to make future videos. I looked at all the guys to make sure we were prepared. We were fortunate to have Joe, our guitarist, that night as he was currently playing the nationwide Peter Andre tour – but as luck would have it they had done the Brighton Centre gig the night before and the following night he would be playing at the Royal Albert Hall in London.

Creeda looked chilled, Joe looked moody, Clive looked like he had taken a load of uppers, and Wama and I were dressed in our ridiculously over-the-top jackets.

"One, two, three, four," said Creeda and we launched into the set by meshing the first two songs together. Seven and a half minutes later we had the moment of truth as the second song came to its conclusion. The crowd went mad. They were really receptive and appreciative, and this in turn made us all a lot more relaxed. I think it is fair to say that from here on in we treated the rest of the set as one big party, as we were not just performing but genuinely enjoying our time on the stage. I knew this size audience certainly wouldn't faze Creeda or Joe as they had done big gigs before and were amazingly comfortable with their instruments. I wasn't sure how Wama or Clive would deal with it, but the truth is they took it in their stride and by the looks on their faces they were loving the whole surrealness of it all. In the set, we did some well-chosen upbeat covers, but also managed to do four of our own originals and it was a truly memorable performance. There was much to celebrate, but I would like to touch on two memories that have a particular place in my heart. As I have already told you, I was now starting to write a few of my own songs, so I had a go at writing a love song of sorts. This was not our usual kind of material, but after a few weeks and lots of rehearsals our new tune entitled 'Tree' was ready to be played in public. What better place to perform this than in front of a few hundred people and the person it was written about? I couldn't see Tree in the audience, but she was out there somewhere. To introduce the song I went through a gushy tale of how this individual had come into my life and had a huge impact upon me. Unbeknownst to me, at the time Tree was in the downstairs of the venue visiting the ladies' loo. Apparently, as she came out of the loo, there were security staff and cleaners standing by a cordoned off area at the foot of the stairs. Apparently, someone had vomited all over the place and due to health and safety reasons no one could go back up until the area had been fully cleaned. So, as Tree waited with a few others downstairs I was going through the verses of my personal love letter without her hearing a word. The song finished and was received well. Tree made it back to the main auditorium and a few friends were asking her how she felt about the last song. There was a lot of confusion as she wasn't aware that her take on the Lenny Kravitz song "Are You Gonna Go My Way" was of such great interest to anyone. Tree missed out on a lot of our so-called big moments and I do wonder to this day whether this is by mistake or by design.

The second great memory I have of this show was our very last song. We performed our signature tune 'Dirty Weekend in Brighton' and had a few added extras. We had persuaded a couple of others to come up onstage and join the band. We had Dave Croissant on tambourine and a wonderful chap called Paul Denton, who was wearing a mad wig and had his own inflatable guitar. The song started, and we were giving it large and rocking it. Paul on inflatable guitar was going mad and Dave was jumping up and down like some sort of demented kangaroo.

Suddenly Wama's daughter Danique ran onstage, wine glass in hand, followed by a collective of like-minded individuals, and proceeded to have her own private party with the band. We carried on playing and a few others were now up with us dancing all over the place. The on-stage sound engineer was frantically trying to take people's drinks from them as he was obviously worried that someone could either damage thousands of pounds of equipment or electrocute themselves. We carried on playing and all around us was some of the best madness as the crowd just partied on. It was surreal, it was messy and it was the best way that we could have brought that set to an end. We are incredibly lucky that the memories of this are all captured on film as the cameras were rolling for this song. We ended up making a full live video of it. Go on to YouTube and put in 'Dirty Weekend stage invasion' to witness what was one of my life's favourite memories.

We came off stage absolutely buzzing and loving life. I then had to get back onstage as I had to carry on with my compere duties. I talked about the charity to try and prise more money from the assembled crowd and then I went on to introduce the last act.

The last band were The Lanes and I don't think I could have chosen a better act. These guys know how to work a crowd and they went on to deliver one of the most electrifying live sets I have ever witnessed. The night ended and in true Dirty Weekend style I got absolutely mashed. The whole thing had been stressful, but by the same token it had also been absolutely exhilarating. Would I do it again? Of course I would, but maybe I'd do it bigger.

* * *

The year carried on with us doing a few more gigs and also with some personal highlights for the band. One that springs to mind is that Latest TV had a sister magazine and in it was published the Latest Music chart. We had positions number 1, 5, and 8 going into Christmas, so you could say we had a Christmas number one. I'm not sure how this chart was compiled, but I suspect that Wama had something to do with it.

We also played the Green Door Store venue where we supported a band by the name of Wille and the Bandits. This outfit were a big deal and toured year after year extensively throughout Europe. A fantastic group of musicians who had an exceptionally large and loyal following, home and abroad. I was particularly proud of this gig as it was the first time the majority of the set was made up of our own material. That's why I liked Dirty Weekend, as that set us apart from your normal pub band. Maybe I was slowly turning into one of those up-their-own-arse musos, but I didn't mean it that way. To me, we had the ability to include an element of fun whilst working on our own vanity projects. I also think this made Creeda and Joe enjoy it more as we weren't just reciting music but creating it as well.

We finished the year by playing our beloved Neptune on the Saturday before Christmas. As always, it was a party and it was the start of a little ritual for, as soon as we finished, Mary had booked us for the next year.

It would come to pass that Dirty Weekend would play the Saturday before Christmas for the next few years.

FOOTNOTES

MY PULPIT – It wasn't until a year later that I fully appreciated the fine detail Wama had gone into in creating my music platform. When we had finished a gig, I was standing against it and was just reading some of the newspaper paraphernalia he had decoupaged on the stand. I suddenly noticed my full name and was reading a story about how I was engaged in some sort of sordid sex scandal.

PAPA DODGE – Sadly, we lost our beloved friend Roger far too early. I have only good memories of the man and expect to see him behind the bar every time I go into the Neptune. I wish I knew where the Papa Dodge character came from, but my best guess was that he had done it as some sort of bet on whether he could do a comedy night. He tied this in with raising money for the R.N.L.I.

THE LANES – A three piece from Brighton who provide one of the most energetic live shows you will see. There is not a weak link in the band as all are craftsmen on the instruments they play. Where they stand out is the way they bring theatre to their performances. They play with the same gusto whether to two or 2,000 people. They set out to be the best band on any line-up and will go all out to achieve this. I admire them as they do it in a way to spur themselves on. Go on YouTube and put in The Lanes 'Dirty Synth' and this will take you to the video that we got the Local TV station to film.

THE OLD MARKET – The Old Market opened in 1828 as a fresh food market. It has been used as a stables, a warehouse and since the 1980s an arts venue.

Its current owners in 2010, Yes/No Productions made various changes in order to maximise potential use for gigs, theatre productions, events and performances.

In 2011 the building was reopened under the new name TOM – The Old Market.

As TOM – The Old Market is a venue in both the Brighton Fringe and Brighton Festival during May.

BIG FOOTNOTE

DISCO PETE – Sadly, this local legend is no longer with us. You would often see Pete at regular music events around the town. He would be dressed in coloured garb busting out dance moves and generally keeping the crowd entertained.

I have read in interviews that he thought age was immaterial and that if you had a passion or a skill you should use it. He was an inspiration, especially to young children, and would often talk about the physical and mental benefits that dancing brought him.

Earlier in his life he had been a radar mechanic, a hospital radio DJ and then a caretaker in an infant school for many years.

He was a regular on the local club scene and would often be found in his favourite, the Pink Coconut, in the 80s and 90s.

He was a talented artist and poet and had some famous ancestry in the shape of W. Turner the artist and Romantic poet Percy Shelley.

He devoted much of his later years to helping with local children's charities, donating to organisations such as NSPCC and Chestnut Tree House Children's Hospice.

On a personal note I would like to say that it was a pleasure to have had the chance to meet the man and the world is a lot less bright without him around. Pete will feature in the next chapter as well as I tell you the story of how we kidnapped him for five hours on what was one of the most amazing and surreal days of my life.

CHAPTER 13 – HAVE SOME PRIDE

We now enter into 2015, a year in which Buckingham Palace first announced Prince Andrew was not a pervert, Stephen Fry got married and Bruno Mars drove us mad with 'Uptown Funk'.

As a band it was a relatively slow start to the year on the surface of things, but there was a lot going on behind the scenes and this would turn out to be a very momentous year indeed. David and I were in the process of publishing our first *Brighton Unsigned* magazine, which was no mean feat as neither of us had any experience in this field whatsoever. I was writing articles and David was teaching himself how to format the actual layout ready for a print run. As well as this I had blagged my own monthly slot on a music show called *B-Music* which was to be broadcast on Latest TV. This was where I would highlight my pick of local bands to look out for under the guise of '*Brighton Unsigned* Ones to Watch'. I would give an overview of a particular band, and then give examples and my opinion of their work in a kind of John Peel style, or at least that was how I saw things. We had also been approached by the organisers of a big food festival event and were being asked which bands to book for their music stage. In the end, I persuaded them to let me do it all, and I saw this as a good way to launch the concept of *Brighton Unsigned* back into the forefront of the local music scene. The event was called Foodies Festival and the Brighton date was just one of many that took place all around the country. It was a big deal for us and we figured if we could impress, this could lead on to bigger and better opportunities in the future.

This was also the year of our shortest ever gig on 11th April at a pub called the Montpellier in Brighton. All was fine to begin with as we did our usual setup and, as we normally did, we had brought a sizeable crowd with us. It looked like we were going to have an enjoyable evening ahead of us, but the problems started after the first song when we were instructed by the bar staff to turn the volume down. This in itself was nothing too troublesome as we were aware that different pubs have varying local noise constraints. We were happy to abide with this and then went into the second song. As we finished, we were instructed by the manager to turn down some more and once more we obliged with no issue at all. The third song went by and I could see him behind the bar running his fingers across his throat in an action that suggested we needed to kill it. I stopped singing and instructed the rest of the guys to stop playing. I then walked behind the bar and asked him to tell me exactly what he wanted us to do, and he then told me that we needed to come down in level again. To my mind we weren't loud, in fact we were embarrassingly quiet as far as I was concerned. So, in my best diplomatic way I told him to go fuck himself and suggested he didn't bother with live music ever again. (We never did get rebooked.)

* * *

In May we did the Robin Hood street party again. We had Theseus as our guest drummer for the day as Creeda was doing some hipster shit with his more beautiful band; this was followed the next day by a performance at the Foodie Festival. As I was in charge of the stage I decided to take full advantage of this opportunity and added Dirty Weekend to the bill.

Next up for us in the merry month of May was the Great Escape – a big international music festival hosted annually in Brighton. It was classed as a celebration of new music from all over the world. As well as an opportunity to see lots of live music at a variety of different venues it also doubled up as a conference. This is where the so-called great and the good of the music industry would converge and basically pretend to be interested in finding the next big thing.

You would have record companies, publishers, promoters, talent agents, etc, all walking around town wearing their lanyards displaying their name and job title. It was a bit of a game reading the lanyards to see how much of a big dick the wearer was within the 'biz'. Dave and I had blagged our way on to the delegate lists, and if I recall correctly my lanyard told the world I was a director/owner/publisher of *Brighton Unsigned*. Quite a lofty title indeed for someone who hadn't actually done anything yet and I wondered where that placed me in the pecking order of the beautiful people. In fact, it has just occurred to me that we even managed to get Richard Wood a press photographer pass and he used this to get into a secret, intimate Paul Weller show where he took photos. To get a band into the Great Escape festival was nigh on impossible as the line-up was basically a done deal, all sewn up by money and self-interest. It was pretty much run by a cartel of the big players so, in all fairness, there was no point trying. But it did have an Alternative Escape fringe festival running alongside it and this we found presented the best opportunity to infiltrate. As *Brighton Unsigned* we were given permission to use the corporate banner and were sanctioned to have our own small stage during the three days. We transformed the Royal Standard pub into our arena and, lo and behold, Dirty Weekend managed to get themselves on to that bill as well. It was shameless, I know, to use my influence, but if I had not, believe me, Wama would have murdered me.

Because of my dual role, I was taking this event very seriously, as to me this was an opportunity to showcase our original material. I think I harboured some kind of dream scenario where an influential delegate walking around the town would decide to go and check out one of the fringe events in the hope of tapping into the next big thing. When they saw us they would slap themselves on the back as they were one step ahead of their competition. (Dream on, Phil.)

I was not just doing this for Dirty Weekend, but for all the bands that I was putting on. Nothing would have given me greater pleasure than knowing a band I had given a chance to would be discovered and go on to bigger and better things. If it turned out to be us then that would just be a happy bonus.

Wama and I had been continuing with our songwriting and by this stage had enough songs to easily carry a full set. Wama's songs were all very punchy and fast paced, and I would counterbalance this with songs that would tell of Armageddon, depression or suicide. I would often rib him about his songs being all about gangsters and living on the edge of some sexy, exotic world in the seedy underbelly of Brighton, and he would counter that by saying that I was just a miserable cunt. (He had a point.) Wama and Clive knew this gig meant a lot to me as I wanted us to gain some credibility from our peers. I didn't know why I felt so strongly about this at the time, as it certainly doesn't bother me to that degree now. Anyway, we had set up the pub to resemble something that at least appeared to be a professional stage and Dirty Weekend were to be the first band out of seven playing that day. Joe and Creeda hadn't arrived at the agreed time, and when they did eventually arrive there was only a couple of minutes to spare. This had really wound me up and was something I didn't need on top of all the other stuff I had been involved in to try and make the day a success. On top of this Creeda was pissed as he had been out until the early hours taking in the festival around town before watching the sun come up and then getting straight back on the party bus.

I was fucking livid as we powered through the set, we were playing poorly in my opinion and I just wanted to get through it. The end couldn't come soon enough for me, and when it was all over I felt personally let down and was embarrassed by our performance. Now, I know this sounds like I am taking this far too seriously and all of this is supposed to be fun, but I felt protective towards our own material, and that Creeda and Joe were not respecting the band fully. Maybe they thought they were the only credible musicians in the band, but to my mind myself, Wama and Clive were every bit equal to them and they should have known better. It took a while for me to calm down and it turned out that no great record company executive had walked in that day, so we didn't squander an opportunity. At the next practice session we thrashed it all out, cleared the air and then kissed and made up.

So, things were patched up quickly and there was certainly no bad blood lingering, as two weeks later we did one of the nuttiest and funniest gigs we had ever done. This brought us right back to what we did this for, and that was to have nights of joy, fun and general stupidity. It was at the Albion, this one situated in Hove and not the one in Fishersgate mentioned previously. It was the usual setup, but with a couple of additions from Wama thrown in. He had arranged for students from a local arts college to come down and shoot some live video footage. He had, as always, set up the stage with the now-obligatory porn backdrop and Maisie had been inflated to her full glory. He had also spent some time and money on Facebook, advertising the details of the gig, and asking people to come down and be prepared to join in the filming. Another new addition was a battered suitcase, which was placed at the front of the stage. He opened the lid and inside were an assortment of brightly coloured wigs, inflatable guitars, saxophones to blow up, and the odd sex toy here and there for no apparent reason whatsoever.

As a band we were incredibly lucky with our hardcore following, as, to put it bluntly, they were completely insane when it came to making the most of a chance to let their hair down. They were always up for anything that smacked of a laugh and a good time, and as soon as they saw the suitcase of goodies it wasn't long before every single prop was in their possession. Paul Denton and Richard Wood were straight into the blow-up instruments, and Dave, Floss, Tree, Janet, Kev, Daiga, Jim and Jackie were loving the wigs. Not sure who went for the sex toys, but I do have my suspicions. As soon as we started playing, the majority of the audience in front of us resembled a line-up of contestants from *Ru Paul's Drag Race* and the whole room went nuts for the next two hours. The crowd were pissed, and I followed their lead, joined in and just got pissed with them. We did 'Pretty Vacant' by the Sex Pistols and it was bedlam. We did a multitude of anthemic tunes and soon had everyone in the whole pub singing along to 'Dakota' by the Stereophonics. I thought Jackie standing in front of me was having an orgasm, she looked so excited. It was apparent that 'Dakota' was a particular favourite of hers. All the thoughts I'd had two weeks earlier of me being all serious and sulky were dispatched to history, as I found myself reconnecting with the main purpose of the band – and that was to have fun. If you watch some of the video footage shot on that night, one thing you would take away was that this band was certainly not up its own arse, and that is what made us Dirty Weekend.

* * *

And, so, this leads me to the biggest, most insane, most fun show that we ever put on. This would be our first ever appearance in the Brighton Pride parade, which we would do a few times over the years and each one has been great. But, as the saying goes, 'You never forget your first time', and this rings true with me.

Although for some, it may be hard to believe, I am aware not everyone is familiar with the Pride event so here is a very brief history lesson. The year we first did the parade was the 25th anniversary of the event. The very first Pride march was held in the city in 1973, when the Sussex Gay Liberation Front organised a small march just seven years after the decriminalisation of homosexuality. The reason Pride was only celebrating its 25th anniversary is that the next event wasn't held until nearly 20 years later in 1991. The 1995 Pride march was the first to attract major sponsorship, and by 2000 the event reported 60,000 visitors. From 2004 the event was awarded charitable status and began to attract many high-profile performers, including Boy George, Fat boy Slim, Alison Moyet and Paloma Faith. Disaster struck in 2011 when, despite record attendance the previous year, the management went bankrupt after running up debts of over £200,000. But under new management, things took off again and since 2012 more than £110,000 has been raised for local LGBTQ+ community groups. The festival, which now promotes equality for LGBTQ+ people, now includes a huge range of entertainment, including an arts and film festival – and even a Pride Dog Show.

When Wama had informed me of his plans for us to apply for a float in the parade some months earlier I must admit I didn't give it a lot of credence and had pushed it to the back of my mind. It wasn't because I was questioning his ability to get it done, but I did have a good understanding of the hoops you had to jump through to get a foot in the door. For starters, it is not a cheap thing to do and we didn't have the advantage of corporate sponsorship to help with the financing. It is amazing the big firms that latch on to this event have managed to somehow suck some of the ethos out of what should be a celebration of the individual spirit overcoming obstacles. It almost seems like if you happen to have a few quid in your pocket you will be made to feel welcome. That is the way of the world though. I suspect this was not the rule when this event was starting out in its more idealistic days. I know many friends from the gay community who cannot stand Pride as they feel that it has been hijacked for all the wrong reasons. I guess I could be called a hypocrite, as in some small way I was adding to this in essence. As the weekend celebrations were drawing ever closer, Wama gave us the official news that we were in. Interrogating him fully, we worked out that the plan involved a tractor, a 30ft trailer, a compulsory colour scheme, as well as us playing live and performing throughout the ride. It all sounded dodgy to me, but if that is what needed to happen, then so be it. We were also going to invite our nearest and dearest to join us, as well as giving some spaces to some die-hard supporters who had helped us out.

Other things were also happening regarding Pride. At this time, I also found out that David and I under our *Brighton Unsigned* banner would be officially staging the music for a three-day chilled out Pride event (Pride Village) that would run on Friday, Saturday and Sunday in the centre of town. So, all in all, it wouldn't only be a busy weekend, but an extremely boozy one by the sound of it. Because of this taking up a lot of my time I didn't have much to do with the planning of the float for the parade so had no clue as to how this was progressing nor indeed what it would look like. I knew Wama was on the case and I was more than happy to just turn up and do whatever I was instructed to do. It wasn't that I didn't care, more a case of not being able to spread my own resources too thinly.

Friday arrived and Dave and I were into the first day of the *Brighton Unsigned* event at Pride Village. It had kicked off in the early afternoon and all had gone well. It almost looked like we knew what we were doing. The event was situated in the throng of Kemptown on a square by the name of Steine Gardens. It was a large, chilled-out area that was dominated at the sea end by a large, magnificent marquee going by the name of the 'Tipple Temple'. This was to be our base for the next few days and our host was a lovely lady called Lindsey. Her 'Tipple Temple' venture was relatively new, and she had taken a big gamble on being able to pull off an event that would complement all the other attractions Pride had to offer. Throughout the day we had a succession of low-key, mainly acoustic bands playing, and this was so chilled out we soon found ourselves basking in the atmosphere, and, ultimately, partying late into the night. Luckily, I had already arranged for the following day's festivities to be overseen by my good friend and sound engineer Roy Weard. I knew that on the day of the parade itself, I would be fully immersing myself into the party atmosphere and that the event we were involved in would be having its quietest day so there was no need for us to be on site.

Saturday morning arrived and my alarm went off at eight o'clock. I felt dreadful, quite frankly, and quickly regretted the amount of pride I had been showing the night before. The parade was due to start at half-past twelve, but I had said I would be down at ten to lend a hand with the finishing touches to the float (not that I was in any fit state to contribute anything meaningful). I made myself a coffee and sat in silence pondering what the day might have in store. I had a mental picture in my head of an old, dilapidated tractor towing 60-odd idiots and a band through the streets, before breaking down somewhere near the start line. I got dressed in a purple Hawaiian shirt and a pair of red long shorts, as bright colours are the uniform for Pride. Our particular float had been allotted the main theme colour of orange, but I was somewhat lacking in that particular shade within my wardrobe selection. I said goodbye to Tree, as she would be meeting us a bit later just before the start, and I popped into the shop next door where I bought several bottles of water. I walked straight down to the seafront and slowly made my way along the promenade to meet the others at the designated starting point. It wasn't a long walk, but it seemed to take forever and a day as I was hungover, dehydrated and extremely hot. Anyone else doing the same walk, would have been chuffed to bits as it really was a beautiful morning, and the sea vista was outstanding to say the least. I had already consumed copious amounts of the water. To be fair, I had had worse hangovers and felt surprisingly well, considering. I began to surmise that I might still be a little tipsy and started to question my preparation techniques.

In the far distance, I could make out a throng of bodies as well as a mass of colours and what looked like thousands of flags blowing in the mild sea breeze. Many others were walking the same route as me and the array of different attire on display was flamboyant in the extreme. In fact, some of the lack of attire was even more eye-catching. It makes me realise why I love this place so much because quite frankly people have the confidence to be who they want to be and overall, no one really cares to be of a critical nature. In fact, if you dress conservatively here, then you are the one who stands out as being a bit weird.

I walked on ever closer to the throng. Wama had informed me that we would be one of the last floats in the parade, so I was awfully close to seeing what sort of shit show I would be parading on very soon. I arrived and had to do a double take to make sure what I had seen was not a mirage.

Wama was busy working away with many members of his family as they were bedecking the chariot we would be riding that day. The tractor at the front could only be described as an absolute beast. If they did an episode of *Pimp My Ride* and they showcased a tractor, this would be the one. It was new, shiny, a beautiful deep scarlet and had a bloody great big scoop on the front. Sitting behind the red beast was the 30ft trailer. It was adorned with rainbow bunting, poles with orange flags fluttering in the breeze, balloons of every colour, Dirty Weekend banners, and a blow-up doll in a blonde wig wearing a Brighton FC shirt with a scaffold pole up her arse.

At the front of the trailer was a generator, the PA system with speakers on high poles – which seemed to be secured by string – a full drumkit and the guitar amps. The rest of the trailer had enough room to house a very snug crowd of approximately 40 to 50 bodies. Right at the back was the banner of the bondage lady facing outwards so the crowd could see her in her full glory.

There were a few of the usual suspects already there. They were dressed in the full regalia of colourful Hawaiian dress with an assortment of exotic headgear as well as an abundance of flowered leis. The atmosphere was one of excited anticipation, with lots of friendly banter permeating through the sunny sea air.

The parade was set out as a long wagon train of floats, intermittently separated by a group of walkers from different societies and organisations. All the ladies and a few of the men in our posse were giddy with excitement as the float that would be following us was that of the Adonis Male Strip Troupe. Milling around at the beginning, we were getting to know the guys and it wasn't long before they were invited on to our float for a variety of photo opportunities. One could have found this intimidating, but I convinced myself that they were probably jealous of us being international rock gods (delusional or what) and were worried about having to follow us. They were a great bunch of guys and I think it's fair to say we had between us two of the noisiest and liveliest floats in the whole parade.

You had to feel sorry for the poor souls who ended up positioned in between us – and if memory serves me right those poor souls turned out to be Amnesty International. Quite what they would be thinking as they marched behind our bondage lady all tied up in front of them is anybody's guess.

We were getting close to the proposed start, but there were murmurings there was a bit of a problem. Word had come through that the start of the event was delayed as apparently the police were dealing with a suspect package that had been found on the route. In the end, they had to call in the bomb-disposal team to do a controlled explosion and as such the route was going to be redirected from its original plan.

Whilst waiting, there were crowds of people walking past us heading into town towards their preferred vantage points. Coming towards us was a familiar face and it turned out to be Disco Pete. We greeted him and asked where he was heading. Naturally, he said he was off towards the park where the parade was due to finish. We said we would give him a lift and, that, ladies and gentlemen, is how we kidnapped Disco Pete.

Now because the route had been recalculated, the time of the parade wasn't going to be the two hours we had planned for, but instead it would now turn into an estimated four hours. It was a baking hot day, and once the parade started you weren't allowed to disembark from your float. There was also a no-alcohol policy adopted for the parade and I would be lying if I were to say this was maintained stringently on our float. The parade was soon under way and because it was so long in length it took quite a while for us to get rolling. But now we were off and travelling at a mind-boggling three miles per hour. We started to play our first song and it sounded good as all the equipment appeared to be doing what it should. Suddenly the tractor came to an abrupt stop, which led Clive to fall into the drum kit and Joe to fall over his amp. We pissed ourselves laughing and wondered – if this had already happened within the first 20 seconds, what would the rest of the day have to give us? We realised this was going to be a very tricky exercise indeed, but we soon adjusted to the stop/start nature of things. The crowds on either side were thin at this point as technically we hadn't even joined the actual route, and by the time we arrived at the Peace Statue, which marked the official start point, it was all rather more amplified.

The atmosphere was electric, for as well as our playing, all the people on our float had whistles and kazoos and were generally going nuts. The crowds were now growing on the pavements either side of us, and the buildings left and right had many bodies hanging out of windows, waving and clapping. We had a prearranged setlist of around a dozen songs, which we perceived to be bangers, and as this was a moving show, we figured we would just repeat them throughout. We also had a few friends on board with us who could give me a hand with singing duties as I would need a break every now and then. This was to turn out to be a godsend as the parade wound up lasting twice as long as first anticipated, and in this searing sunshine it was hard work. We had our good friend Jimmy Slag, as well as Satch (then the lead singer of a band called Frankie Furlow) and Clem (singer of Kudu Blue).

Going along Western Road towards the main shopping area of Brighton the crowds just kept growing and growing, and then the whole parade came to a complete standstill at the shopping centre, Churchill Square. This is the main shopping area of Brighton and it had literally thousands of spectators crammed into the large space. We were stationary there for around six minutes and this gave us the chance to play two songs to their full length. We had the whole crowd dancing and singing in unison to 'Sex on Fire' by Kings of Leon and 'Play That Funky Music' by Wild Cherry. Not particularly my favourite songs but the right ones for this time and place.

We had never envisaged that we would be able to perform whole songs to a captive crowd that day, and this was repeated several times along the route. Two personal highlights were singing 'Take Me to Church' by Hozier, and 'Pretty Vacant' by the Sex Pistols to thousands of eager and appreciative partygoers. You couldn't have asked for a better crowd. They were drunk, happy, engaging and, above all, captive. Amnesty

International behind us were beginning to look a little tired and the Adonis boys were running low on baby oil as we soldiered on through the throng of revellers.

By the time we were approaching the most populated part of the route, my voice was beginning to go and I was thankful I could let others take over the singing duties. This gave me a chance to really soak up the atmosphere. To see the general mayhem going on all around us was surreal, but at the same time truly magical. Disco Pete was still going strong and the sheer energy of the man was something to behold. It appeared every single vantage spot available was taken, with every window of every building having countless bodies draped out of them, as well as every bus stop roof crammed full of joyful party people. The whole road ahead was just a sea of colour and happiness, and it appeared that everyone had made a real effort with not only their outfits but their attitudes as well. It is a beautiful thing to see a contagion of happiness spreading from person to person.

By the time we had come to the finish I figured I had sung 'Sex on Fire' roughly 15 times, 20 for 'Play That Funky Music', and all the others on our small setlist at least six times each. To this day, if ever I hear the intro to 'Play That Funky Music' I break into a sweat and shake a little, and it is with a heavy heart that I must admit I have grown to hate the bloody song.

We had reached the finish point of the parade at Preston Park. This was the location of the main activities and was a ticketed area that had all the big acts. That year I think they had the Human League and Fat boy Slim on. We let everyone off the float and poor old Disco Pete looked like he was regretting his decision to hitch a lift with us. He, being the party animal that he was, headed to the park for another six hours of dancing. We had other plans. A fair few others and I arranged to head away in the opposite direction from the mayhem to find a pub where we could just chill out and celebrate the madness of the day. We decided to rendezvous in the World's End pub. I stayed on the float for a little while as I gave Wama a hand unloading all the equipment into his van. As soon as the tractor was free from the constraints of the parade, our driver put the pedal to the metal and we found ourselves bombing up the road at 40 miles an hour. Wama, Clive and I were hanging on for dear life whilst trying to make sure we were holding the PA, drumkit and amps down, as they were in real danger of flying off the side. Everything was safely stored away in the van and it was time to say goodbye to our red beast. I felt like a little boy who was having his favourite toy taken out of his hands, and it was sad to see it bombing up the road and disappearing into the distance.

Clive and I made our way through the crowds and headed to meet the others. We were going against the tide as the hordes were heading to the park, but I'm sure we had made the right choice in trying to escape the madness. We met up with the rest of our crew and just whiled away the hours swapping stories of our own separate perceptions of our day. The night ended up with some obscure drunken Hawaiian pool championship somewhere in Hove for some reason that escapes me. It was estimated we had played to 200,000 people that day and I was proud we were the only live band in the whole of the parade. A huge sense of pride came over me when I read reports of the parade in the papers. There were a couple of comments giving our float for a special mention and it was satisfying to know we had made an impression on a few strangers.

* * *

The following day was hangover hell. My voice was gone, and I ached in places that should not ache. We still had the small matter of running the third day of our Pride Village event and, as well as several different bands I had lined up for the day, Dirty Weekend to do a stripped-down acoustic set. I met Dave early, and we went into autopilot mode and got back into the groove of things. We made the decision to just push on through and deal with the obvious consequences the following day and, as such, we were straight back on the beer. The day was gorgeous. We were in the most ornate large marquee you could imagine, surrounded by friends and listening to the most laid-back and technically brilliant music imagine. The entertainment of the day was finished by the enchanting spectacle of an artist by the name of Joe Black. Joe is a cabaret/drag artist of the highest calibre and quite frankly this was the best way we could have finished off such a magnificent weekend.

* * *

With Pride done and dusted, next up for us were a couple of street parties. We had done the Robin Hood a couple of times in the past and I had always enjoyed the general vibe at these events. We had been asked to perform at the Stirling Street party in Hove, which was very local, and we were also aware it was a fundraiser gig as well. Once again, we were blessed with decent weather and as I approached, there looked to be a good-sized crowd. The street had been decorated with bunting adorning the lampposts. There was an array of long tables that had various little stalls like tombolas and cake selling, etc. There was a small gazebo right in the middle of the road. The road had been closed off for the day and the gazebo in the middle was to be the stage area, housing a PA system and just enough room for a band setup. It was situated right outside the pub on the corner and the whole area was a sea of colour. It really had a great community feel, as people of all ages were enjoying the various activities and the company that was on offer. We were greeted by our host, a lovely lady called Pippa Hodge. She first thanked us for agreeing to play and then went through the plans for the day. There was one other musical act on before us and they were a small rock 'n' roll outfit whose name escapes me.

All our mates turned up and it was an idyllic day kicking back in the late summer sunshine. We were due to do our set, but just before we started there were a few announcements over the PA system. There was a raffle, and a couple of the kids pulled out the tickets and announced the winning numbers over the microphone. A youngish chap with learning difficulties was interested in the mic and asked me if he could do something. I asked him what he would like to do, and he told me that he was a rapper. I said, "Go for it," and introduced him. He then started doing a rap that he had written and, without having to be prompted, Creeda started accompanying him with a rhythm on drums and Joe came in with some punchy guitar riffs. The young lad was not only excellent, but as the crowd were getting into the whole groove you could visibly see him grow in confidence and stature. He came to an end and received thunderous applause as he made his way back to his friends with a look of absolute joy on his face. We started our set and, in all honesty, just had one of those joyous times that money cannot buy. The rapper chap had a mate called Harry. He had Down's syndrome, fancied himself as a bit of a singer and wondered if he could join in. Of course, he could, and so we both did 'Sex on Fire' with gusto and feeling. Singing with him was an absolute pleasure as he got the shear enjoyment of the music, and was belting out every word with meaning and enthusiasm. Our last song in the set was 'Comfortably Numb' by Pink Floyd, and to witness a large group of young children doing a choregraphed balletic routine in front of us was not only bizarre but also beautiful. The whole street was joining in with the choruses and as the sun slowly set behind us, we couldn't have asked for a more perfect finish.

We followed this up with another street party at the Ancient Mariner pub, where we went down well, but I am not sure the organisers were completely aware of what they were booking. We followed a masterful musician called John Crampton who did what he called foot-stomping blues. It was beautiful and fitted in with a truly chilled-out afternoon. I got the impression the residents were not overly happy with us as we were the complete opposite. We were loud, brash, crude and over the top. Once again Creeda couldn't make this one as his other band were playing the Love Supreme festival, but we were able to call upon the services of yet another top drummer by the name of Cameron Spence. At the time he was on a break from being the drummer of the official Iron Maiden UK tribute band. We went down a storm with the street and pub crowd, but those living in the area made their feelings known to the pub that we were not their cup of tea.

* * *

As we approached the end of the year we were in and out of the studio recording an album of original material. A particularly exciting time for the rest of the guys, but a complete ball-ache for myself. We had one last big gig coming up and this was an event at the Latest Music Bar. It was a ticketed event as we had decided to try to raise some money for the Shoreham Airport Disaster Fund. Wama was approached by his friend, Mick Robinson, to see if there was a chance he could use the gig to do a single launch for a young band he was helping at the time. Wama, being a great supporter of local music, was more than happy to have them join. To make the evening even more of a spectacle, Mick offered to do a DJ set in between the bands, which was great as Mick was a very accomplished DJ.

The event was sold out, admittedly mainly down to our friends and followers, but there were a few followers of the other band. It was agreed we would go on and do around an hour, followed by Mick and his DJ set. Then the young guys would come on, do a set and it would culminate with the release of their brand-new single.

What transpired next was odd. This is an honest assessment of what I was thinking and feeling on that night, and it is how I saw things and reacted to them at that moment in time. We had all arrived early and were in the process of getting all the equipment downstairs. Whilst milling around, the young lead singer/guitarist from the other band was standing directly behind me when his phone rang. He answered and started speaking to a mate of his. He was using a bit of a 'street' accent and was saying "bruv" a lot. He then went on to say, "Yeah bruv, we won't be on til a bit later coz we're fucking headlining mate, yeah fucking headlining."

Now, this quite frankly really pissed me off. I thought it was a total lack of respect and a pointless fucking comment. There has always been this thing about being called the headliners – and I will now let you into a little secret. If you are a famous band at a festival, it is probably a feather in your cap, or a great honour to be called a headliner as you have been given this accolade due to the years of work that you may have put in. At a local level being the headliner is not all it is cracked up to be. On a gig with a few other bands, you will find headliners tend to be the ones who supply most of the gear as they are the last ones on. And, once the fans of the bands on before you have seen them play, they tend to fuck off and leave you with the smallest audience of the night.

So, with the words of the young upstart pounding in my head, I vividly remember going up to every member of our band and instructing them that we were about to do the best performance we had ever done, and the mission, quite simply, was to be so good that when they came on, they looked stupid. Looking back, I know that this was childish and pathetic, but I was incensed that we were not given the full credit from other bands that I thought we deserved. It was this gig that pushed me onto a new level in performance, as I really did, for the first time, develop some sort of alter ego and adopted a character. Every song was not just sung but performed, as I gave it everything that I had. We finished our set, and I knew instantly that we had reached a whole new level. The atmosphere in the room was electric and we went into the break with Mick now ready to deliver the DJ set.

Unfortunately, there seemed to be an issue, as the equipment Mick had wasn't compatible with venues. There was a small period of panic, but as far as I was concerned it just meant that the bright young things would be going on a little earlier and would have longer for their set. The trouble was they didn't want to go on yet as a couple of their friends hadn't turned up, one of whom was some chap who had been the lead character in their video for the new single. With a room full of punters, something had to happen – so Wama said maybe we should do another set. I, for one, was well up for this as I saw it as another opportunity to make them look like bigger pricks than I already thought they were, and with that we did another hour. This was to an even higher intensity than the set we had already done and by the time we finished the room was on fire. We finished at around 11.15 and that left the stage clear for the headliners to close the show.

Their missing mates finally turned up, and the superstar of their video was working the room and showing himself to be a complete and utter cock. Talk about acting like rock stars, these guys were complete stereotypes of what you would imagine prima donnas to be. It was now midnight and most of our friends were getting a bit fed up waiting for the bright young things to start and, as such, were slowly started to make their way out. The band finally bestowed upon us the privilege of actually hearing them play and, by the time they got under way, there was hardly anyone in the room apart from their knobby mates and us. I took great pleasure in watching their car-crash of a 20-minute set and made a promise to myself to never treat others as they had treated us, or the assembled audience. I also remember thinking to myself at the time that the person they had let down the most was Mick. He had done so much to get this opportunity for them, and he had a complete belief in what they were about, yet they had no understanding of exactly what that man had done to progress them.

It had been a gig that taught me many lessons. As a performance, it was one of our best, I felt, and at least it raised some money for the Shoreham Airport fund as well. We would finish the year in party mode with our usual Christmas gig at the Neptune where, for some reason, we opened with Charlie Chaplin blasting through the speakers doing the speech from *The Great Dictator* film. We also had support from a couple of 18-year-olds under the band name of Kavity, who had emailed us for gig opportunities. We, being the champions of new emerging music, were more than happy to oblige and I remember it being a bit of a baptism of fire for the young hopefuls. They were grateful, though, and joined us in true Dirty Weekend style by getting completely trollied. It had been a year of some tremendous highs, and we had grown our circle of friends as well by getting to meet and play with some amazing people. Onwards towards 2016 with whatever we could conjure up along the way.

FOOTNOTES

FOODIES FESTIVAL – A large gathering spread over three days on Hove seafront. A remarkable event where rich people persuade not-quite-as-rich people to pay an entrance fee, so they can walk around and spend even more money buying overpriced food supplied by rich people. We ran the music stage, as they kept ringing me up asking for bands and, in the end, I thought it would be easier if I just organised the whole thing. I agreed, with the intention of giving local bands an opportunity to put their stuff in front of a large audience. I supplied 90 per cent of the bands but did have a couple of novelty acts foisted upon me. One was a Marilyn Monroe tribute act who was a friend of the organiser. Her total disdain for other performers was quite something to behold and she gave me an important insight into exactly the sort of individual I would never tolerate again. My advice if you are approached to play at this event is to decline politely as they certainly place no value in musicians.

JOE BLACK – Dark cabaret drag darling, musical comedy misfit and Vintage Vaudeville Villain.

Living somewhere between the stages of music, theatre and comedy, Joe Black takes an audience firmly by the hand and guides them into a place where the strange and unusual reign supreme. No stranger to the absurd, Joe Black creates a world where the shocking is the sublime and the ridiculous is the beautiful. One of the leading figures in the dark cabaret genre, Joe Black has toured extensively across the UK, Europe, Australia and America for more than a decade. Dubbed "Charismatic and downright filthy" by *Broadway Baby*; "More seamless than a Venusian onesie" by the *Belfast Telegraph*; "Indecent hilarity" by *Time Out Melbourne*; and "Nothing can detract from his blood-curdling brilliance" by the *Reading Chronicle*.

Joe Black is a constantly evolving cabaret chameleon, blurring the lines of decency within entertainment, and continues to drive music and performance into strange new realms.

B MUSIC (**LATEST TV**) – This show was a monthly feature on the local TV station and covered a wide spectrum of genres, with features, interviews and live performance. One presenter in particular was one of the most supportive of the local scene. Ellie Talebian had her own show on Juice FM as well as being a journalist for *BN1 Magazine*. I always found her to be a real champion of new bands, even if it was not really her thing. Currently a presenter on Gaydio.

STIRLING STREET PARTY – This event is beautifully run and has over the years helped to raise funds for local charities that support the community. Great fun and very inclusive.

MICK ROBINSON – Previous owner of the famous Pelirocco Hotel, Mick has been one of the more visible supporters of Brighton music. He has been a manager, promoter, DJ, as well as having his own shows on various radio stations, one being the Monty Platters show on Totally Radio. One of those individuals who follows his passions and puts his money where his mouth is. The young band he was managing in those days was a band called Dirt Royal. After speaking with Charlie, the lead singer later, I realised that he was in fact a top bloke and bore no resemblance to the impression that I had the first time I met him.

BIG FOOTNOTE

THE GREAT ESCAPE – This a three-day event held annually in Brighton in May. Founded in 2006, it hosts over 300 bands in around 30 venues throughout the city. It is also a music industry convention attended by over 3,000 delegates.

Alongside the main event you will find a fringe festival called the Alternative Escape. Events are mainly run by the smaller promoters and it is a way for bands to play and feel part of the wider festival. Under the guise of *Brighton Unsigned*, over a period of three years, myself and Dave were able to put on a stage where we were able to showcase more than 50 local artists. The whole thing was a lot of hard work, but it didn't seem it at the time because we had so much fun.

We went at it using, what some would call, guerrilla tactics in trying to entice someone higher up the food chain to wander in and see the best that Brighton had to offer in the undiscovered music scene. Looking back, we were a little naïve to think we could attract the corporate musical illuminati away from their professionally stage-managed love-ins, but alas we had a rather more romanticised view of the scene than perhaps we should have.

As delegates we had the opportunity to go to an array of different networking events that the conference had to offer and, looking back, I didn't make full use of this. I found these events difficult as I didn't really sense I had an awful lot in common with the other attendees. I found the general ethos a little soul destroying as I hated the fact that, to me, the music side of things seemed secondary to the cosmetic dressing of an act. I began to fall out of love with the music scene, and it took some time to rediscover the value and joy in something that had become a big part of my life.

I imagine many thousands of people say the Great Escape was an important part of their musical journey. Whether they are musicians, producers, promoters or any number of professionals in the business, you will have many voices extolling the virtues of what it did for them. I must admit I was no good at the networking bullshit that went with it and, as such, lost some faith. But there are plenty of ways of having your faith restored and later on I will drop in a few examples for you to ponder.

CHAPTER 14 – MONTY FLIES IN ON CONCORDE

The life cycle of a band will have many twists and turns and will go through periods of prolonged stability peppered with occasions of great upheaval. I had reached a stage with Fingered By Aliens where I wasn't enjoying it as much as I used to. Having to practise with both bands twice a week was starting to become more of a chore than something to look forward to, and unfortunately some of my fellow bandmates weren't very flexible when it came to offering some alternatives to make things a little easier for me.

With this in mind, I decided to concentrate solely on Dirty Weekend and gave the other band notice that I had decided I no longer wanted to continue with them. The split was amicable, and they found themselves a new lead singer quickly as Tony had a friend who was up for the challenge. Wama was well chuffed as I think, deep down, he considered the other band to be like a mistress and he was the devoted wife hoping I would come to my senses and return home full time.

Dirty Weekend were also about to embark on a period of change as Creeda informed us he would have to leave the band soon because of other commitments. We knew this day would come at some point, and we bore no malice at all as it was done in the proper way – quite simply, we always wanted the best for him. Creeda and Joe were in a different situation to the rest of us as they always saw themselves making a living and a career out of music. They had the skills, they were young enough and they saw this as, hopefully, a job for life. Creeda had been playing in several function bands that would do weddings, birthdays and corporate gigs. On top of this, Kudu Blue, his originals band, were finally beginning to take off and it looked like they were on the verge of making a breakthrough with some of the bigger players in the business. He did the decent thing and gave us plenty of notice – and on top of this said he would spend time with the new drummer to go over every single song in our repertoire. We knew this was not the last we would see of him as he had become a very dear friend and would always be a Dirty Weekender. I like to think we had been good for his progression as well, and I am sure if you asked him he would say we made him a better drummer. Joe was doing some session stuff and around about this time was accompanying Fleur East in Germany, as well as performing with Larissa Eddie as she was supporting Lionel Richie on his UK stadium tour. Joe was playing to packed venues in some of the finest establishments in the land. We would be fitting in the few gigs we had around his schedule, and I would listen with interest to the stories he told about his adventures. Some elements of the stories really annoyed me though as I realised how the talented young dreamers were being taken advantage of by the large group of charlatans who work within the industry. For example, we would play a pub gig and split the fee. The proportion that Joe would receive from us would be far more than he would receive for the Lionel Richie tour, which to my mind is a fucking piss-take. The people who run these tours know that young musicians would do anything to play these venues and so they play on this and basically rip them off. I am sure that, higher up the food chain, the bigger acts must be aware of this, but they simply turn a blind eye because the reality is they just don't care.

Wama was sort of trying to do some work within the music business. This saw him opening a stall in a Saturday street market in the centre of Brighton. He had the notion that it would be fun as he had a romantic vision of himself and his faithful dog Betsy selling soft furnishings that depicted icons of music legends, as well as asking local bands to bring down their EPs, which he would promote and sell for them. Every Saturday morning he would get up early to set up his van that had a converted awning attached to it. Being the early months of the year, it was wet and bloody freezing all the time. He did this for roughly six weeks and in that time Clive's wife Linda would pop by to say hello and end up looking after the stall whilst Wama went off to warm up. My better half Tree bought a cushion from him that had the face of John Lennon on it with the words "Give peace a chance". Also printed on top was "A Dirty Weekend product". He decided to give this little goldmine up and I would imagine if you were to root through his garage you would probably find hundreds of cushions emblazoned with images of Bowie, The Who, The Beatles and Bucks Fizz.

* * *

We had done a couple of small gigs and were in the process of finishing up some recording. Wama wanted to get a sax sound on to a track and I suggested a sax player I knew who might be able and willing to do some for us. This was the introduction of Jon Le Serve into the fold. Wama loved the sax, and it was not long before Jon was invited down to rehearsals. Jon informed us his daughter Jo was a bit of a singer and straight away Wama was extremely interested as he had always wanted another voice in the band. Within a couple of weeks our band of five had become a seven piece.

It was interesting initially as the whole sound had a completely different dimension to it. It was good to have some decent backing vocals (sorry Wama) and the sax worked for some songs, but not, to my mind, for all. One example where it definitely did work for me is in a song I had just written called 'What Have We Done?'. The parts Jon added to that track were sublime. As you can imagine from what you know about the songs I write, the subject matter is never really uplifting and listening to Jon's sax work it brought true emotion and meaning to the feel of the piece that would not exist without it. Whilst I am on this tack, I should also give credit to friend of the band Paul Wanders who has done some video work for us. Paul was a school friend of Wama's and lives in Holland. Wama would send him songs and Paul would cobble together some videos with ideas he had. I think he did the video for 'Drugs & Sin' and when the video was returned for 'What Have We Done?' I honestly couldn't have asked for anything better. It is the song I am most proud of and it just goes to show there are many others who play a big part in what we do.

So, with two new members and we had to go through a period of transition as we embarked upon teaching them all the stuff we knew. Selfishly, as a singer, I can find this a bit repetitive and boring at times, going over the same lyrics, time and time again.

The first gig we did as a seven piece was the Robin Hood Street Party and we went down well as always. Our setlist now contained more of what you might consider crowd-pleasing party songs and judging by the audience interaction this was proving to be a success.

I was progressing with *Brighton Unsigned* and once again found myself organising stages for the Foodie Festival as well as videoing our own interview sessions with bands. Whilst doing this I was introduced to an extraordinarily talented musician and filmmaker by the name of Pilar Onaris, who was an accomplished composer as well as being a sublime and imaginative filmmaker. She agreed to work with me, and we organised a day where we had a large number of bands come to the studio to be interviewed by my good self. I think I was harbouring dreams of being Brighton's very own John Peel, and I saw this as being a way of infiltrating the scene that was controlled by the infamous Brighton music mafia. On the day of filming, I picked up Pilar and she directed me to also fetch a young chap who would be helping on the day with some of the camerawork. I pulled up and was greeted by a young, long-blonde-haired hippy-looking dude by the name of Jye Whiteman. "G'day," he said, in an Australian accent and immediately I sensed the guy was stoned out of his head. He was pleasant and charming and came across as a laid-back surfer dude who didn't seem to have a care in the world. We made our way to the studios, where Pilar went through some ideas and made plans for the shoot. Whilst waiting, Jye picked up a guitar and started playing a selection of his own compositions whilst staring into space. There were several of us in the room and we all stopped what we were doing and just sat there mesmerised as we all realised that we are witnessing brilliance in action. Jye was completely oblivious to us as an audience and seemed to be very chilled in his own little world. Once again, it was another example of how music changed a stranger to a friend. I mention Jye as very soon he was to play a part in one of our greatest days.

* * *

We had our first big gig for quite a while coming up and there were one or two small problems to be sorted out. We had been asked to play at an event called FyneFest, which was to take place on the shores of Loch Fyne in Scotland, approximately two hours' drive from Glasgow. Problem number one was that Creeda was unavailable, and problem number two was that Wama was going to be in Germany for two weeks as his upholstery business had a contract doing some repairs to a big ship in dry dock. We really didn't want to turn this down as not only would it be our first big festival, but it would be fun and seemed like an adventurous holiday as well.

We persuaded our friend Theseus to join us on drums and I asked my new friend Jye if he would like to come on a little adventure as well. He was of the opinion that this sounded like a bit of a laugh and exactly the sort of thing that he would like to do. So, he agreed, and with that we had yet another line-up of Dirty Weekend. Arrangements were finalised and we figured out the logistics of what was technically our first tour. Wama was gutted deep down that he was missing out and this ended up being the only gig that Dirty Weekend ever did without him. So upset was he about this prospect that he even looked into the possibilities of flying into Scotland for the weekend just for the gig, regardless of the time and money involved. In the end this wasn't possible, so with a heavy heart he accepted defeat.

We all assembled at the studio. Tree simply loves to drive and had volunteered to be the driver of our chariot. We loaded up with equipment and personal belongings for the weekend and set off on our merry road trip. Theseus had been up all night and crashed under some covers at the back, and Jye appeared to be stoned out of his box again. The minibus was not all we had wished for – there a few drawbacks. It wasn't the most modern of chariots and it seemed to lack one or two of the creature comforts you might expect. It had also been fitted with a speed limiter that wouldn't allow us to go over 58 miles per hour and this was something we only found out about on the day. We set off at half eight in the morning, full of vim, vigour, and jollity. We arrived on the shores of Loch Fyne at half nine at night – cold, tired, and desperate for a beer. We found a pub on the shores of the loch and with beers in hand we gazed out on to one of the most beautiful panoramas. It was still light, and as we slowly chilled out after such a long drive, I was thinking to myself that it didn't get much better than this. It was at this point I had my first introduction to the local residents, and they were complete bastards. They were not human, they were certainly not big, but they are the evillest creatures that a so-called God had placed upon the earth. These were the thoughts going through my head as I was being eaten alive by midges. They really are the meanest little bastards and there is no way of escaping them.

We had been put up in a quaint cottage, or bothy as it's known locally. It really was the most idyllic place set in between the surrounding hills. A walk of approximately two miles led us down to the festival site and during the daylight hours it was simply beautiful to stroll past the free-roaming Highland cattle that resembled a young Justin Bieber. Finally, we arrived at the festival site where there were a number of concession and food stalls dotted around the main stage area in the middle. There was a massive marquee, which by my reckoning would hold upwards of 2,500 bodies. At the front was a huge stage that ran pretty much the whole width of the tent. At the back ran the bar, which had a selection of 100+ pumps of ales and ciders of varying strengths.

We were the first band of the first day and we went through a soundcheck that was professional by our standards. Considering Theseus had only played with us twice and Jye had never played with us at all, it was hard to gauge what sort of performance we would put on. We tried a few of the local brews and I, for one, was feeling merry. Theseus and Jye appeared to have been trying something completely different to me, but for some reason they looked merrier.

It was hard to tell what size audience size we pulled as, although the place looked empty, it was bloody huge and, as such, there were probably more people in there then you would have thought. We started the set and I have to say we were not shabby at all. Our sound was great. Theseus and Jye were master musicians, so the fact that they hadn't played with us much or at all didn't seem to have any detrimental effect. Jo the singer got a bit upset when one song she was doing lead vocals for got mucked up, but all in all we were fucking good. As we came off stage and were milling around, quite a number of people came up to me and were asking what time we would be on the next day. When I informed them that we wouldn't be performing again I was made up with their disappointment. There were others who hadn't been in the marquee at the time, but had heard us from across the field, who were upset as, in their words, they had probably missed the best band of the weekend.

The next couple of days were just a mixture of listening to good music in the company of friends surrounded by the most amazing vistas. Jye managed to get himself a solo set on a smaller stage and watching him was one of the many highlights of the weekend for me. I remember thinking of Wama, how much he would have lapped up the whole experience and hoped that he would get the opportunity to experience this in the future. We all over indulged and by the end of the night had lost Jye completely. He was last seen heading off into a field with some new friends he had made. On the morning we were leaving, we found him aimlessly walking down a dirt track completely oblivious to where he was or where he had been. Once again, he was living in his own little world and he slept for the whole 12 hours on the drive home. The whole experience had been a lot of fun and I hoped this was something we would be doing on a regular basis from now on.

* * *

Next up was a farewell gig for Creeda down the Neptune. This was a most joyous occasion as we were celebrating having known him and not dwelling on losing him. The place was packed with well-wishers and that was when it hit home that even the audience were part of the whole process. They were right behind him in everything he was going on to do. He wasn't just the drummer of the band, he was 'Creeda', one of them, and they had come to say thank you.

Now, we had been looking for the replacement for Creeda for some time and there were a few names being bandied about. I knew who I thought it should be and at first there was a little bit of opposition. My choice was Monty, who has been mentioned briefly in previous chapters.

I had got to know Monty a bit over the last few years as he was the drummer in Clive's other band, Blind Ammo. They had been practising every Monday night down at PA Studios which was the rehearsal space I had built with our former drummer Tony and it was a running joke that for some reason, they had only ever done a handful of gigs over the course of several years. Every Monday they would meet up and spend three hours playing what sounded like the same song over and over again. They seemed to enjoy themselves, though, and I did wonder whether they used the band as an excuse just to get out of the house for an extra night each week.

Monty was like the rest of us in that he was a similar age and had come to the world of music at a later stage in his life. The thing I really liked about him was that he would come down to the studio a lot on his own and would spend hour after hour trying to improve his technique. His work ethic and dedication were second to none. I knew he wasn't the best drummer at the time, but I also knew that no one would be more committed or work harder than him. If you add on the fact that he had been playing with Clive for several years I figured that his joining us would have many benefits.

Not all were convinced by my recommendation, but we did get him in for a few practices to see how he fitted in. He was a top bloke, and he gave the impression of someone who had won the lottery. He wasn't to Creeda's standards, but no one was at the time. Speaking of Creeda, he was absolutely true to his word and spent time with Monty going over the various nuances of the setlist.

For the next couple of months, it was a case of no gigs but plenty of practice, as we once again had to start the process of going through our catalogue of tunes to get Monty up to speed. I found this a bit tedious as I was singing the same stuff repeatedly, but I did understand it was a necessary evil. We had Jo the singer doing the lead on a few more songs and this suited me fine as it meant that I could shy away from some of the songs that I hated. It became something of a running joke that I would disappear every time they practised 'Valerie' by Amy Winehouse (I preferred The Zutons version) as the mere sound of the intro would send a cold shiver down my spine. It was certainly a song that the crowd got involved with, but to me it was another in a long list of tunes that belonged in a wedding band setlist. Mind you, when we did these songs at a gig it also meant I could bugger off for a fag. It was definitely a different band now that we had extra vocals, a saxophone and songs in the set that were more crowd-pleasing. For me personally it wasn't really the direction I was inwardly enjoying, but it was still bloody good. What was to be very surprising though was that this line-up would go on to do what I will always consider to be our best live performance.

* * *

I had been involved in running the music for a new open-air mini festival that went by the name of Tyefest and, as such, I had made Dirty Weekend the closing act (perk of the job). This would be Monty's first gig and the news of this made him nervous as hell as the reality of having to actually play live kicked in. Added to this Wama told us the following week he had managed to get us a support slot playing at the famous Concorde 2 venue in Brighton, and we would be supporting Dr Feelgood. THE fucking Dr Feelgood.

Now for anyone of our level, to be playing a show at the Concorde 2 in Brighton is the pinnacle. For some it wouldn't be that big a deal, but for us it was everything and for me personally it was just the setting to finally show what we could do not as a pub band but as serious artists. We discussed different options as to how we would play the set, and I managed to convince everyone that this was the perfect platform to put all of our original material on display and stand or fall with it. We weren't going to get this opportunity often and I thought we might as well indulge ourselves.

What we did differently, though, was deciding to do a choreographed show as opposed to a set. I thought we had to grab the audience from the very first note until the very last, and as such I devised a strategy that would make every song flow. The intros, links between songs, banter with the crowd and even the silences were worked out to the finest detail. At one practice session we spent a good hour just on the intro to the first song and for the next month we covered every eventuality you could think of. I am sure at times some of the others were getting a bit bored with it all, but I believed in what we were doing, and I was taking a lot of enjoyment in seeing ideas I had come to fruition.

I thought Monty was doing great considering his level of experience and ability and would imagine he was starting to get incredibly nervous as the date edged closer and closer. At least we had the Tyefest gig next, and although we would be doing a completely different set it would give him a little bit of experience playing live with us. It was a low-key fun event and as such there wouldn't be any hard critics there to judge him. So, the day of Tyefest arrived and we all headed off for a day of fun. I was looking forward to playing in front of a live audience again. The day itself was overcast and windy, but this hadn't deterred a reasonable crowd from turning up to enjoy the day's festivities. I was up on the stage doing my compere duties, introducing a variety of musical acts. The clouds gathering over the coastal cliffs were beginning to get darker and darker, and the wind was getting somewhat fresh. I began to worry there was a chance things might not pan out too well. As well as the multitude of electrical equipment that was exposed to the elements we also had to contend with the fact that the huge stage we had hired for the day was a massive inflatable construction and we were situated in a field overlooking the cliffs on the edge of the English Channel.

The next act on was a local lad by the name of Sam Hughes. He had approached me to ask if there was any chance he could get on the line-up as he lived in the local area and would love the chance to play in front of his home crowd. I asked him what sort of stuff he did, and he informed me he was an Elton John tribute act. As this was a family-friendly festival, I figured this might be a bit of fun and as such added him to the bill.

Meeting Sam for the first time on the day, my first impression was that he was a very polite, quiet young man who in no way struck me as an Elton John tribute act. Inside I was thinking this was going to be an absolute car crash, but I had given my word that he could play and so be it. Sam came onstage dressed up in full Elton mode, sat down at his keyboard and played. At first, I thought the transformation in appearance was indeed impressive, but you cannot fake confidence, stage presence and talent. He had some backing tracks doing some instrumentation and backing vocals, but the piano and lead vocals were all him and he was outstanding. He went through a number of tracks and the crowd were loving him. He really was quite a performer, and I would highly recommend his act for one of the most entertaining evenings you could have. The sky was ominously getting darker and darker as he went into a superb rendition of 'Don't Let the Sun Go Down On Me'. As he belted out the chorus, it heralded some kind of celestial practical joke as the heavens opened, and what follows is two hours of the heaviest rainfall I have ever been exposed to. Consequently, it was the end of the show and we quickly scurried to turn off all the electrical equipment and frantically deflate the stage before it was blown away. Monty, who had been psyching himself up for the last month, wouldn't be playing his debut with us today. Instead, his debut would be at the Concorde 2 supporting Dr Feelgood, so no pressure there then.

* * *

Concorde day was upon us and even by our standards we got to the venue ridiculously early. We were all in agreement that this was a day where we wanted to take everything in and savour every last second of the experience. We knew we were probably not going to have this opportunity again, so we embraced it and enjoyed every single second. The Concorde 2 to us has massive relevance. All around the world many cities have their own equivalent. In Liverpool it might be the Cavern Club, New York had CBGB's, London has Brixton Academy. These are all examples of venues that hold iconic status in their local music scene. So, there we all were outside drinking a beer and looking out towards the beach and the sea. There appeared to be no obvious signs of nerves, although Monty had a look of a man who was not really sure what was going on. We hadn't met the Dr Feelgood guys yet and it transpired that they had already set up, done their soundchecks and were milling around the town somewhere. We had to bring all of our own equipment as we weren't permitted to share any of the Doctor's gear. Naively at the time I didn't fully understand this, and thought they were just being mean, but at the time I had no idea about the etiquette of these things.

With the help of the excellent sound engineer and the stage technician, we went about the job of how the setup would take shape. Wama had brought his gorgeous dog Betsy along and she was having a nose around the stage. She sat centre-stage and stared out into the large empty hall. I quickly grabbed my phone and took a photo as she was at the perfect angle with the large Concorde sign emblazoned above her, so even if the gig was a disaster, I'd have a photo that would live with me forever. Who knows, maybe I would make it the front cover of a future book. We went through the process of the soundcheck and to Monty this was an alien experience as he had to go through the routine of going through every single piece of kit, bit by bit, with the engineer. Just doing the drums takes forever and I could tell by the look on Monty's face that he was loving every single second. One by one, all of the other members of the band were put through their paces, until we were all checked and ready to go through a few numbers together.

It is hard to describe the feeling of looking out from the stage into that large empty room. I imagined that in a few hours there would be a mass of bodies in front of me eagerly awaiting what we were about to deliver. Then I realised that, as we were the support band, we would more than likely just have our die-hard friends and followers watching as the majority of the audience would probably still be in the bars waiting until the Doctor himself appeared. Just our crowd would probably make the space seem very empty, but so what, we would have the best sound, stage and lights we could ever wish for and would enjoy it all. We ran through a few tunes and the noise that we generated made me feel immensely proud.

Monty was solid, he stuck to what he had to do and didn't get carried away with doing anything that might be a stretch for him. That is all I wanted him to do at the time, as it would provide a solid base for us to work from. Clive had a constant grin on his face. He really was the kid who had been put in charge of his own sweet shop. Jon on sax really looked the part and he had come dressed for the occasion wearing an all-red outfit, dark glasses, black trilby and tattooed sleeves that he wore on both arms. On guitar Joe was practising all of his best rock star faces and it came as a bit of a relief when I realised he wasn't in control of his volume. Jo the singer was looking more confident than I could ever remember and her harmonies were sublime. Wama and I were dressed in our now-customary outlandish jackets and Betsy the dog had a pretty neckerchief on as well. Finishing the soundcheck, I had a feeling it would be hard for us to do any better and just hoped we could transfer that to the show.

We had a few hours to kill now and this was spent with a few bottles of beer outside staring out to sea. Betsy the dog had been picked up by a family member, which was a shame as I thought she would have been a good addition onstage. We had our own dressing room backstage, and it was funny to walk past large screens with the stage times and our band logo on them, just underneath that of Dr Feelgood. In the main, we had a lot of goodwill from people who were coming to support us. The tickets weren't cheap, but they knew this was a bit of a one-off for us. Musicians in other bands were fairly supportive that we had got this gig but, as is always the way in life, you get the odd prick who makes comments and cannot bear it when good stuff happens to others. Let us call this person 'The X Man

We finally met the Dr Feelgood guys, who came across as pleasant. They were in the middle of a nationwide tour and were playing a different town every other night. It was interesting looking at the lead singer sitting dressed in a cardigan, doing a crossword and drinking a cup of herbal tea. A few hours later he would turn into an absolute animal and his energy levels for a man of his age were simply phenomenal.

It was 15 minutes before we were to go on and I decided to take a quick look out the front. As I suspected, the main room was empty, but the large bar at the back looked like it was throbbing. The promoter popped back to wish us good luck and informed us that the gig had sold out so it would be a full house. The question now was how many would come in to see us – and more importantly how many would stay? We were going to do the full set of all-original material so this meant much of the crowd would be hearing this stuff for the very first time. We could have done a load of covers to make it easier for us, but I didn't see the point as this was a test to see if we were more than a pub covers band. We started out with a song called 'The Sea'. I had choreographed the opening to be a slow build up with the start of a solitary bass drum, which gradually over was joined by all the other instrumentation piece by piece. The plan was for this to create an atmosphere that would give the punters in the bar time to drip feed into the main room. It gave an element of building suspense, which in turn made the crowd curious to see what was about to occur. This whole intro built up for over two minutes before exploding into life with the song. We had meshed the first three songs of the set together and so the opening foray didn't stop for roughly 12 minutes. The room was mobbed and when we finally finished the third song, I screamed the words "Hello Concorde, we are Dirty Weekend!" The room went mad with cheers, whistles and applause. I was on a complete adrenaline rush and had no nerves whatsoever, as I knew the practice we had put into choreographing the show was all going to pay off.

I had what can only be described as another out-of-body experience as I went into character and was delivering all the songs with true meaning and was not merely reciting the words. All the others had obviously picked up the vibe of the crowd and were also going about the set with no fear and playing to a level that was higher than I had witnessed before. Monty was loving it, but to his credit he wasn't getting carried away with it. His dedication in the practice he had put in paid off as he remained the solid bedrock we needed for the whole performance. We played for an hour, but it seemed like it only lasted about ten minutes as the whole experience went by in a flash. As we reached the climax and struck the final notes, we were greeted with the explosion of some confetti cannons going off in the front of the crowd. The applause was huge and we basked in the adulation of the crowd for a few minutes. It is to this day the best live performance we had ever done. We had the venue, the crowd, the sound, the lights, best personal performances and our own material. This to me was the pinnacle of Dirty Weekend.

We came off stage and were greeted by Dr Feelgood, whose lead singer was very complimentary of our performance. We sat in the dressing room, had some beer and just sat there for a while just grinning at each other. It had been some night and it was not over yet, as now we could get out front to enjoy the rest of the gig with our mates. When we got out front we noticed a friend of Wama's daughter was up onstage with a hoover. It turned out the Concorde weren't great fans of confetti cannons as it gets into all the equipment and makes a right mess of the stage. We stood there watching with laughter as the interval show was one of ours doing the hoovering for ten minutes.

Dr Feelgood were excellent, and you could see they were utter professionals. I think we had the better night though, not because we played better, but you could see we enjoyed it more and it meant more to us. Many friends came up to us to say how good we were, and the really pleasing thing was so many strangers coming up to us l and saying how much it had meant to them. My own personal favourite comment came from a chap we knew by the name of Mick de Stripp. He is a great lover of music and he can be found in many bars supporting the scene. He is also the singer in a local outfit called The Gastric Band, and when he came up to me, he said, "No other band I have seen in pubs could ever do that set of original songs to that standard. You are the best band in Brighton." He then looked me in the eye and said, "I really mean that. I really do."

As you can imagine, by now the rest of the night lasted a long, long time and many drinks were consumed.

So how do you follow up a gig like the Concorde 2 then? At this point Monty must have been thinking we would be playing Wembley Stadium next if he were to progress upwards from his first appearance, but alas Monty was brought crashing back to the ground in a blaze of realism.

* * *

Next up was a little charitable number that we had been roped into for WaterAid. It was to take place on a Saturday afternoon at the Unitarian Church slap-bang in the middle of a busy part of the town. On paper, this looked like an event that would attract a decent-sized crowd and we also had the feeling we were doing something worthwhile for the planet. The building itself had a grand outside façade with multiple steps that made for a natural staging area, which in turn overlooked a large pedestrianised space that had a busy and constant footfall of traffic. What a great place to play, I thought to myself. The reality, unfortunately, was that the entertainment would actually be taking place inside on a small stage.

Standing on this stage, looking out at a few rows of completely empty chairs was a different vista to the one I had at the Concorde. The only noise resonating in the room was coming from a serving hatch in the corner where an elderly gentlemen was buying a cup of tea to go with his slice of carrot cake. Our good friend Janet turned up to support us and we then played what to her must have seemed like her own private gig, as she was the only one there. The only sounds to be heard between songs was the occasional, "Do you want sugar with that love?"

It wasn't a complete waste of time, as we all saw the funny side and actually started enjoying the whole thing. I was giving it full on rock diva in the church and Joe on guitar played as if he was onstage at the Royal Albert Hall. We finished the gig and waited for the shouts for an

encore, which never arrived. Over the road we went to the Mash Tun
pub, where we spent a few hours planning the next big thing.

We finished the year off with another first, as we organise a gig in
London with another local band. We hired our own coach and sold
tickets to not only attend the gig but have an outing in the big city. All
tickets sold quickly, as I imagine most people were interested in a cheap
way of going shopping in London.

It was reminiscent of a school coach trip, with the only difference being
that the kids on board were of a more mature vintage. Mature in years,
but certainly not in attitude as our assembled travel companions were
complete nut jobs and ready to start the party early. It was only ten in the
morning and already Mad Al and Mad Daz were off their tits. Jackie and
Bob were high as kites, and everybody seemed to have either a can or
bottle in their hands. We were sharing this adventure with another band
called Tenderhooks and would be picking up their crowd at the next
stop. Their crowd appeared to be slightly artier and a bit posher – and to
my mind didn't have an awful lot in common with our posse. The
journey towards the city was loud, boisterous and fun, and I realised that
the two groups weren't so far apart in their pursuit of a good time after
all. By the time the coach arrived everyone was half-cut and of not much
use in helping us to cart the gear into the venue. Our home for the day,
the Fiddler's Elbow in Camden, welcomed us and must have been
thinking their ship had come in as they gazed upon the clientele
disembarking from the bus. It was a large traditional-looking boozer that

converted into a live music venue in the evening, and to me was exactly the kind of unpretentious place that I like.

There were many hours to kill before the gig, and the gathered masses split off into groups and ventured out into Camden to soak up some of the vibe of the place. Some were there to visit the famous market nearby, whilst others wanted to see what kind of exotic herbs could be found in the local area. I decided to hang around the Fiddler's Elbow as there was an impromptu open mic taking place. A few others and I whiled away the afternoon, and I got up to do a couple of tunes on acoustic guitar, which was a lot of fun. As the afternoon drew to a close, bit by bit, our coach crowd returned to base in dribs and drabs, with some noticeably the worse for wear. The building was now closing as a pub and was reshaping itself to become a venue as showtime was drawing near. We were first on that evening, which suited me as we could do our bit and then just get slaughtered for the rest of the evening. It was also ideal as the rest of the band had been on it a bit too much by the looks of them, and I knew from bitter experience that Wama and Joe were fucking useless on guitar when they got to the point of no return.

We did our set, and all was good with lots of high energy and, surprisingly, very few mistakes. It was a great little venue for authentic live music with good sound, an intimate feel and the right-side-of-shabby decor. It felt more like a party than a gig as none of us were feeling any pressure at all – and the audience was the ultimate home crowd as it was made up of all our mates on a jolly.

We finished and it was cheers all round as we reached the interval before Tenderhooks did their set. But before this, we had an extra little nugget of the show to come. I had always assumed, along with many others, that this was arranged by Wama, but years later I found out he had absolutely nothing to do with it. It turned out it was organised by Markus, the lead singer of Tenderhooks, and he was obviously the Tenderhooks equivalent of Wama. Both nuts, both dedicated to the show and both old enough to know better. I knew in advance that something had been arranged where some sort of cabaret act was to appear. They went by the name of Sirona Thorneycroft and Dollie Dore and were a couple of burlesque dancers. Quite what anyone thought this would add to the show, only they will know, but I do know not everyone had the same thought process as them. As soon as they started there were lots of differing reactions in the room. Mine was, "Oh no, Wama's really fucked up this time," others were thinking, "My god, this is sheer filth." Others were thinking, "This is pure art," and I am sure Gill (Wama's wife) was probably mulling over how she was going to murder Wama when she got him home. The art (stripping) went on for a good 20 minutes. Lots of very arty feather-boa action was on display, as well as a lot of saliva from various men. I was glad we weren't following this and felt a little bit sorry for Tenderhooks. Wama was pretty oblivious to any dissent or criticism at the time and didn't really know what all the fuss was about. They finished their show to a mixture of light applause from half the audience and rapturous cheering from the other half. The night carried on with Tenderhooks up next and everyone joined back in with the party atmosphere. If I remember rightly, they had the whole pub singing the chorus to a song called 'Doghouse' where everyone was just going "woof woof". I was so pissed that I thought it merited an Ivor Novello Award. The greatest accomplishment of the night, though, was actually getting everybody back on to the coach for the journey home and I was amazed no one was left behind.

As always, we finished the year off with the annual Neptune Christmas gig where we did a rocked-up version of 'Silent Night', Wama was dressed as an elf and we launched our own album. It had been a year of change and there was more to come.

FOOTNOTES

KUDU BLUE – This is the originals band that Creeda is a member of. They are brilliant at what they do, but not necessarily my thing. This is good for them, as you wouldn't want an old git like me being into your band as this could be considered brand damaging. Made up of Clem (vocals), Owen (keys), Tom (bass) and Creeda (rhythms), Kudu Blue give you a refreshing snapshot of contemporary music in the UK, a back-to-basics postcard from the underground club scene. Their distinctly fresh sound brings on a new wave of progressive modern dance-pop, encompassing influences from across both time and space. From 1990s trip-hop and sound-system culture, all the way through to Buddhist chanting, and back around to old-school hip-hop and R&B.

THE X FACTOR – Around about this, time Joe Colburn was not only appearing on tours with Lionel Richie, but he also did a performance with another Ritchie that deserves mentioning. This was Stevi Ritchie, a contestant on *The X Factor* who sand 'Bohemian Rhapsody'. I don't know how Joe got the gig, but his job was to dress up like someone out of *The Matrix* and, along with another guitarist, strut around the stage looking mean and moody. They were surrounded by an army of dancers performing some exotic choreography, whilst Stevi was in full Freddie Mercury mode. They weren't plugged in and were pretending to play, giving it the full rock-god guitar performance. The climax was both the guitarists standing either side of Stevi holding their instruments aloft as pyrotechnics exploded from the neck of the guitars. The trouble was, Joe was such a diva he forgot the choreography and was so caught up in his own little rock world that he was inches away from burning poor Stevi's head off. It was bloody hilarious to watch, though, and you can find it on YouTube.

FYNEFEST – Great beer, great food and great music, all amid stunning Highland scenery: FyneFest has all the ingredients for a fantastic festival. It is a cracking festival, with over 160 beers on offer, food from local producers and a line-up of live music that is guaranteed to get you dancing. This was to be my first experience of Scotland and it was stunning. The only downfall were the midges, which in my opinion are the evillest animal to ever set foot upon this planet.

PILAR ONARIS – She is one of the most talented individuals I have ever met and an incredibly generous artist. Look at the artists she has helped out on her own BrighTunes YouTube channel. Pilar is a music composer and pianist. She started her musical career at the age of seven. I met her through a mutual friend and had the benefit of her many skills when she kindly helped me out on a music video project. She has worked with a multitude of local musicians and they will all testify to her beautiful, generous spirit.

JYE WHITEMAN – This is his stage name, Jye Albert is his actual name. Hard to describe, but the words that spring to mind are 'funny as fuck'. He describes himself as a "van-dweller and musician". To me he is like an Australian Bob Marley, but that would be doing him a disservice as he is much more laid back than Bob was.

He went off around South America on a bike, as I think he was about to be deported from England for overstaying his visa somewhat. Concept of time was not one of his strong points to be fair. I do miss just being able to bump into him as he is one of those people who just makes your day brighter without trying. Great musician and worth looking up the stuff he has done online. Last I heard he was doing lots of stuff to raise awareness to the damage the Great Barrier Reef was undergoing.

CONCORDE 2 – Brighton's multi-award-winning live music venue and nightclub. Nationally recognised as one of the UK's leading live music venues. Concorde 2 has played host to a continuously diverse cross-section of events for many, many years.

With its perfect dreamy seaside location, Concorde 2 is a firm favourite on the UK's touring circuit with many bands returning on a regular basis.

CHAPTER 14 – MY WEEKEND COMES TO AN END

We started the following year with even more upheaval, as Joe gave us the news he had been asked to join a touring band aboard a cruise liner and this entailed an initial contract of four months. We knew this was an opportunity he couldn't turn down and I for one was genuinely pleased he had finally managed to find an opening to build a career around what is undoubtedly his passion in life. It was only six months ago that we had lost Creeda and now here we were faced with a similar dilemma. It wouldn't be straight away, though, as Joe's ship was not sailing until March, so this should give us ample time to find a replacement. Mind you, this wasn't as easy as you might think. Wama has always thought the two hardest things to replace in a band are a lead singer or a lead guitarist as, to his mind, these two elements tend to shape the identity of a band. Joe and I had a close love/hate relationship. My god, he was good; but, my god, did he piss me off a lot as well. I was very protective of him in many ways, but I was also his harshest critic and would certainly let him know if he was being a knob, which was quite a lot, actually. I was made up for him with the news of the cruise ship job, but I also knew selfishly that I would be losing one of my biggest assets in performing at a gig. I know I had joked about his rock star faces and turning the volume to 12, but I also realised the benefits of having such a talented player and showman in the band as well.

So, the search was on for the next Joe Colburn, and I knew that Wama was particularly worried we wouldn't be able to find anyone close to his calibre. I was concerned, but not as much as Wama, as I was in the fortunate position of knowing a lot of guitar players through the stuff I had been doing with *Brighton Unsigned*. The hard part would be in persuading someone to commit, but I knew that if we could wait a little longer for the right person I would easily be able to secure the services of some top-notch guitarists for one-off gigs.

The first gig of the year turned out to be Joe's leaving gig and this was at the Three Graces pub in Hove on 3rd February. We spent the weeks leading up to this in the rehearsal rooms doing our usual practice, as well as trying to find the next member. On one of these occasions Wama told us a chap had been in touch through an advert he had put out and he would be joining us to have a bit of an audition. Adrian arrived, and he was nice and extremely pleasant. We were in the room getting ready to practice and anticipated that Adrian would join in as well. Adrian had a guitar with him and a bag that resembled something you would pack a tent into. Unzipping the bag, he placed the largest pedal board I had ever seen in my life on to the floor. He delved back into the bag and produced a variety of add-ons that were then connected into various bits of the monster board. Once set up, he went through the process of making sure it all worked and spent an eternity checking myriad different connections as it transpired that all was not functioning as it should. This went on for a good 20 minutes and Adrian was very apologetic for taking so much time. Eventually he appeared to be happy that all was good, and he was ready to jam with us. We chose one of the more straightforward songs to play and Adrian joined in, but was stopping and starting a lot as he was not quite getting it. Now I must point out that he was a nice chap, but he was nowhere near the standard we were going to need. I was estimating that at this rate our first gig with him would be in roughly another five years. It might sound like I had turned into one of those judgemental musical cocks that I so hated, but I was just being realistic, and we wouldn't have been doing him or ourselves any favours by not being honest. He knew by the end of the session that he was not going to be joining us and we left on friendly terms. In fact, I admired him a lot for putting himself out there to try and later I believe he started a band which was more suited to him. The real measure of the guy was when we performed our first gig with our new guitarist, Adrian was in the crowd supporting. I had been spending some time looking at message boards on social media to see if there were any potential new members and, eventually, I found one on Gumtree. Under the section of bands there were listings of musicians who wanted to join a band. Most of these weren't suitable, but one did intrigue me. I delved deeper and this is where I found Marcos Gonzatto.

An exotic name, I thought, and on more detailed analysis it turned out he hailed from Brazil and was now living in Newhaven. There were a couple of video links that took you to YouTube, where you could see a bit of his performance. His guitar skills were excellent and, by the looks of things, it would appear he had played some high-level gigs back in his homeland. I messaged him and received a response the next day, so we then went about arranging a meet-up the next week down at the studio. I told Wama that I thought I may have solved our problem and showed him the footage I had uncovered.

* * *

The following week I had my first meeting with Mr Gonzatto. He was roughly mid-30s, so not too young and not too old. He had long black hair with a moustache and goatee beard and looked like the stereotypical swarthy Latin lover that this band had been missing. His grasp of the English language was basic and as such communication between us would prove to be a little tricky. We went into one of the rooms, and both he and Joe decided to have a low-key kind of jam session in order for me to see if he had any potential for us. For the next two hours we went through a variety of different songs that covered a multitude of genres. He was particularly keen on more rock-orientated music, although his personal favourites appeared to be anything influenced by the Beatles. He was an exceptional player and was so different in style to Joe. He played with a style that appeared to be more relaxed and laid back, and I could tell straight away that he would be easy to accompany as he was more about the whole sound of the band. I wouldn't say he was better or worse than Joe, as the truth is they are both excellent but just have different ways of playing. At the end of the two hours, and after a chat that took longer than it should have, I asked him to come along to the next practice session.

He agreed, and so the following Tuesday he was in a room with six strangers, staring at him, to put him through his paces. We played a number of tunes that were familiar to Marcos, and it was a joy to watch him and Joe playing together and taking turns doing a variety of lead parts. The session ended and we said goodbye to Marcos. I informed him that I would be in touch soon and thanked him for coming along. Going back into the room the rest of the band look a bit perplexed.

Wama said, "How the fuck did you find him?"

Joe said, "He's the one, mate."

A very quick unanimous vote then ensued, and Marcos was installed as the next Dirty Weekender.

Much the same as Creeda's send-off, the one for Joe followed a similar vein. It was, again, to be a celebration of all the good stuff we had done together. As it was his send-off, I think I even left his amp volume up a little bit. It was pleasing at the time to know that Joe was finally going away to do what he loved. I was confident that things would work out alright for the band as well, because we had discovered a bit of a gem in Marcos. Bearing in mind that Monty hadn't been with us that long, we had over a truly short period made some major changes. Monty was fully involved with the band and he continued to do extra practice on his own just so he could keep improving and stretching his own standards. The downside of having the upheaval of a new guitarist, though, was that we were going to have to go through the tedious process again of bringing Marcos up to speed with everything in our setlist. I'm sure this was the start of me losing a little love for the band, as it just didn't grab me in the same way that it used to. Marcos was a very quick learner, which was a bonus, and he and I would spend extra time down the studio to speed things up for the main rehearsal. In these sessions, as well as working through the setlist of covers, we would also just muck around coming up with original material. This is something I found really satisfying and I was becoming a prolific songwriter during this period. It was good to have Marcos being instantly capable of putting my ideas to melodies in front of my eyes. But this would lead to new frustrations with the band as I didn't really see how the songs I was beginning to write would fit into the sound that Dirty Weekend currently had.

* * *

After a short hiatus we announced our first gig for a while in which we were performing with our new lead guitarist. It was at a pub called The Blue Anchor in Portslade. There was a lot of interest as, firstly, we hadn't performed for a while, and secondly, people were curious to see how we would get by without our excellent Joe. The place was packed, which came as no surprise and we were confident we wouldn't let anyone down. Marcos was very laid back and this shouldn't have surprised me as, on reflection, the guy was used to performing to audiences in their thousands back home in his native Brazil. Good friend of the band Janet remarked to me that it was great to see the band with a bit of eye candy in it and I assume that is why she was at the very front. The next two hours of playing were excellent, and it was as if we hadn't been away for very long at all. The band sounded like it did before, in the main, with only a few discernible differences. We weren't as rocky, but the overall depth of sound was much more balanced. Jo was now singing a few more lead numbers, as we were finding stuff that fitted her style and voice. A lot more party numbers were creeping in, which was great for crowd participation, but I must admit they were not really my thing (miserable sod). The feeling we got from the audience as regards the new guitarist was positive, but we expected this as we knew how bloody good he was.

Now that Marcos had lost his Dirty Weekend virginity, we followed this up with a string of shows in quick succession. We had another boozy day trip to London with the band Tenderhooks. Wama and their lead singer were embroiled in some kind of bromance, as they saw themselves as the leaders of two allied tribes. They were like the Jon Snow and Daenerys Targaryen of the Brighton music scene at the time, and it was customary to see both bands on the same bill around the town. We once again did the Robin Hood annual street party in May and this was followed up by one of the funniest gigs we ever did – and the bonus was that it was on my birthday as well.

* * *

We had been asked to play at the Brighton Trades & Labour Club on Lewes Road. I am not exactly sure how we got the gig, but I knew this one was certainly not through Wama as I was pretty confident he had zero ties with the Trades and Labour club at the time. As it was to fall on the same day as my birthday we decided that a small group of us would get together to celebrate the day and we would attend the gig in the evening. As it was a members' club we were given a set amount of people we could bring as not just anyone could roll up and see us. We were being paid by the club, so this was not really a gig as such but us being booked as the entertainment. I had passed this place many times over the years, but had never been in. From the outside it had a very nondescript frontage and you got the impression it couldn't be particularly big inside. You would be very wrong, though, as we found out it is huge once you pass beyond those deceptive front doors.

We had decided to get down super early as the plan was to load all the gear in, do soundchecks and then fuck off into town for the afternoon to celebrate my birthday. Perhaps not the most professional approach, you may think, but I wasn't considering that at the time. So, we arrived in the early afternoon and were told to go around the back to load in. We entered through the back door, which then led to the stage and the main function room. We were all completely taken aback by the size of the room and acted like schoolchildren when we saw the setup of the staging area. Not only was the size of it impressive, but the array of professional lighting and sound equipment made us realise we had the tools to put on a truly outstanding show. The guy that had shown us in gave us a quick tour and talked us through the equipment we had at our disposal. There was a bar to the side that stretched the length of the entire room and I couldn't help noticing that the beers were sold at ridiculously low prices (priorities).

We took a while to set up as there was no rush – and also when you do have a proper stage you tend to relish these moments. Clive's face was a picture as he was used to being squeezed in right at the back, tucked in between drum stands, but now he had space in which to run free (not that he would). Once prepared, we then started the soundcheck. We would normally, on average, do about two minutes at the most. But here in this empty room with the stage, sound and lights, we did nearly half a set. It was fun and we were all lapping up every second as we churned out one tune after another. Above all, we sounded awesome as well. I had a mic lead at the time that could go out for a good 40ft, and I remember standing off stage far out into the room singing and looking back at all the guy's onstage playing. It looked great and sounded magnificent, and I knew that the audience tonight was in for one of the best night's entertainment they had seen in a very long time.

We wrapped up the soundcheck and it was time to meet a few friends in town for a birthday drink. I went into Brighton with Dave and Floss, and we met up with Tree in a pub called the Brighton Tavern. As the day went on, we were joined by Wama, Kev and Janet. Drinks were flowing all afternoon and a laugh was had by all. We were chatting about the gig in the evening and were all in agreement it would be a night to remember. We made our way to the Labour Club where we re-joined

Clive, Monty, Kim, Linda, Marcos, Jo and Jon. They were all sat in the smaller front bar. It wasn't a small bar, but in comparison with the main room it could only be described as such. I was in a particularly jolly mood, due to alcohol and birthday vibes, and I wasn't the only one as the whole group appeared to be in 'hair let down' mode.

We were due to go on at nine o'clock and, before us, a few other club activities were taking place. My memory tells me this consisted of a quiz, a raffle and a game of bingo. As you looked into the main room through the windows of the doors you could see this huge auditorium was full of nearly every single seat at every table occupied. It appeared the long bar was doing a roaring trade as well and you sensed this was to be a special evening. We carried on in the small bar chatting, laughing, singing and generally winding each other up. The humming sound that was being generated from the main room was electrifying and it was certainly tapping into the adrenaline levels being generated in my body. The time was now half-past eight and very soon we were going to have to get into full show mode. The bingo caller in the main room had just announced the last number of the last game and the winner was being given a generous round of applause from the fellow players. The compere said a thank you to everyone for playing, and before saying goodnight he urged everyone to stick around for the entertainment. The door of the main room opened into the smaller bar and a trickle of people made their way through to leave. We sat there at the table drinking and chatting but finding it harder to hear our conversations as the noise from the hordes walking through was making quite a din. This went on for approximately 15 minutes and then the crowd started to slowly dissipate into just the odd lingering soul.

Fifteen minutes to go to the start, and so I gathered the band members and ushered them to get ready. We finished our drinks and made our way to the doors of the main room. I opened the door, walked in and immediately started to piss myself laughing. In the far distance I could see two bodies propping up the bar. There was a table at the front with maybe another three and then dotted around the room I could see roughly another five groups of two. The others joined me and looked somewhat mortified. We made our way to the stage, and you could literally hear a pin drop as we took our positions and did some last-minute adjustments. The rest of our gang from the smaller bar came through and looked kind of shell-shocked as they managed to secure a prime table at the front facing the stage. It was at this point that I was glad we had gone out all afternoon and early evening and decided to take it for what it was and just enjoy the occasion. I was out with my favourite people on my birthday playing music on a brilliant stage. Wama was gutted and looking a little sorry for himself. Marcos gave him a pep talk in his broken English. He told Wama of how he had played in front of thousands, but he had also played in front of no one. He told him that the important thing was that he must play for himself and do as good a performance for even one person who bothered to listen, as this one person deserved his best.

I would estimate that at the start of the show we had around 50 people in a room that held around 500. Within 30 seconds of the first song we lost about six as the noise generated had most definitely messed around with their hearing aids. It was probably the fastest that these people had moved in years, as they scurried to find the nearest possible exit. I found this amusing and decided that tonight was an ideal night to become the full-on entertainer. Armed with my extremely long mic lead I jumped off stage to use as much of the room as I possibly could. The rest of the band appeared a bit shocked by this at first, as they were watching me atop tables 30ft in front of them. I went on a little tour of the audience and tried to engage with the patrons and get them to participate with me. I followed someone on their way to the loo and serenaded them on their journey. We played bloody well and the whole band was completely relaxed and enjoying the whole occasion. The small crowd that stayed with us thought it was the best thing they had seen in years and the atmosphere of the evening had turned into one in which I could not have had a better birthday party. We spent the whole evening having our own party. The guy who booked us came up to us at the end and said he would be in touch to book us again. We never heard from him though.

* * *

Practising continued as ever and on one particular occasion I was there earlier than the others just mucking around with some of my own songs on guitar. Clive and Monty arrived and were getting set up, and I asked if they could accompany me with a new song I had. I gave them the basic chords and we started to jam. The song in question was called 'Appletree' and I was in the early stages of trying to work out how I wanted it to progress. Wama arrived and started to get his gear ready and was listening as we played. No one really seemed to show much interest in it, and we wrapped it up as the others arrived. We then went on to go through lots of covers we had done hundreds of times, and then went about looking at some new party covers that were being considered. At the time I was finding it hard to rouse any enthusiasm for what we were doing and realised I wasn't getting the same buzz that I used to get. As such, I found I wasn't really feeling the love with practice nights anymore and was inwardly becoming frustrated with what we were playing. I had carried on going to open mics and, on most Monday nights, you would find me attending the one compered by Theseus at The Neptune. Near the end of the night Theseus asked me to come up and do a couple of numbers. He asked me what I was going to play, and I said I was going to try out a new song I had written called 'Appletree'. He asked if I wanted any accompaniment and I replied that no one would know how it went as I had just written it. He told me it wouldn't be a problem and called up Chris Hookway to play bass. He then persuaded a brilliant young guitarist called Jed to join us. I very quickly went through the chord progression of the verse and chorus and explained to Jed that there was a lot of space in between in which he could go off on a tangent whilst I just went through the chord progression.

I started to play and, with Theseus now joining us on an electric drum pad, I soon realised that what was being played all around me was not only of a genius standard but was also giving me a satisfaction that I had been missing lately. It drove me to play better and once the performance of the song was finished, I was bowled over by the reaction of the crowd. I had a real feeling of accomplishment, and a renewed love of the music and performance. I didn't know if I was now turning into a musical diva, but I did know that I was on cloud nine. Walking back from the pub that night was when I decided that doing the stuff with Dirty Weekend was not fulfilling me, and it was time to go and do something else. Having known Wama and Clive longer than the others, I contacted them and told them that my intention was to leave the band at the end of the year. This would give them a good six months to push things in the direction they needed. Wama tried to change my mind and to this day still cannot understand my reasoning, but there was no bad feeling from his end and no remorse from mine.

The rest of the band were informed at the next practice and I think they had a separate meeting later to decide the direction the band would take going forward. They had a great singer in Jo, and she had come on a lot in her confidence with performance. It was a weight off my mind knowing that the decision had been made and I wanted the next six months to be fun. I was determined to finish with a bang.

We did the Stirling Street Festival again and this was, as per usual, a day of great fun and celebration. Joe Colburn had come back from his cruise ship contract and was waiting to be offered another posting. He came down to the street party and was going to do a guest guitar slot for a couple of numbers. Unfortunately, he overindulged a little at the bar that day and by the time he came to play with us he was slaughtered. As we got to the end of one particular song, he decided, for no apparent reason, to go into the longest and most meaningless solo I had ever heard. It went on and on, and at one point I was in front of him on my knees with my back to the crowd. I was drawing my finger across my neck and, looking up at him, I was telling him I was going to fucking kill him if he didn't shut the fuck up. He knows how I felt about him that day and I found him totally disrespectful towards us as a band and to the event as well. It made me realise that Marcos was a lot easier to play with as he was more about the overall band sound.

We had a few gigs lined up for the rest of the year and, maybe because I knew that I was on my way out and had a definite end date, I began to embrace the fun side a bit more. We did one called the Undercover Festival and this appealed to me as it was one of those where the emphasis was on our original material. Marcos had by this time fully integrated into the band and our singer Jo was doing more and more of the front work with every show. I believed Dirty Weekend would carry on as the guys simply loved it, and with Wama's never-ending enthusiasm there was no reason why it would come to a halt. The work and dedication that went into this band was astonishing. Obviously, Wama was a large driving force in this, but every single member had a love and loyalty that you would find others couldn't replicate. Every single person that performed with us was considered one of us, and this also extended itself to those who came to listen and support. The whole thing had become a family, and it mirrored the best and worst of that concept. From time to time, we would have fallouts, but these were worked through as quickly as they had arisen. You never really left the band either – as I would find out later, as I performed with them again from time to time in the future.

One unexpected honour we received was when we were told about a famous mural in town that was being redone and updated. This particular piece of art adorns the large side wall of a pub in Brighton called The Prince Albert. It is famous to music fans all around the world and depicts portraits of musical legends who have shaped the lives of generations, as well as some iconic imagery centred around popular culture.

To my utter amazement just to the left of John Peel and the Banksy that depicts the 'Kissing Coppers', and just to the right of Tom Petty, you will find us. Not a picture of us but our Dirty Weekend band logo. It makes me proud to have a little imprint on the music scene and it makes me laugh when I realise that everyone else on that wall is dead. One happy night, I remember bumping into Wama by chance, who for some reason had been out taking Betsy for a ludicrously long walk. We ended up having a couple of beers at The Albert and talking about the old days, before going around to the mural and staring at it in disbelief. We persuaded a passing Japanese tourist to take a picture of us. I was on one side, Wama was on the other and Betsy was standing on top of the bin in the middle wearing a cravat. We are both raising our glasses and have the biggest smiles possible as we toast the fact that we are just two chancers that had fun doing things that people of our age should apparently not be doing.

* * *

And so, to my final gig as the frontman for Dirty Weekend. It couldn't have been a better time or location as we were about to do the annual pilgrimage to The Neptune at Christmastime. Everyone who had followed and supported us appeared to have turned up and the atmosphere in the place was one of excitement, happiness and anticipation. As always, we had arrived early and, seeing as this was my last gig, I was going to treat the whole night as the party that it was. By the time we were to start, I was in extremely high spirits, and was in full rock-star, piss-taking mode from the outset. Because it was my last performance, I had been given the main say on the setlist for the night, and I relished the fact that we did more of the hard rock and punkier tunes. It was nice to resurrect a few that we had done years previously and for some reason discarded, and I felt it brought back a bit of the angst that I had liked about the way we performed.

We did the first set, which went down well, and after a few fags and some refuelling at the bar we were ready for part two. Just before we were about to start, Wama grabbed the microphone. He wanted to say a few words. I stood there as he went on to tell the crowd about his mixed feelings on this night. He thanked me for all we had been through as a band and then ushered someone to bring something to him. He handed me two large parcels.

I opened both. The first was a photo of the band performing onstage at the Old Market. This had been blown up and printed on to a giant canvas. The second was of us performing at Concorde 2. I literally had a lump in my throat, and I could sense I was watering around the eyes. All the band had signed it and these two pictures are amongst my most treasured possessions. I am not a material person by nature, but these two items are not material. They are spiritual to me. So much in those two images encapsulated everything that was good about life in a band, and I suddenly realised I was going to find it extremely hard to fill the space left behind.

We launched into the second set, which whistled past in no time at all. The music was pumping, and the venue was rocking as we reached the climax and finished the last song to what can only be described as complete euphoria from my point of view. I took a bow and was dripping in sweat as I took a second to soak it all up for the last time. The crowd were baying for more and Tree had sown a seed in my head to get Creeda and Joe up to play a tune. I checked with Jon, Jo, Monty and Marcos to make sure they didn't mind, and asked for Creeda and Joe to join me onstage. I knew exactly what we were going to do.

Technically, Dirty Weekend started on 10th July 2011. But to me, the real start was the first gig we did at the Neptune on the 26th of February

2013 – with Creeda and Joe. On that occasion, if you remember, they were introduced to the world when we did a rendition of the Jimi Hendrix song 'Hey Joe'. So here we were, back at the same place, with the same line-up and in all honesty I couldn't have planned a better way to finish my time with the band. As soon as we started, memories came flooding back and I was completely lost in the moment, as for the next seven minutes we just jammed away to our hearts' content. Joe was soloing, Creeda was soloing. I was making shit up, and Clive and Wama were relentlessly driving the whole thing on. I had plenty of time to study the faces of all the guys onstage whilst they played, and all I could see was pure fun and enjoyment. I had plenty of time to look out into the crowd and gauge the reaction from our audience, and to me it looked like an outpouring of pure love for the band. We eventually brought the song to its conclusion, and once the final notes had gradually lowered in volume, I remember going straight up to Clive and Wama and giving them a heartfelt and loving hug.

I have a lot to be thankful for and I certainly wouldn't have done anything differently. My mid-life crisis rumbles on in different directions, and if you are going through one I would highly recommend that you embrace it. My Dirty Weekend is over for now and I don't know what is around the next corner. It doesn't worry me though, as I have collected an assortment of friends to share it with and I wouldn't have found these people without going on this strange musical ride.

Thanks to all who have indulged my madness and may the power of music live on in your lives.

Printed in Great Britain
by Amazon